Blue
THUNDER

THE **JOCK WALLACE**
STORY
Blue
THUNDER

JEFF HOLMES

First published by Pitch Publishing, 2014

Pitch Publishing

A2 Yeoman Gate

Yeoman Way

Durrington

BN13 3QZ

www.pitchpublishing.co.uk

A CIP catalogue record is available for this book
from the British Library.

ISBN 978 1 90962 632 4

Typesetting and origination by Pitch Publishing
Printed in Great Britain

Contents

For my wife, Elaine

Thanks

IT was testimony to the popularity of Jock Wallace that I received so much help and assistance in writing this book. Many of the Barcelona Bears were only too happy to chat about Jock and recalled, with great fondness, memories of their time together both on and off the park. The Barca Bears are heroes to many thousands of Light Blues supporters who still remember the European Cup Winners' Cup success with great fondness.

A good friend, Bobby Roddie, put me in touch with the Bears and I was able to grab relaxed and informal sit-down chats with Alex MacDonald, Peter McCloy, Tommy McLean, Willie Mathieson, Alfie Conn and 'Captain Fantastic' John Greig. A special thanks also to Pam Jackson, wife of 'Bomber', who co-ordinated the interviews that day, and helped make it one to remember for a lifelong Rangers supporter.

A day out in the Ibrox Members' Lounge, again courtesy of Bobby, brought further chats with Willie Johnston, Colin Jackson and Derek Johnstone. I tracked down Bill McMurdo, Jock's one-time agent, who was fantastic and open and put me in touch with Willie Henderson.

Likewise, Graham Clark, Jock's friend and work colleague, who was only too happy to share details of their close working relationship. Graham was fantastic – although there was just one secret that he couldn't spill! But even just getting to use material from Graham's 1984 book on Jock, *Football is the Wallace Religion*, was a great help.

When I managed to track down Nicky Walker, who kept goal for Jock at Leicester City, Motherwell and Rangers, he was just the nicest guy. Warm, friendly and very candid, he held a genuine affection for his former boss.

A real breakthrough arrived when my daughter Carey stumbled across Paul Friar at his place of work and they got talking about football. She called me that night and said, 'I was talking to this guy today who played for Leicester City in the late 1970s and early 1980s.' I met up with Paul and he was another of Jock's former players who had nothing but good things to say. He put me in touch with Alan Young, Jock's main striker at Leicester, and the man tasked with looking after a young Gary Lineker. Alan was a joy to talk to.

I was invited through to Falkirk Football Club by Alex Totten to talk about his relationship with Jock in the early to mid-1980s, when 'Totts' was assistant to Jock at Ibrox. I could have sat talking to Alex for hours, and it wasn't just the tea and excellent shortbread!

Journalists Fraser Elder, Kenny McDonald and David McCarthy were also a big help. Veteran sportswriter Fraser was able to fill in many blanks on Jock's Berwick days and was a constant source of enthusiasm during our many chats. Kenny regaled me with tales of Jock and very kindly helped edit the manuscript. David Williams proved an invaluable source of information from Jock's days at Bedford Town.

And last, but certainly by no means least, is Ally McCoist, the current manager of Glasgow Rangers. 'Super Ally' took time out from his hectic and demanding schedule to welcome my son Derek and I to Murray Park for a lengthy chat about the manager who showed great faith in Rangers' greatest ever goalscorer. It was another wonderful experience, and a special thank you to Laura Tarbet for arranging.

To everyone who helped out – you're simply the best!

And a special thanks to Paul, Jane and all at Pitch Publishing – a real winning team on and off the park!

Introduction

I T was September 1977 and I was the luckiest kid alive. I had just turned 17 and was working as the 'boy' in Scottish Television: the 'do this, do that' lad who helped keep each department ticking over.

No two days were ever the same and in just one calendar month this young and excited 'star spotter' had met movie greats Charlton Heston and Sophia Loren – and secured their signatures. Others would follow – Paul and Linda McCartney, Sylvester Stallone, Cliff Richard, but they would mean very little compared to a number of autographs I got one very ordinary Monday morning.

I was ambling past reception when a security man happened to mention that 'The Rangers' were coming in to use one of our conference rooms to view tapes of a forthcoming European opponent. 'What time?' I asked excitedly. '10am.' Enough time to nip down to the locker room and get my brand new autograph book, or so I thought.

Off I went down to the general stores and couldn't believe it when I was packed off to Central Station with one of the drivers to pick up several crates for the film library, off the London train, if I remember right. We were gone for half an hour and on the way back up Hope Street to STV, and with the traffic lights stuck at red for an eternity, I jumped out the van and made straight for the front desk. The look on the security man's face said it all. 'You missed them, they're already in the room.'

Dejectedly, I started to walk off, when he shouted me back. A taxi had drawn up at the front door and out hurried Jock Wallace, manager of Rangers. Obviously late, and wary of setting a bad example to his players, he started bounding towards reception. It was now or never. But was it a good idea to stop this giant of a man in his tracks for a request so futile? Go on, you only live once.

'Excuse me, Mr Wallace,' I said with a mixture of nerves and excitement. 'Can I have your autograph please?' 'MY autograph,' he smiled. 'Of course son. You a Rangers fan then?' he asked. 'Absolutely, and I hope we beat FC Twente next week in Holland.' 'So do I son,' he said. We were having a conversation!

He turned to the security man and asked if all the players were in. 'They are, Mr Wallace,' and with that he looked at me, and then at my barren autograph book, and said, 'It doesn't look like you've got many autographs. Did you not get the players when they came in?'

After I recounted my tale of woe, he said, 'Come on, we'll get them now.' The security man asked me to show Mr Wallace to the conference room. Me! We walked along the corridor and he asked who my favourite player was. 'John Greig.' 'Aye, he's no' bad,' he said, and with that we were inside a room full of heroes.

The manager said, 'Before we get started today, I want you all to sign, eh, what's your name son?' 'Jeff.' 'I want you all to sign Jeff's autograph book, 'cause the pages are blank,' and he let out a small chuckle. 'We'll fill them up for you son,' and with that he was off. But I wasn't.

One by one the players signed my book: Tommy McLean, Colin Jackson, Derek Johnstone, Peter McCloy etc, and the one and only John Greig.

I was speechless. Once I had secured each and every signature, I walked up to the manager and said, 'Thank you very much Mr Wallace.' He turned to me and said, 'You're welcome son. I would invite you to watch the film with us but you might get the sack,

12

so you better get back to your work,' and with that he smiled and I toddled off.

Mr Wallace, you made a young man very happy that day, and it's something I'll never forget. You were one in a million.

Jeff Holmes,
April 2014

Foreword

THERE was far more to big Jock than his gruff, sergeant-major type image: far more substance than the way he was portrayed in public. He was both clever and shrewd, and one instance stands out from all others. I was going through a bit of a bad patch and he called me into his office one morning and said, 'I've had Cardiff City on the phone, what d'you wanna do', and he looked at me. I said, 'What do you mean?' He said, 'Cardiff, d'you wanna go?' I told him I didn't want to go anywhere. 'Okay,' he said, 'I'll tell them.'

I left the office determined to make my mark at Rangers, but the more I thought about it the more I reckon he was kidding me on. I'm convinced he just wanted to see my reaction and find out if I was ready to fight for my place or take the easy option and leave.

To this day, I still don't believe Cardiff had called about me, but I thought it was a fantastic example of his man-management skills.

How would I describe my first impressions of big Jock? I hate to use the word fear, because it wasn't fear. I was more in awe of him. He was a big, powerful man, and commanded total respect. When you meet someone like Jock for the first time you certainly don't forget him.

His first game in charge was a 3-0 loss at Aberdeen and we soon found out that he liked a wee bit of 'music' on the away trips. I recall him smacking the odd player who wasn't singing, but he loved Jimmy Nicholl, because he knew all the words!

He didn't have any favourites as such, but he loved when all his boys were together, having a few drinks and enjoying a wee sing-song. He was big on camaraderie and team spirit, building a good solid unit, which I thought was fantastic.

His first trophy back at Rangers was the League Cup, and I scored a hat-trick in the final. I'll always remember seeing Jock bursting with pride. After the game, he gave me the biggest bear hug possible and I was dangling in mid-air for what seemed like an eternity, but there was this classic moment when a reporter from STV tried to interview him. He kept the big man waiting and Jock was becoming irritated.

There is a clip of it on YouTube and it's the funniest thing, but in Jock's defence, he was desperate to get into the dressing room to celebrate with his players. That just summed him up. He didn't suffer fools gladly and expected people to do their job to the best of their ability. He refused to accept anything less.

I firmly believe he was unlucky in his second spell at the club. We were sitting having a cup of tea a few years later and he told me that he had wanted to sign Gordon Durie and Craig Levein, two top, top players at the time, but said he wasn't given the money. It could have been very different had he got guys like that in.

I remember Jock taking us to Iraq on a mid-season tour, and Baghdad Airport being bombed the day after we left. I think big Jock was just looking for a fight – but that's only my opinion.

We played the Iraqi national team in Baghdad, and Jordan in Amman. That was definitely a proper adventure. It was another classic Jock tactic because it helped take the sting out of what had been a bad period for us. It might have been easier to take us over to Torremolinos to play a couple of games, but going into some of the places we visited on that tour really brought us all together.

I was very sad when Jock left. I remember very clearly him coming in and telling us what had happened. The players were genuinely gutted and no matter what anybody says, the vast majority of managers leave a club because the players haven't done their job well enough, and we all felt a massive responsibility.

Jock is up there with the best managers I ever worked under. He won two trebles, as well as a host of other trophies, and will rightly go down in history as one of the great Rangers managers. Our club, more than most, has been blessed with some fantastic people and big Jock certainly comes into that category.

His man-management skills were brilliant and something I learned from him is that, as much as you might like to, you can't treat all players the same, because while some need a kick up the backside, others perform better with an arm around them, because individuals are different. There are different ways to manage different people, and he was exceptionally good at that as well. The big man's legacy certainly lives on at our club.

Ally McCoist MBE
Manager, Glasgow Rangers

Prologue

THE day Rangers clinched their second treble in just three years was the pinnacle of the Wallace career, but it was also arguably the day that his time in football flatlined. Of course, there was success of sorts at Leicester, Rangers (again) and Colchester United, but the great man would never again reach the dizzy heights of his first spell in charge at Ibrox.

Before reaching the hallowed ground of Govan, Wallace had tasted one-off glory days at clubs such as Bedford Town, Hereford United and Berwick Rangers. It was the ability to transform the ordinary into something extraordinary that clinched the initial move to Rangers, where he showed leadership beyond the norm to create not one, but two super teams.

The first of these was responsible for ending Celtic's domination of Scottish football, while the second showcased another side of his talents; this time the construction of a talented football side containing the silky skills of Davie Cooper, Bobby Russell and Gordon Smith.

But the beginning of the end arrived on the afternoon of Saturday 7 May 1978, at around 2.55pm, when Wallace warned his captain, the Greatest Ever Ranger, John Greig, not to return to the dressing room without the Scottish Cup.

Rangers had already secured the Scottish League championship by two points from Aberdeen, while an extra-time winner by Gordon Smith against Celtic had claimed the League Cup. A Scottish Cup Final win over Aberdeen would complete the set and merely cement Rangers' position as the greatest club in the country.

But Wallace was no forerunner of your modern-day egotistical boss, who cared only about the 'honours won' column on his CV. He wanted the success alright, but it was for the players, the supporters and everyone connected with a club he had supported as a nipper. He was a driven individual, as was his skipper. So when Greig burst into the Hampden dressing room after a pulsating 2-1 victory over the Dons, and shouted, 'You wanted it, well here it is,' and launched the cup across the room, Wallace was forced to show all his old skills as a top goalkeeper to catch the famous old trophy and, as he did, an ironic smile broke out across his face.

I was fortunate enough to interview Greig as part of my research and we got chatting about that particular afternoon. He said, 'Jock told me not to come back in without the cup. He was underlining the importance of winning another treble, and knew exactly what it meant to our supporters. Of course, we won the game and I remember coming back into the dressing room and throwing the cup at him, which maybe wasn't the cleverest thing to do, considering he was an ex-goalkeeper! But it was an historic moment because it was our second treble in three years and it turned out to be my last game for Rangers, and also Jock's last game, because he went to Leicester after that.'

Wallace and his players had been under enormous pressure to deliver following the abject disappointment of the previous campaign, in which the team had won absolutely nothing. Supporters demanded a return to the glory days of 1975/76, in which Wallace had steered the club to a stunning treble. On that occasion Rangers fans craved a period of dominance to rival Celtic's nine-in-a-row success under Jock Stein, but it had failed to materialise and they were left to endure a miserable time of it when Celtic won back the league, and added the Scottish Cup to their list of honours due to a controversial penalty award in the final at Hampden against the Light Blues.

It would perhaps be wrong to suggest that Rangers were a club in turmoil, for just 12 months previously they had swept the boards in Scottish football and Wallace had given the supporters back their swagger. It was clear, though, that surgery was required for the new campaign and the fresh challenge that would surely follow. Of course, the manager would have key players such as Tom Forsyth, Colin Jackson and Derek Johnstone – who had all missed large chunks of the ill-fated 1976/77 season – back in the side as Rangers prepared to go head-to-head with Celtic, as well as 'emerging' forces such as Aberdeen and Dundee United.

Greig, more than most, took the barren season to heart and, at the time, said, 'I know people are looking for scapegoats because we lost everything. I am an obvious target because of my age but I certainly won't quit because of public opinion. I've enjoyed my last three years with Rangers, so why should I leave now?'

But he did reveal that should he lose his place in the side the following season then he would hang up his boots. He wasn't for sticking around to play reserve football, while moving to another club simply wasn't an option.

But Wallace had players in mind who could revolutionise his team, and help drag them kicking and screaming into the modern age, but there was also a major role for Greig. The manager set his sights on capturing three players, and while he splashed the cash on Davie Cooper and Gordon Smith, it was another youngster, Bobby Russell, who arrived on the scene minus the fanfare, but who would go on to create quite a noise for his new boss.

It wasn't quite a changing of the guard which brought Wallace and Rangers the treble in 1977/78. It was a mixture of old and new, and a fresh dose of drive and determination within the squad. Oh, and a large helping of 'character' – the buzz word around Ibrox while big Jock was in charge.

So, as Wallace caught the Scottish Cup from his captain, little could he have known that the side he had so expertly pieced together would be no more than a one-season wonder, as far as he was concerned. And that Scottish Cup would represent a metaphorical baton, as Greig traded in the hallowed piece of silverware for the keys to the office which had housed great managers such as Bill Struth, Scott Symon and Willie Waddell. Greig would be installed as Rangers boss shortly after Wallace packed up his belongings, walked down the marble staircase and on to pastures new.

When Wallace left Rangers, he insisted he was leaving behind the best Rangers team he had ever worked with. A few years later, he would say, 'All the ingredients were just right. Every man in the squad could play football. I had a good keeper in Peter McCloy. Sandy Jardine and John Greig were full-backs who could come forward. Tom Forsyth and Colin Jackson were the central defenders. They weren't great passers of the ball, but they had pace, were good in the air and just wouldn't let anyone past.

'Tommy McLean could put a ball on a sixpence, but preferred to put it on the head of Derek Johnstone, and Gordon Smith provided the thrusting pace behind Johnstone. Bobby Russell was industrious and had great control. Alex MacDonald had bite to his industry – and Davie Cooper was pure magic on the left.'

Wallace may have pushed his charges to the absolute limit during pre-season training, with his penchant for total fitness on 'Murder Hill' at Gullane, but it was done for a reason, and there isn't a player around today who would criticise him for doing so. It wasn't there to be enjoyed. It was a means to an end and when you consider that in his time as manager of Rangers, Jock Wallace won ten major domestic honours, then those means were well and truly vindicated – and blazers at the Scottish Football Association, proprietors of the Scottish Cup, can rest easy knowing that any dents on the famous old cup didn't get there as a consequence of the actions of captain and manager on Saturday 7 May 1978!

1
It's Early Days

JOCK Wallace was as proud and as passionate a Scotsman as anyone born north of Hadrian's Wall. While managing Leicester City and Colchester United, a constant companion was a foot-high statue of legendary Scottish freedom fighter, and namesake, William.

In Alan Ball's excellent biography, *Playing Extra Time*, England's 1966 World Cup winner – Wallace's assistant at Colchester – talks of the time the Us were staying at Stirling University while on a pre-season tour of Scotland. One night, Wallace was perched on the end of Ball's bed and both were enjoying a dram. The curtains were closed and Wallace got up to open them. Moments later Ball drew them shut again, and this continued like a pantomime sketch until Wallace pinned the diminutive Ball to his duvet and bellowed, 'I put you in this room so you would have to look at that statue of William Wallace, and you keep closing the fuckin' curtains!'

Ball admitted to being both frightened and amazed by big Jock's outburst, and obvious passion for his country, but thought better of arguing and, after straightening the lapels on his pyjamas, said, 'Boss, I had no idea that the guy out there meant so much to you – I didn't even know who he was', and with that, the two men continued to drink. As is patently clear from his book, Ball held Wallace in tremendously high regard, as does everyone you speak to who was acquainted in one way or another with the former Rangers manager.

Wallace was born in September 1935, the son of John and Catherine, and everything pointed to the 'bairn' being a native of Wallyford, a small village just six miles east of Edinburgh city centre.

Wallace senior, a professional goalkeeper, had just been transferred from Raith Rovers to Blackpool, and was playing for the Lancashire side at the time of his son's birth. Several sources, therefore, suggested that Wallace junior was born in Blackpool, although the local registry office had no record of a birth for John Martin Bokas Wallace on 6 September 1935. Can you imagine how Jock would have felt about being English? It was soon confirmed, however, that young Master Wallace was indeed born at 10.40am on Friday 6 September at 146 Forthview, Wallyford, in the Parish of Inveresk.

The middle name of Bokas was a square peg in a round hole, though. While Jock's dad, John Martin Wallace, played for the Seasiders, a team-mate was Frank Bokas, a Bellshill-born half-back who had started out his career at Kirkintilloch Rob Roy. One can only assume that the pair became best buddies during their time at Bloomfield Road, and that the unusual middle name was a nod to Jock senior's team-mate. Bokas died in 1996, the same year as Jock senior.

Wallyford Primary School and Musselburgh Grammar offered the youngster a solid educational grounding, as well as his first taste of organised football, but it wasn't as a goalkeeper that he starred for the latter. Young Wallace turned out at centre-half while the keeper's yellow jersey remained the property of Bert Slater, who would go on to keep goal for Dundee, Liverpool and Scotland. John White, a future Spurs and Scotland star, was also part of a rather talented school team.

One of Jock's teachers, Alex McGillivray, helped run the school team and remembered how the youngster had to be handled with kid gloves. Speaking in 1975, he said, 'I had a soft spot for Jock, but

I was scared to drop him from the team. Most players would accept being left out now and again, but not Jock. If I didn't choose him, it wasn't long before he was hammering at my door and demanding to know why he wasn't playing.

'Jock was our centre-half. He couldn't get a game in goals because of Bert, who was better at the job. We also had another youngster, John White, who was a great player, but at that time, out of the three lads, I would've tipped Wallace to make the top. White was small and slight, while Wallace was tall and well built. He also had character and was both reliable and very determined.'

In the early 1970s, Bert Slater said, 'Both Jock and I had a mining background. Life was hard but we enjoyed our football. When the school bell rang at four o'clock we dashed to the gasworks pitches for a kick-around. In those days Jock didn't like playing in goal. His build helped him to be an ideal centre-half. Before joining the Army, Jock worked as a steel bender and the story went that he used his teeth to bend the steel!'

But it seemed that young Wallace was destined to play between the sticks, although only after an inauspicious beginning. After moving from Wallyford Boys Club to an Edinburgh juvenile side, he turned up for a match only to discover that the regular goalkeeper hadn't showed, and as Jock was the tallest of the outfield players he was shoved in goal. Later that night, he visited his aunt's house and she said to him, 'How did the football go today, son?' He replied, 'We got beat 10-1.' '10-1?' she said. 'For goodness sake, who was in goals?' 'Me', he replied sheepishly.

As a youngster, Jock and his pals played every night on the pitches at the old Musselburgh Gasworks – later to be used as the Loretto rugby grounds. Wallace also regularly watched local favourites Wallyford Bluebell, with whom his dad had played when he was starting out in his career.

And when he was just nine years old, Jock would make the long and arduous fortnightly pilgrimage by train to Ibrox Park which, according to his dad, used to worry the youngster's mother sick.

Jock senior said, 'My son would think nothing of going alone by train from Musselburgh to cheer on Rangers. But his mother was unhappy. She used to worry herself sick when young Jock set off on his own, so he joined a Rangers supporters' club and travelled by bus.' Years later, Jock junior would say, 'I was nine when I started going to games and asked men to lift me over the turnstiles so I could see the Rangers.'

The majority of school leavers in Wallyford, and surrounding villages, found employment at the local pit. Owned for the largest part by the Edinburgh Colliery Company, the Old Pit at Wallyford had witnessed many disasters, with one, in 1901, taking the lives of two local men when a pit wall collapsed. It was a tragedy that cast a giant shadow over the small town and its inhabitants.

Wallace, though, was desperate to follow in his father's footsteps and become a professional footballer. He signed for Blackpool on apprentice terms but was freed shortly after when he became homesick. He headed back to Wallyford, where he took up a job as a delivery boy with a local bakery, while also having a spell as a motor mechanic. But it wasn't long before he was itching to get back into football and he received a break when he signed for Workington. He joined up at Borough Park just after the Cumbrian side had been voted into the Third Division North of the Football League.

Wallace combined playing part-time for Workington with toiling away in a local pit, but sadly his team had also plumbed new depths and finished rock bottom of the league in their debut season. It also turned into a nightmare move for the young goalkeeper and he was released after making just six competitive appearances, including a match against Tranmere Rovers in which he suffered a broken hand.

Wallace moved on but Workington remained one of the league's perennial strugglers and finished second bottom the following season. They received a new lease of life in 1955 when a young manager by the name of Bill Shankly arrived from Grimsby Town. Workington were eventually voted out of the Football League in

1977 and replaced by Wimbledon, and have played non-league football ever since.

Wallace, though, was determined that the early setback wouldn't be the ruin of him and after the broken bone in his hand had healed, he was picked up by Ashton United, who were based just east of Manchester, and plied their trade in the Lancashire Combination. Floodlights were installed at Hurst Cross the year Wallace made his debut for the Robins although his stay in Ashton-under-Lyne was a short one. Six years after Wallace left Ashton, the club signed a young Alan Ball, who would go on to work with Jock in the twilight of his career.

For Wallace, though, the move was anything but a success and although trials were later arranged at both Hibs and St Johnstone, neither came to much and it was a disillusioned young man who opted for a change of career. He decided to fulfil another ambition by joining the Army and moved to Berwick where he signed a 'three-year contract' with the King's Own Scottish Borderers in 1954, a proud regiment which had been based in the Borders town since its inauguration in 1689.

While undergoing rigorous army training with the 'Kosbies', and playing for his army team, he caught the eye of Berwick Rangers, and duly signed a part-time deal with the Wee Gers. He made a solid debut in a 4-0 win over Montrose and a further highlight was a match against English cracks Aston Villa, to mark the official opening of Berwick's Shielfield Park.

Wallace played several games for Berwick before landing his first official posting with the Kosbies. He was off to Ireland for three months, which put the brakes on his career, but his latest football experience had at least been a positive one.

On returning from Ireland, he presumed he would be able to pick up where he left off, but was told that he would soon be on the move again – this time to a posting slightly further afield. He was off to the humid and dangerous jungles of Malaya. Later on, Wallace would say, 'One lasting memory of hearing that news was that we soon realised it would take us four weeks to get there by boat!'

But far from wrecking his burgeoning football career, the spell in Asia boosted his confidence – and his medal collection. He said, 'I played for the Borderers, for the Combined Services and, in all, about seven different teams while we were out in Malaya. I also did quite well in the athletics where I specialised in the quarter-mile and the high jump. But we had a very successful football team and ended up winning various cups and trophies during my three years in Malaya and Singapore.'

A guerrilla war, the Malayan Emergency – as it was known – took place between Allied forces and the Malayan National Liberation Army between 1948 and 1960 in an attempt to halt the spread of communism and the defeat of the Commonwealth government.

In the 19th century, Britain claimed Malaya and parts of Borneo as colonies. Many local Malayans were against their country being colonised by the British but were too weak to remove the colonial power. This continued through to the Second World War when, in 1941, the Japanese invaded and defeated the British. They immediately occupied the area, 'liberating' it from colonialism, but imposing their own often brutal form of martial rule instead.

During this period the British trained and equipped many local Malayans and Malayan Chinese as guerrilla groups to fight the Japanese. The Chinese in particular despised the Japanese because of a previous invasion and brutality in parts of China in the 1930s.

At the end of the Second World War, the British urged non-communist Malayans to take control, but the Malayan Chinese, many of whom were communists, were hell-bent on ensuring Malaya's future was as a communist country, and started to fight the British. The King's Own Scottish Borderers was one of several crack British battalions sent over to fight the communists, who were eventually defeated in 1960, and it was in this conflict that Wallace played his part.

Former Rangers star Derek Johnstone remembered his old gaffer talking about his time in the Malayan bush, and recalled, 'Jock often told the story of being knee-deep in the jungle while wondering how Rangers were doing on a Saturday afternoon. Apparently he got a few of the guys to rig up a radio mast high up in the trees so they could tune in to the BBC World Service, and get the football scores as they came in at 5pm British time.'

Rumour has it that when Wallace signed up for the Kosbies, and was asked his religion, he replied 'football!' And that was big Jock turning his back temporarily on the game to hunt communist bandits in Malaya. The officer in charge of his battalion, Major Richard Hill, once said, 'Jock was a steady, reliable soldier. In those days a good footballer was usually kept at HQ to play for the team, but I don't think Wallace was interested. Anyway, I always said he had two left feet.'

Wallace admitted that his time in south-east Asia had a profound effect on his character, and said, 'Up until I joined the Army I was a bit of a loner. I was never short of friends but tended to keep myself to myself. That all changed in Malaya.

In the Army you quickly realise that you have to become a team, and that your life depends, quite literally, on the people around you. I was only 20 but I learned more in Malaya than at any other time in my life.'

After three years in the Army, Wallace found himself back on Civvy Street, out of work and with little prospect of finding employment. But while those in a similar position preferred a pint and a visit to the dogs, Wallace decided to keep himself fit until something came along. That something was a job as a labourer, digging drains for a living, which proved easy enough for a man with his build and athleticism, but he yearned for a return to the game he loved.

And it wasn't too long before he was re-introduced into the Berwick Rangers squad. Wallace was soon turning in impressive performances on a regular basis and, having served his apprenticeship in the game, he was starting to make a real name for himself.

Following his stint with the Kosbies, Wallace started the 1957/58 campaign at Shielfield, but the first few months turned into a bit of a nightmare. The Borders side lost all of their League Cup ties and were shipping goals right, left and centre. The big keeper lost ten in his first two games – and was named man of the match in both!

As he 'celebrated' his 21st birthday, Berwick's dismal form continued but Wallace's stock was rising, as reports read, 'Berwick owed a lot to their brilliant keeper Wallace', 'Wallace's ability to cut out the wing crosses kept the score down'. There was a pattern emerging and it was only a matter of time before a bigger side moved in for the talented keeper.

2

Learning His Trade

AIRDRIEONIANS were the First Division equivalent of Berwick – rock bottom of the table and struggling to keep the ball out the net. Manager Willie Steel was desperate for a new keeper and parted with £2,000 to sign Jock Wallace. He made his debut against Third Lanark at Broomfield in October, 1958, and after a 3-2 loss, the match report began, 'It's little wonder Airdrie are wallowing at the bottom of the League. Their display against Thirds was pathetic.'

Slowly, the Diamonds managed to reverse their fortunes and secure their First Division status. Wallace was a key figure in their revival, but dropped a clanger at Celtic Park – a ground he would visit many more times in the future – in a 4-2 loss, and was jeered mercilessly by home supporters.

One of the characters of that Broomfield era was trainer Bobby Reid, of whom Diamonds star Gibby Ormond once said, 'I've never been fitter. There's none of the old track-lapping routines at Broomfield. Bobby uses all the modern methods – and some of them are murder!' Did Reid harvest big Jock's future lust for total fitness?

Wallace started the 1958/59 season on top form and helped Airdrie to a 5-4 win over Rangers. The Diamonds were on the up, although the loss of Ian McMillan to the Light Blues – after 66 goals in 64 games – should have stunted any progress. But when asked why Airdrie had suddenly shaken off the tag of also-rans, gaffer Steel answered, 'The eagle eye of trainer Bobby Reid. The season previous, he was studying Jock during an evening session and noticed the big man had a limp. Further investigation uncovered a thigh injury.

'Bobby got him on the treatment table and found his muscles in a bad way. It was weeks before the cure was complete but what a difference it made to the player. Today there is no denying that Jock's form has inspired a new confidence in our defence.'

A 2-1 win at Falkirk – in which one newspaper insisted, 'Wallace had inspired his colleagues by bringing off several brilliant saves' – was followed by victories over Raith Rovers and St Mirren, which put the Diamonds top of the table alongside Rangers and Hearts. It was joy unbridled for the long-suffering Airdrie fans.

But despite their lofty league position, Broomfield crowds had plummeted, with around 1,000 knocked off the 5,000 average since the departure of McMillan. Another reason for the dwindling gates was the advent of the bookmaker. Supporters were lapping up the comfort of the bookies' shops and opting to watch television screens in plush surroundings.

Airdrie carried their superb form into 1959 and Wallace was hailed as one of the best keepers in the country. The Diamonds finished fifth in the league – above Celtic – and Wallace started the new campaign with a shut-out against Partick Thistle – no thanks to the referee. In the first half, Davie McParland hit a low shot from an impossible angle and it went straight into the net.

Was that 1-0? Not a chance. Wallace chased the ref all the way to the centre circle to tell him that the ball had slipped through a hole in the side netting. He arrogantly waved the keeper away but, as many will testify, big Jock could be mighty persuasive. The humble ref trotted back to the goal for a quick peek. The net was indeed loose at the post and the goal was chalked off.

Tragedy wasn't far off though, and when Partick Thistle visited Broomfield for a League Cup tie, a 4-0 home win was overshadowed by the death of Thistle manager Davie Meiklejohn. The former Rangers great had suffered a heart attack in the directors' box just moments after the final whistle. He was rushed to hospital but died on the way.

Wallace's stunning form was finally recognised at representative level when he was named as travelling reserve for Scotland's league international against Ireland in Dublin. Big Jock was understudy to Rangers keeper George Niven, and looked on as the Scots won 4-1. As a result, Swansea took more than a passing interest and manager Trevor Morris travelled north to run the rule over the big keeper, but Diamonds gaffer Steel issued a stern 'hands off' warning to all would-be suitors.

Morris met with Steel after the 1-0 win over Aberdeen and was told that their prized asset, valued at £12,000, wasn't for sale. The following Saturday, Wallace played his last game for Airdrie, against Hearts, and just four days later signed on the dotted line… for West Brom for £6,500.

Of his move to The Hawthorns, Wallace, who was 24 at the time, said, 'I'm happy to sign for West Bromwich and realise my ambition of becoming a full-time player. When I re-signed for Airdrie, I asked that if a full-time club came in for me that I be allowed to leave. I am pleased that manager Willie Steel kept his promise.'

Bert Thomson took over in the Diamonds' goal but shipped 11 at home to Hibs in just his second match. Wallace, hoping for better fortunes 300 miles south, was determined to grab his opportunity in the English top flight with both hands.

He made his debut at Bolton and despite newspapers describing him as 'Dour Scottish goalkeeper, Johnny Wallace', he managed a shut-out – and with a smile on his face. The game finished 0-0 and he left his mark on the opposition – literally. One report read, 'It was no game for weaklings. The hefty keeper stood up manfully to the barging of the Bolton forwards and during one heavy assault, inadvertently knocked out Stevens when attempting to punch the ball!'

Wallace made his first home appearance for the Baggies at The Hawthorns against Luton Town at the end of October 1959, and was instrumental in a 4-0 win. The Baggies had a host of big names, including future England boss Bobby Robson, and Don Howe, who would go on to manage Arsenal, and played the kind of attractive football that earned many plaudits from within the English game. It was continental-style football before its time. The players loved nothing better than to pass the ball, and had been likened to the great Tottenham team of the same era.

Wallace said, 'Dick Graham was our coach and I remember beating Spurs at their own game in the year they won the Double. It was a bit of a golden era for football down south and when I think back to some of the players I played with, and against, I was proud to be a part of it.'

Wallace labelled Don Howe 'the best professional I ever met', and added, 'Don had the right attitude to football and it didn't surprise me that he went on to do so well when he finished playing.' The pair would talk football for hours on end and it was crystal clear, even back then, that both had great careers ahead.

But while most players in a similar position would have been living the life of a top footballer, Wallace was different. He lived for football and, to him, a Saturday afternoon was the culmination of a week's hard work, and his reward for putting in the hours on the training field. But even football had to take a back seat on Monday 4 April 1960 when he married the love of his life, Daphne Martin, in Berwick Parish Church.

Wallace had met Daphne while playing for Airdrie. He was part-time at Broomfield and worked in the steel mills, but was spending a lot of his time back in Wallyford as his father was unwell. It was a tough time but Daphne was the silver lining in his personal cloud. She was a tower of strength, as were his aunt and uncle, Ruby and Bert Winters.

After the wedding he was to remain at The Hawthorns for another two and a half years, but the introduction of new boss

Archie Macaulay, a fellow Scot, just before Christmas 1961, would eventually prove the catalyst for the keeper to leave the Midlands.

At the end of the 1961/62 season, Wallace had an issue he needed to discuss with the manager, but found to his dismay that Macaulay's door was never open. It was a source of great frustration for Wallace, who believed he was at the peak of his career. He would later insist that it was through a point of principle that he decided to leave the club, and not a disagreement over money.

Macaulay – a former Rangers player – paved the way for Wallace's departure but slapped an unrealistic price tag of £12,000 on his shoulders, which the big Scot insisted was akin to pricing him out of the game. It was then that he invoked a little-used English league rule – and walked away for nothing. A transfer fee would only have to be paid by another Football League club, but Wallace was free to join a non-league club. When word got out that the highly-rated keeper was available free of charge, a disorderly queue formed, with Bedford Town at the front.

Managed by former Falkirk boss Reggie Smith, Bedford made their move and Wallace happily signed for the club who played to decent crowds in the Southern League. The move to the Eagles would also kick-start a love affair with giant-killing.

Bedford supporter David Williams recalled seeing Wallace's debut against Chelmsford City in August 1962, and said, 'Chelmsford were thought to be much stronger on paper but in front of our best crowd, 4,300, for several years we won 2-0. Jock made several key saves and soon became the most popular player on the books and the one whose autograph we all wanted!

'I saw a lot of his games, though not as many as I'd have liked because I had to play school rugby some Saturdays. As a keeper he could be spectacular and courageous but would occasionally let in a real sitter, sometimes appearing to lose a ball in the air. I never met him personally but those who did found him friendly.'

Wallace was the first-choice keeper throughout his two seasons at Bedford – 1962/63 and 1963/64 – and missed only three first-team matches. He made 106 appearances in all, but the match that sticks in the mind of most Eagles supporters has to be the 2-1 FA Cup defeat of Newcastle at St James' Park in January 1964.

David, who runs the Bedford Old Eagles website, recalled, 'Jock's display that day was probably the longest and best sustained spell of excellent saves I have ever seen by any keeper. Without him, Newcastle would have had five or six. Towards the end, his goal was under continual bombardment and that was when the odd incident of the lost contact lens occurred. At least we all thought it did at the time, because there was a story that he wore glasses when not playing, and years later claimed he'd not lost a lens but got one stuck!

'I'm sure, however, that the players all joined in the search, hence the injury time in which Anderson finally beat Jock and got it back to 2-1. We did wonder if his tendency to misjudge aerial balls had anything to do with eye problems.'

Following two fairly successful seasons at Bedford, Wallace decided to leave The Eyrie and sign for Hereford United, which David thought strange at the time. He said, 'We were all surprised that he moved to Hereford, especially as they had just been relegated to the Southern League's lowest division, although he helped them come straight back in 1964/65. I suppose they just offered him better terms. He gave another great display against Bedford at the start of 1965/66 when we came back from a goal down to win a league match.

'A lot of Bedford fans followed his career after that and were chuffed to read about Berwick's famous defeat of Rangers not long after Jock had gone there. He was popular at The Eyrie and I don't think he had an especially hard reputation when he played for us, although not many would have argued with him I suspect!'

Hereford had been struggling prior to the arrival of 'Big Johnny Wallace' but the move paid instant dividends when he helped them win the title with a record number of points and goals. The promotion was gained not only as a result of some outstanding displays by Wallace, but also due to the prolific Albert Derrick – a firm favourite at Edgar Street – who led the way with 37 league goals.

The following season, Hereford, a club with a penchant for FA Cup upsets, created another when they shocked Third Division leaders Millwall. The result left only two non-league clubs in the cup and, almost inevitably, they were drawn against each other in the next round. It was the tie that pitted Wallace and Hereford with Bedford Town. On a snow-covered pitch, it was Bedford who progressed.

In Wallace's third and final season at Edgar Street, Hereford signed the 'Gentle Giant', John Charles, and his debut drew the largest opening day crowd for many years, 4,869. Neither Wallace nor Charles let the fans down, with the latter scoring in a 5-1 thrashing of who else but Bedford. The former Leeds United and Juventus star was the ultimate Welsh icon and his presence at Edgar Street brought the type of attention normally reserved in the 1960s for The Beatles.

Wallace set another record during the 1966/67 campaign – and one that may never be equalled. He left Hereford in December 1966 for Berwick Rangers, and played in their historic Scottish Cup meeting with Rangers. Having already turned out in the English and Welsh FA Cups for Hereford, he became the only man to play in all three national competitions in the same season.

So the big keeper moved back to the town where he had successfully combined a career in the Army with a stint at Shielfield Park, but how would he fare second time around, and with the added responsibility of being manager?

3

Ripping Up The
Form Book

THERE was little fanfare when Jock Wallace left Hereford
United at the beginning of December 1966, for the manager's
office at Shielfield Park.

While England's World Cup win of some six months previous
was calming down to a frenzy, in a pretty little corner of England –
Northumberland, to be exact – a football revolution of its own was
about to take place.

Berwick Rangers had been plodding along just fine under Danny
McLennan, but little of note had been achieved and Second Division
mediocrity seemed the predetermined lot of the Borders side. There
were some decent players at Shielfield, so perhaps they were just
lacking one final piece of the jigsaw.

The appointment of Wallace was an early Christmas present for
Berwick fans and with it being his second spell at Shielfield, it was
hoped he would hit the ground running, although his first match
in charge, against Queen's Park, wasn't a happy affair. Wallace
pulled off some fine saves in a 2-0 loss but was badly at fault for the
clinching goal. A correspondent for the *Berwick Advertiser* said, 'To
hope for any goalkeeper to keep a clean sheet with this sort of panic
in front of him is beyond reasonable expectation.'

Wallace got to work on the fitness of his players and had them running up and down sand dunes – and there were plenty of them in the seaside town. He put them through an army-style training programme, something else he had picked up on his last visit to Berwick.

Following a particularly tough session on the dunes, one of his players remarked, 'That wisnae as bad as we were told it would be!' Wallace said, 'Aye mibbe so… but now you'll do it carrying a telegraph pole up and down!' The torture prompted one player to remark, 'They say he was a gaffer in the Scottish sodgers, but I reckon it's more likely he was in the Gestapo!'

By the time the Scottish Cup arrived in January, the players were in tip-top shape. A visit to the amateurs of Vale of Leithen posed little problem and Berwick stormed to an 8-1 victory. Wallace pronounced himself happy with their fitness. Forfar were next up and made the long journey over the border. Ken Dowds sent the Station Park side packing with two early goals.

When the draw pitted the Wee Gers with the Big Gers, the town was buzzing and Wallace struggled somewhat to fan the flames of enthusiasm – and expectation. 'Will it be Jock the giant-killer again?' screamed the headline in the *Berwick Advertiser*, given his propensity for slaying dragons during his time in the south.

The week before the tie, Wallace travelled up to Aberdeen to watch the Ibrox men in action and spotted what he believed to be a chink in their armour, and one that his part-timers could perhaps exploit. With more than a hint of bravado, he said, 'Why should I worry? Let the Rangers do the worrying.'

As townsfolk awaited the great occasion with bated breath, the manager took his players to the cinema before packing them off to bed early on the Friday night. Perhaps Wallace's Warriors went to see George Peppard in *The Blue Max*, or Charlton Heston's new film *The Agony and the Ecstasy*. On the Saturday morning, black and gold adorned a town which had switched allegiance between Scotland and England many times. On this occasion, there was no doubt which side the locals were on.

If you fancied making some money from the bookmakers that Saturday – 28 January 1967 – there was no point in looking to the football for profit. As far as the bookies were concerned, the Scottish League First Division was a one-horse race. Celtic were 1/6 to win the title, with Rangers next best at 4/1. John Banks, the Glasgow city centre bookies, quoted the remainder at 'Up your Jumper the rest!'

The odds were even shorter on the day's Scottish Cup ties. Bookmaker Tony Queen wasn't offering single bets on either Celtic v Arbroath or Berwick Rangers v Rangers. You had to stick them in an accumulator with Partick Thistle, Clyde and Queen's Park for the 'Glasgow accy'. Perhaps the best way to make a few bob was to bet on the outcome of the Glasgow Pollok by-election, especially if you fancied the Scottish National Party to lose its deposit.

Rangers, while supremely confident, were treating their opponents with every respect and travelled south the day before, staying overnight at a comfortable hotel in Dunbar. Under the managerial guidance of Scot Symon, the Rangers party were taking nothing for granted, especially with their opponents in the midst of an eight-game unbeaten run.

A few miles south in the town of Berwick-upon-Tweed, an air of nervous expectation was present. Six years previous, when the teams met in the same competition, widespread rowdyism had left a sour taste in the mouth, long after the victorious Rangers team had departed for Glasgow. So much so that when the third round draw was being made for the present competition, Berwick chairman Dr James Sadler said, 'We don't want Glasgow Rangers!'

Rangers it was, though, and all sides were hopeful of erasing those painful memories. The Berwick directors decked out their boardroom in royal blue irises, and before the match, plans were drawn up to present the Rangers Supporters' Club with a painting of the town.

Wallace asked his players for nothing more than 90 minutes of honest endeavour – and sounded a warning to his opponents by saying, 'We will come out fighting. There will be nae surrender! We appreciate the power of our opponents, but truly believe we can give the cup holders a hard game.'

And boy how Wallace got the honest endeavour he had demanded, because come 5pm it was the home supporters in the full house of 16,000 who were celebrating the most incredible upset since the competition began in 1877 – Berwick Rangers 1 Glasgow Rangers 0.

The only goal of the game was scored by former Celtic starlet Sammy Reid. The player had required permission to leave work early, and was back at his full-time job as a gear cutter with a Motherwell engineering firm the following day to make up the lost time! The £8-a-week player was naturally jubilant, and at the time he said, 'It's all down to Jock Wallace. He is a wonderful manager and we really want to win for him. He told us that we would win, and now it has actually happened.'

Over the years, fact has become interwoven with fiction, and many reckon the victory was achieved somewhat more easily than it actually was, but Berwick came under enormous pressure in the first 20 minutes, a period which saw them concede eight corners. But with Wallace supreme in the Berwick goal, and Doug Coutts dominant in defence, they dealt with everything Rangers threw at them.

Throughout the 90 minutes, Rangers never once varied their tactics and Wallace was forced to make two outstanding saves from George McLean and John Greig. But as the game progressed, Berwick grew in confidence and began to carve out chances of their own. Local boy Alan Ainslie hit the post, while others made Norrie Martin in the Rangers goal earn his corn. However it was Reid who scored the only goal of the game, and released a generation of pent-up frustration when the final whistle sounded. While bedlam broke out around Shielfield Park, one man more than most showed his class – Rangers class. Skipper John Greig sportingly applauded each Berwick player off the field.

And as those jubilant players surrounded manager Wallace in the tiny Berwick dressing room, Dr Sadler spoke of the wee club's greatest fear. He said, 'I don't think we will be able to keep Jock much longer. Believe me, this man will become one of the greatest managers in football. He has worked miracles since taking over. He is able to spot hidden talents in every player – and then get that player to play so much better than before. He is so good we are bound to lose him. Remember the name, Jock Wallace, because he will become BIG.'

Wallace said, 'Everyone in Scotland laughed at me when I said we could win. Well, I was right. We've won – and I knew all along that we would. Remember this, we had more clear-cut chances to score than they did. It should have been 3-0 for us. We missed easier chances than the one Sammy scored. I don't care who we get in the next round. I'm only looking as far ahead as our next game. That'll do me just now – but we aren't going to be scared of anyone.'

Scot Symon called the result, 'the worst in Rangers' history' and lambasted his forwards for failing to put the ball in the net. He said, 'This will scar the record books forever.' Two days after the defeat, Rangers chairman John Lawrence said, 'There is no doubt in my mind that the only people who can be blamed for the defeat are the players. The play of some of them made me sick.'

It was estimated that defeat cost Rangers in the region of £100,000. From their semi-final and final ties alone the previous year they had drawn £40,000. They also lost the guarantee of European football – and that was where the big money lay.

It was indeed a black day for the club as asides from defeat, they also lost talented forward Willie Johnston with a broken ankle, after he had come off a poor second in a 50/50 challenge with Wallace. Perhaps goal hero Reid, who was given a lift back up the road on the Rangers team bus, took Bud's seat on the coach. En route, he said, 'It's not the best goal I ever scored but it's certainly the most important. I just happened to be in the right place at the right time.'

More than 100 supporters' buses and a special train left the town immediately after the game and there was little trouble, even though it was the first time Rangers had been beaten by a Second Division club.

Not only was Wallace lauded for guiding Berwick to their finest hour, but the goalkeeper with the telescopic legs was also commended for putting the shutters up on the Ibrox side's vain attempts at procuring an equaliser. Newspaper reports described it as 'the game of a lifetime for Wallace'. The big man made several class saves but one in particular, from a McLean header, was described as 'outstanding'. Willie Henderson was praised for getting in a large number of crosses, but criticised for putting them too near Wallace who, at times, looked as if he had giant suction pads for hands!

A few days later, Wallace said, 'If I had a team of full-time players in my charge, we would all have gone for a Turkish bath. It's a great way of relaxing. We would've had some laughs and talked over Saturday's game in every detail before getting down to some hard work. But I haven't got full-time players, they are all at their ordinary jobs today. We have, for example, a miner, a PT teacher, an engineer, a civil servant and a joiner.

'I've worked the boys hard, but they believe in me and I believe in them – and everything is done in that spirit. I've had to talk them into what they've done. As full-timers I'd just have taken them on to the park and they would have done it themselves. But they have the intelligence to absorb all I tell them and to apply it on the field. Every man knows his job.

'Berwick have given me my chance in management and I'm grateful. It's what I've worked towards. I've been to all the courses I could in England. I've served my time all right – and now I've got the chance to put a lot of what I've learned into practice.'

At a football-related function after the victory, a Berwick player, slightly inebriated, met Wallace and his wife on a staircase and shouted, 'How's it goin' Jock?' It is said that Wallace laid him cold with a swift jab square on the jaw and once he had recovered the big man looked him straight in the eye and growled, 'Boss, aye. Mr

Wallace, aye. Sir, aye, but Jock, never!' The player involved had faced Rangers on the historic day – and soon knew who was boss.

But the players were rewarded by a Berwick director, who paid for them to travel to Wembley for Scotland's famous 3-2 win over England. While down south, the Wee Gers also took part in their first ever friendly match with an English League club, Southend United. The party also visited a nightclub and on trying to gain entry, a bouncer refused admission to one of the younger players. Wallace went chin-to-chin with the officious club steward and growled 'He's wi' me, okay.' The steward stepped aside.

A steady flow of congratulatory messages from all over the world arrived at Shielfield. One of the first letters of congratulation was from the Rangers FC Supporters' Association, which included the words, 'There is no denying the result was a tremendous disappointment to us, but we do not in any way grudge you a well-deserved victory, and wish you the very best of luck in future rounds.'

The following Saturday, Rangers dropped strikers Jim Forrest and George McLean and thumped Hearts 5-1 at Ibrox, with young 'Willie' Jardine making a big impression. Berwick, meanwhile, confidently travelled to Clydebank and won 4-2 – without Jock Wallace. The inspirational player-boss was in Edinburgh, spying on Scottish Cup opponents Hibs.

When the big day arrived, more than a dozen supporters' buses – and a trainload of black-and-gold-clad fans – made the relatively simple journey north to Easter Road for the fourth-round tie, and once again, Wallace's wonders fought valiantly against supposedly superior opponents, although photographic evidence would show that they were robbed of at least a replay.

With 30,000 fans in the ground, and 12 minutes on the clock, Ken Dowd hit a shot which Hibs keeper Thomson Allan clawed out to apparent safety – although pics showed the ball had clearly crossed the line. One could feel the agony of 5,000 travelling supporters as the referee rejected the protests of the Berwick players. It was a cruel twist of fate, and another arrived three minutes before the break when Jim Scott scored the only goal of the tie – with the aid of a massive deflection.

Wallace enjoyed an afternoon of sheer brilliance, culminating in a penalty save from Scott. While the big keeper calmly moved several rolls of toilet paper from his goalmouth, Scott waited impatiently, and then looked on in agony as the master of mind games dived to push the ball to safety.

Berwick left Edinburgh with a bumper cheque for £2,650 and continued to do well in the Second Division. They finished tenth, and lost just four of their last 18 games. Wallace had put them on the map.

Rangers lost the league to Celtic but reached the final of the European Cup Winners' Cup, where they were unfortunate to lose to Bayern Munich in Nuremberg on the last day in May.

The following season, 1968/69, Berwick were handicapped by a spate of injuries and misfortune and, despite the remarkable consistency of Wallace in goal, the team definitely underachieved. Ken Bowron returned to the fold and while managing 20 goals, didn't quite seem the player who had graced Shielfield four years previous.

One player who did prove something of a success was Mike Harris, signed from Wallace's previous club Hereford, although when the Wee Gers went two months without scoring a home goal, it was clear where the problems lay. Wallace signed the prolific Eric Tait from East of Scotland League side Coldstream, and said, 'He has more shots at goal than the rest of the players put together.'

But while Tait would go on to become a real hero of the Berwick faithful, Wallace wasn't around to see the fruits of his last ever signing, as he moved on to become a coach at Hearts. He was replaced at Berwick by Harry Melrose, a former Scottish Cup-winning player with Dunfermline Athletic. For Wallace, though, he was moving up the chain of command in Scottish football, although his new life at Tynecastle would be relatively short.

Berwick revisited

As January came to a close in 1978, exactly 11 years after Berwick had rocked Scottish football with 'that' 1-0 success, Rangers were faced with another daunting trip over the border. And with a real touch of irony, Wallace returned as Rangers manager – with Dave Smith, one of the Gers' fall guys of 1967, in the opposing dug-out. Such was the interest in the tie that 600 police officers were drafted in from all over the north of England, while inside a packed Shielfield, mounted police were on duty to marshal the 10,500 crowd.

One player who sampled the atmosphere on both occasions was Rangers pivot Colin Jackson – and he recalled the fear in the Rangers squad in the build-up to the 1978 return. He said, 'While Jock was now boss at Ibrox there was still a great deal of nerves around as the 1967 result would never be forgotten regardless of what happened in the second game.

'I was only a 20-year-old travelling reserve at the time of the first match but never got to see the end of the game. I had to accompany Willie Johnston to hospital, after big Jock had clattered into him in the box. I remember taking stick at the hospital from staff when news filtered through that Berwick had knocked us out.

'When I returned to the ground, Jock and his players were going ballistic, but the atmosphere in our dressing room couldn't have been more different, and nobody, from the manager Scot Symon down to the players, could ever have imagined how that result would come back to haunt us for many years to come. John Greig and I were the only two survivors from the first game and were probably the most concerned running out at Shielfield for the second match.'

But it was 'Bomber' Jackson who eased the pressure with two headed goals in the first half and while Ian Smith cut the deficit for the battling Borderers, Derek Johnstone headed a third. Jackson, however, was stunned when the Wee Gers pulled it back to 3-2.

He recalled, 'I looked at big John and said, "here we go again". But Derek got us out of jail with another brilliant header. Looking back we never actually looked like losing although all the publicity and hype definitely affected a number of our younger players.'

And the final word to Wallace on a chapter that is now officially closed. 'After the match in 1967, Scot Symon knocked on our dressing room door and said, "Is your groundsman about?" I quickly showed him through to Dick Dunn, and Symon said to him, "Your park played well," and he turned to me and said, "And so did your team." To me that proved he was a class act.'

4

Hearts And Minds

WALLACE turned up at Tynecastle for his first day at work desperate to show what he could do in the cut and thrust of the top flight. The Edinburgh side were hovering around mid-table and manager John Harvey reckoned big Jock's impressive apprenticeship at Shielfield Park had earned him the move.

Wallace was assistant to Harvey and responsible for training, although he wouldn't be taking up his seat in the dug-out for a few weeks, as he was still managing Berwick. The unusual arrangement was set to stay in place until the Wee Gers' involvement in the Scottish Cup had come to an end.

The committed coach would put the Hearts players through their paces at morning and afternoon sessions before switching to Victoria Park, home of junior side Newtongrange Star, where he trained his part-time Berwick players hard two evenings a week. He was also a regular attendee at board meetings in Berwick on a Monday night. It was in the capital, though, where players such as Roald Jensen and Donald Ford were training as if their very lives depended on it. Wallace, then 33, took his first-team stars straight to the gym at Redford Barracks and gave them their first serious work-out in weeks. When he emerged from the army barracks, he said, 'I didn't want to hammer the lads too much this morning. After all, at this stage of the season they ought to be fit enough.'

Wallace added, 'I've several ideas of my own which I want to put into practice, not only in training but in coaching as well. But I'll wait a bit. Let's face it, I've only been here a couple of hours!'

Wallace's arrival allowed Harvey to concentrate on other matters, although he said, 'I'll continue to pick the team, of course, so obviously I'll need to remain in the thick of things. But with regards to training, coaching and tactics, Jock has a free hand. He will dictate where, when and how the players train and will be assisted by John Cumming.'

For his second day at training, Wallace stepped up the routine for his new players, who emerged from Redford Barracks complaining of exhaustion. Wallace trotted out straight behind them, and said, 'At the moment they are having things easy. In a month's time, once they are broken in, I'll start to work them really hard.'

While Hearts were at Ibrox at the end of Wallace's first week at Tynecastle, he was 'down the coast' at Ayr with his Berwick side. Both lost 2-0 and next up for the Wee Gers was their Scottish Cup trip to Pittodrie. Wallace was given the lowdown on Aberdeen from within when Hearts beat them 3-2 in a league match, with centre-forward Donald Ford outstanding.

Beforehand, though, he certainly wouldn't have won any popularity contests at Tynecastle when he insisted on putting the players through a punishing training routine – just hours before they went for a game of golf as a reward for beating the Dons! He said, 'I really put them through the hoop. A few of them were complaining but I think they are now coming round to my way of thinking and will be in great shape for Saturday's tough cup tie at Dens Park.'

But the Edinburgh side suffered a blow on the eve of the Dundee match when skipper Jim Townsend, who had been out for four months due to an ankle injury, picked up a dose of flu, although his absence didn't stop Hearts edging through against Dundee by the odd goal in three. Manager Harvey paid tribute to Wallace's part in the victory, and said, 'I feel the boys are beginning to benefit tremendously from Jock's tough training regime. They were still going all out at the end of the game and I think we will be even stronger when the next round comes along.'

Meanwhile, Wallace took his Borders minnows to Pittodrie and one man still smarting from his last brush with the big man was former Rangers striker Jim Forrest, who had been made chief scapegoat for his side's 1967 loss in Berwick. But the game finished 3-0 to Aberdeen and Forrest, as expected, scored twice. However, the former jungle fighter enjoyed a slice of good fortune when an early free kick hit the bar and cannoned off his head to safety. Full-time training told in the end as the Dons grabbed two late goals to seal victory.

After the match, Wallace said his goodbyes to Berwick players and staff, and looked ahead to his job at Tynecastle. Meanwhile, Hearts' reward for a job well done at Dens Park was a trip to Ibrox to face Rangers in the next round, which meant Wallace was in charge for the club's next match – against Celtic at Parkhead – while Harvey took the opportunity to cast a beady eye over Rangers. Ironically it would be the first time Wallace had seen his side in action, as he had been off playing for Berwick each Saturday.

Harvey said, 'Appointing Jock has been a dream come true. I've been looking for the right man for a while now, and just to illustrate how badly I needed an assistant, I was forced to send my older son Alec to spy on Dundee at Shawfield. Fortunately his report helped us win the game. Now that Jock is full time, we can get down to some real work. Although I will continue to pick the team Jock and I will have regular conferences where we can thrash out various viewpoints.'

But taking charge of a top-division team for the first time was anything but fun as Hearts were thrashed 5-0 at Parkhead. The pitch may have resembled a quagmire but it was stick-in-the-mud winger Jimmy Johnstone who ran the Hearts defence ragged to leave Wallace nursing a thumping headache. Wallace would no doubt have been impressed by Celtic's incredible stamina and strength and that was something he hoped to add to Hearts' woefully weak armoury in the weeks and months ahead.

He made sure his players were straight back on to a snowbound Tynecastle for training first thing on Monday morning. They had a Scottish Cup tie to prepare for and his routine read: training session followed by a straight-talking 'pep' chat, more training, a light lunch and then a trip to the movies. Although it was a film with a difference, as the coach had arranged for the squad to head through to the BBC studios in Glasgow to watch a re-run of their humbling 5-0 defeat at Celtic Park – as well as the previous week's victory over Dundee.

Wallace said, 'For the first hour against Celtic we gave as good as we got, then Celtic changed their tactics and we made mistakes. I've had a chat with the lads, though, and I think some of the despondency has been lifted.'

Wallace was a firm believer in football psychology and made sure the Dundee match was shown last, 'to ensure his players left the studios in a positive frame of mind'.

Hearts full-back Davie Holt gave an insight into how the players felt about their new coach. He said, 'There is a tremendous spirit at Tynecastle at the moment. Since his arrival we have learned to take each game as it comes, and on its own merits. For instance, last Saturday's defeat at Celtic is in the past, and all we are interested in now is beating Rangers. That is the way we are thinking.'

Donald Ford, a chartered accountant, added, 'It's quite amazing how confident the boys are of beating Rangers, and I think a lot of this stems from Jock Wallace. He's an astonishing character who seems to have the happy knack of getting players into the right frame of mind. In the space of a few short weeks he has everyone on the staff fully convinced that we are professionals in the fullest sense of the word.'

Like most Scottish Cup ties that weekend, the Ibrox match was a victim of the big freeze, which held Scotland in a vice-like grip. The thaw arrived just as quickly, and the tie was cancelled due to a waterlogged pitch. Back came the freeze, and Hearts' league match against Dundee was called off the following Saturday.

With training on conventional surfaces also ruled out, Wallace took the players to Portobello Beach for a session, and Holt said, 'It was really wonderful. It was bitterly cold at first but when the sun came out it got quite warm. We had a first-class work-out.'

With no game for three weeks, Harvey and Wallace decided to take their players to Largs for the weekend in the hope that their scheduled league match with Kilmarnock would go ahead and, if not, they would at least be able to train on the 'milder' west coast.

The match against Killie was one of just two top flight matches to beat the freeze – although Hearts couldn't beat their opponents, and lost 1-0 to remain ninth in the table. Hearts then lost 2-0 at Ibrox in their Scottish Cup tie. It was the end of the dream for another season. A 5-1 defeat at Partick Thistle followed and Harvey and Wallace vowed to sort their team out.

Hearts wound up their league programme with a 2-1 win over St Mirren at Tynecastle, a result which pushed them up to sixth in the table, but still almost 20 points shy of league winners Celtic. Still, a positive end to the season represented mild success and the management duo could begin to prepare in earnest for the following season.

The new campaign kicked off with a friendly against Carlisle United at Brunton Park, but it turned into a nightmare as the English Second Division outfit won 5-0. In fact, a quick peek at Hearts' next two warm-up games, against high-flying Newcastle and Tottenham, and one could have been forgiven for thinking that the players were going to need all of Wallace's positive psychology in the coming weeks.

When the players turned up for training on the Monday morning, they were locked in the 'tea room' for 90 minutes while Wallace told them exactly what he thought of their performance against the Cumbrian side. It seemed to work and the players were back on song for the midweek match against Fairs Cup holders Newcastle United and were unfortunate to slip to a single-goal defeat.

The final preparation game – and arguably the toughest – was the visit of Spurs to Tynecastle. Tottenham included the likes of Jimmy Greaves, Alan Mullery, Martin Chivers, Alan Gilzean and Pat Jennings. But it was Jim Townsend and Roald Jensen who stole the show as Hearts claimed a deserved 1-1 draw against the London giants.

Hearts were then hit by a number of injuries on the eve of their opening League Cup match against Dundee United, although character was in no short supply as they ground out a 3-2 win at Tannadice after being two down at the break. Were the fruits of a tough close-season paying instant dividends? At the end of the match, Wallace congratulated each player individually and all 11 would have appreciated the stamina and strength they had shown to come back from a seemingly impossible situation.

Granted, Hearts fans brought up in the halcyon days of free-flowing football might not have approved of the manner in which the capital side had eked out the win, but Wallace was operating in an era when results were king, and performance played second fiddle.

But when they lost their opening league match to Morton, the players were booed off the field. Harvey was disgusted by his team's performance, and said, 'We were disgraceful and I can scarcely recall us playing anything of value in the game. I could rectify the situation today if I could go out and buy but we simply don't have the cash.'

They won their next two, but lost the one that mattered – the Edinburgh derby at Tynecastle, which helped Hibs move top of the table. Hibs played the better football but also won the physical battle and were described as having 'too much fire in their bellies for Hearts to handle'.

The following week, it was the Hearts players who had too much fire in their bellies as the police were called to give the referee an escort off the pitch after the Edinburgh players had fought out a 0-0 draw with Ayr United at Somerset Park. The tackles were flying in thick and fast and Hearts keeper Jim Cruickshank was the target for missile throwers.

Several mediocre performances followed, before Hearts pulled the big one out the bag – a dazzling 2-0 win at Celtic Park. The intro to the match report said, 'This was without doubt Hearts' best display of the season. They tackled the league champions like a navvy tackles lunch, showed no respect for the Parkhead display cabinet, and never let up in a game which had the Celtic fans fidgeting in their seats all afternoon.' Goals by Jensen and Ford clinched the win, which left Hearts just four points adrift of leaders Hibs.

Harvey and Wallace were given enormous credit for the manner of the victory at Parkhead. They knew it wasn't about Celtic having one eye on an impending European tie against Benfica. Hearts were the better side and the better organised of the combatants. There was praise for the discipline of the defence and the way they broke forward with menace whenever the opportunity arose – and there was hope that the Edinburgh side had finally turned the corner.

Two of the best players on the park were Jensen and Rene Moller, but Wallace revealed that he had noticed certain flaws in their game. He said, 'Both players have been working overtime in the past month or so. Moller has been coming back in the afternoons to improve his heading and shooting, while we kept Jensen away from the ball for several weeks to concentrate solely on track work to improve his speed and physical condition. We are as fit as any team and feel that we will be at our best now that the heavy going is here.'

Meanwhile, trouble was brewing at Ibrox and manager Davie White was sacked in the wake of catastrophic home and away European defeats by Polish side Gornik Zabrze, with Willie Waddell appointed boss. However, Waddell decided to overlook what was technically his first game in charge – against Hearts at Tynecastle – to take in the corresponding reserve match at Ibrox.

And what a game he missed. Hearts scored in 40 seconds, Rangers equalised on the stroke of half-time and grabbed the winner late on, but in between there was action aplenty. They called it the 'Battle of the Brawn', as 'bodies littered the playing surface at regular intervals due to as many off-the-ball clashes as on it'.

Despite the defeat, Hearts had proved they had the stomach for a fight and showed the exact same qualities seven days later when they faced Morton at Cappielow. Outclassed by the Greenock men for the first hour, they looked dead and buried when Morton scored a second goal, without reply. With ten minutes remaining, and on a pitch more suited to mud wrestling than football, Morton visibly wilted and Hearts scored three times to claim both points. It was a victory that had Wallace pumping his fist in the air when the referee sounded the final whistle.

Hearts then thumped Airdrie 5-0 – with Donald Ford scoring twice – and beat Dunfermline to move up to sixth spot. Dundee United were next to fall, at Tannadice, as the Jambos' bandwagon gathered momentum. Teenager Andy Lynch was the latest player to emerge from the production line and his late winner in Dundee showed that the players were capable of going the distance.

By the end of January 1970, Hearts had extended their unbeaten run to seven matches, which moved them up to fourth, on the cusp of a European slot – and with a squad that had an average age of just 22. When Harvey had taken over at the club three years previous, he had put a four-year plan in place, and was well on schedule to getting Hearts back into the big time, with his able deputy at his side, of course.

As the season drew to a close, the main battle, in the capital, was for third place. Hearts kept on winning, but so too did Hibs, and as we entered March, the Easter Road side held a slight advantage. Celtic were well in front at the top, with Rangers in second. Hearts were certainly the most improved side in the country since the turn of the year, and much of it was down to a steady defence, which had conceded just two goals in ten games. In front of keeper Jim Cruickshank stood Dave Clunie, Alan Anderson, Eddie Thomson and Peter Oliver.

But one match – a midweek encounter at Ibrox – proved a microcosm of Hearts' entire season. Three goals down to a Rangers side who had lost three games in a row for the first time since 1926, they were awful for the first 80 minutes. Then, Ernie Winchester scored, Jim Irvine snatched a second and only some fine work by Peter McCloy ensured Hearts would travel east with nothing to show for their efforts.

The Tynecastle side were then charged with trying to prevent Celtic clinching the title in Edinburgh. No mean feat but while Cruickshank put up the shutters on Jimmy Johnstone and co, a dropped point by Rangers at Ibrox against struggling Airdrie saw Celtic crowned champions – and the champagne corks popped within earshot of Wallace and the Hearts changing room.

Hearts kept alive their slim hopes of an Inter-Cities Fairs Cup place with a battling 1-0 win at Aberdeen, courtesy of a Winchester goal. The player, who had walked out on Aberdeen to sample soccer in the US, had the last laugh after being taunted throughout by the home fans. He said, 'I would have given my bonus to get this result.'

But disaster struck when Dundee visited Tynecastle for the final league game of the season. A win for the home side would clinch a return to Europe but Dundee left with a 3-1 victory, and with it went Hearts' chance of continental action. Rather worryingly for Harvey and Wallace was that all three Dundee goals came late on.

Manager Harvey vowed to track down and sign a proven goalscorer in time for the following campaign, but it was a search he would tackle alone, as on Thursday 16 April, his assistant Jock Wallace quit his post at Tynecastle to join Willie Waddell's backroom team at Ibrox. In a week that saw Celtic reach their second European Cup Final – at the expense of Leeds United – Waddell was desperate to wrestle back power from Jock Stein, and saw Wallace as an integral part of his team.

Twenty-four years after first travelling through by train from his home on the east coast to watch his beloved Rangers, Wallace became one of the lucky few who get to make the transition from supporter to employee.

5

The Promised Land

FOR Jock Wallace, the road to Ibrox began in October 1969, when Rangers took on leading Polish side Gornik Zabrze in the second round of the European Cup Winners' Cup. Typically, the Scottish press expected Rangers to brush aside a team crammed full of internationals, and the weight of expectation landed on the shoulders of relatively inexperienced manager Davie White.

The away tie meant a flight to Warsaw, then a four and a half hour journey to Katowice. The city of Zabrze is just 13 miles from Katowice, in the southern Polish district of Silesia. Katowice has an international airport but as the foundations were built upon minefields, the airport was a no-go area for large aircraft.

The local paper, *Trybuna Ludu*, cranked up the heat ahead of the match by suggesting that Rangers fans were 'dangerous'. They wrote of fighting after a Scottish Cup tie against Celtic and how three people had died after suffering heart attacks, with 40 more injured. All a bit rich considering three Gornik players were serving suspended sentences for attacking a referee during a Polish League game!

At the beginning of October, former Gers midfield powerhouse Harold Davis had returned to the club – where he had played for eight years – to take charge of the youth system, under the tutelage of assistant manager Willie Thornton. Davis had managed Queen's Park for four years.

Prior to the first leg against Gornik in the Slaski Stadium, gaffer White, who was just 36, said, 'I have a feeling this will be the hardest match I've had since becoming manager.' Prophetic words indeed.

In fact, the Gers boss was at the centre of a food storm when the party arrived at their posh Katowice hotel. On the advice of Manchester United, Rangers had taken their own provisions and chef – Jimmy Martin, brother of Rangers keeper Norrie – and as they unloaded crates of food from the team bus, the hotel manager refused to allow them use of the kitchen. White immediately threatened to leave the hotel and the manager backed down. It proved a recipe for disaster, though, as Rangers were outplayed in the Slaski and despite a valuable away goal by Orjan Persson, they lost 3-1, with a killer third in the final minute by the inspirational Wlodek Lubanski.

The day before the return tie, Willie Henderson and Jim Baxter failed to show for training after sleeping in and both were disciplined by White. With John Greig a major injury worry, White, a qualified draughtsman, didn't have his problems to seek.

Greig, Baxter and Henderson played in the second leg but the match soon turned into White's own private hell. Baxter gave Rangers the lead in 18 minutes and 70,000 supporters started to believe, but an 18-minute second-half spell, in which they lost three goals, sent them crashing out of Europe before Christmas.

The following morning, the former Clyde boss, just two years in the job, was relieved of his position by directors John Lawrence, Matt Taylor, George Brown, David Hope and Ian McLaren. White, on £4,000 a year but operating without a contract, sped from the ground in his bronze Ford Capri to his Mount Vernon home. Thornton was immediately appointed caretaker manager, and one contemporary journalist suggested that Thornton would be installed as boss without delay. Others reckoned Dunfermline manager George Farm and Aberdeen's Eddie Turnbull were the front-runners for the position.

But Thornton was merely keeping the seat warm and Rangers were searching for only their fifth manager in 98 years. Despite this, the reporter insisted that Thornton was the man for the job, and said, 'The guessing game on the new Rangers manager can cease forthwith. The man who picks up the pieces from White is already in office – Willie Thornton!' He then named Davis as assistant.

At the beginning of December, Waddell was announced as the new boss. 'Deedle' had been a star player at Rangers, before moving to Kilmarnock as manager and guiding them to the first division title. He then retired from football to become a sports writer. He was 49 when he accepted the top job at Ibrox and confessed, 'I would never have returned to football for any club other than Rangers.'

And perhaps as a nod to those who suggested that neither Davie White, nor his predecessor, Scot Symon, had been in complete control at Rangers – and that both managers had altered team selections at the behest of the Ibrox board – he added, 'I have the conditions I wanted for the job.'

Following the appointment, the smile returned to the Rangers man in the street. Everyone was upbeat. Surely Waddell was the man to restore the glory days to this slumbering old giant. Some suggested that he would have to lay down the law in the Ibrox dressing room, but any player worth his salt would soon know who was boss.

Waddell announced that Thornton would be staying on as assistant manager and the day after a second XI match against Hearts, he contacted the secretary of the Rangers Supporters' Association and asked him to invite a delegate from each supporters' club to Ibrox for a meeting. The manager laid out his blueprint in front of the fans and asked them to buy into it. It was a shrewd move from a shrewd man.

His next task was to get the team ticking again and he opted to use John Greig in a more advanced midfield role, next to Baxter. Waddell said, 'I would like a set-up with Davie Smith as sweeper and John Greig in a more forward midfield role. The urgency of Greig in such a position could prove a great asset to this club.' That was the way of it in the coming weeks. Waddell knew that Celtic were favourites to win the title, and was already planning for the future.

But as the campaign fizzled out, and apathy began to kick in among the Rangers support, Waddell's ruthless revolution began in earnest. In the middle of April 1970 he axed his entire backroom team. While many viewed Waddell's move as extreme, it showed the former wing king's absolute determination to follow his success as a player with similar results in the dug-out.

Out went chief trainer Lawrie Smith, physio Davie Kinnear and Davis. For the latter, it was a major blow as he had only been back at Ibrox a little over five months. At the time, he said, 'It was a real shock to us all. After training, Mr Waddell read out the statement that dismissed us. I am annoyed that I was coaxed into coming to Rangers from Queen's Park as I was happy there. Now five months later I have been sacked.'

Kinnear had been connected with Rangers for 26 years – 12 as a player – and said, 'It was a real shock when Mr Waddell told me that he wanted to re-organise his coaching staff.'

Waddell then set about replacing the deposed employees with gusto. The first move he made was his most significant. He said, 'There has been a major re-organisation of the Ibrox training staff. Jock Wallace, the assistant manager of Hearts, will take over as head trainer and coach, and an announcement will be made soon regarding the appointment of an assistant trainer and a physio.'

Wallace was overjoyed at the appointment. The 34-year-old, who lived in Tranent, East Lothian, said, 'I can't describe how happy I am. This is a great job, a great challenge and I can hardly wait to get started. I know I was an assistant manager at Hearts, and now I'm just a trainer/coach with Rangers – but when you get the chance to join such a great club titles don't matter. I'm very much looking forward to working with Willie Waddell and Willie Thornton.'

Wallace, who held an English FA coaching certificate, added, 'Nobody can deny that Rangers are a great club, despite their comparative lack of success recently, and what I'm looking forward to is regular European competition.'

The duo won their first piece of silverware – the Scottish Second XI Cup – against Aberdeen, before Wallace flew out to Amsterdam with the Rangers 'babes' for the prestigious Insulinde Cup, at the home of Ajax. Rangers were drawn in the same section as Bayern Munich plus Dutch sides Ado and Go Ahead Deventer. The squad included kids such as Derek Parlane (freshly signed from Queen's Park), Alfie Conn and Graham Fyfe. The youngsters beat Bayern Munich but lost 2-0 to Deventer to miss out on a final place against Ajax.

In the final league match of the season, Rangers lost to Morton at Ibrox, although Waddell seemed more occupied with what lay ahead than the embarrassing defeat. He promised his team would have 'a right go' the following season, words aimed at the many thousands who had deserted the Ibrox terracing rather than the 15,000 who had bothered to turn up for the game. He added, 'In recent games we have experimented with young players and I have learned a lot – but I am not sad to see the back of this season.'

At the end of May, another name was added to the Rangers backroom team. Stan Anderson was just 31, and had been playing for Clyde after a free transfer from Ibrox earlier in his career. Anderson was installed as assistant trainer, and his duties included working with the reserves and the first team, under the guidance of Wallace. He immediately gave up his job as a clerk with Lanarkshire County Council, and said, 'It's a great challenge for me, especially as I was freed by the club after three years as a player.'

But the management team suffered their first blow when Conn was injured playing for Scotland against France in a European youth tournament. A week later the 18-year-old attended hospital as a precaution and x-rays showed up a hairline fracture just above the ankle. The Prestonpans teenager said, 'I got a bad kick during the match against France but thought it was just a nasty bump. I got the surprise of my life when the doctor told me it was fractured.'

When Waddell allowed Dennis Setterington to join Falkirk for £10,000, it was the cue to call up 'S' form signing Derek Johnstone into the first-team squad. Waddell said, 'We had young Johnstone with us in Holland for the youth tournament and he looked good.'

Next to declare his intention to leave was 1966 Scottish Cup Final hero Kai Johansen, who had just bought a bar in Majorca. He also had business interests in Glasgow but was keen on a permanent move to the Balearics.

But there was good news for Waddell and Wallace when they completed their backroom team with the acquisition of physio Tom Craig. The former Clyde trainer and physiotherapist said, 'I'm delighted. I applied for the job when the vacancy arose and kept my fingers crossed throughout the process. I'm sorry to leave Clyde but an opportunity like this arises just once in a lifetime.'

In the middle of June, Waddell jetted off to sunnier climes. For the boss, it was destination Majorca, and an opportunity to re-charge the batteries for the season ahead. Holidays weren't for Wallace, though, and he passed up the opportunity for a stint on the beach to remain in Glasgow, and the Albion training ground in particular. He was busy putting players such as Alex MacDonald and Colin Stein through their paces. Press-ups and abdominal work-outs were just some of the 'pleasures' enjoyed by the players. Others, including full-back Sandy Jardine, had been sent through to Edinburgh to work with a specialist sprint coach.

But when Wallace did allow himself a foreign break, it was to Berlin for a coaching seminar organised by the West German FA. Before flying out, he said, 'The close season so far has been the ideal opportunity for the players to get to know me, and vice versa. I like to vary the training programmes. There is no point in the players turning up at the Albion knowing exactly what they're doing. Monotony is a bad thing in any job and for highly trained athletes it's even worse.

'This course will give me new approaches and I will hopefully be able to utilise them when we get down to work again before the start of the season. In fact, the ideas I learn could be put into practice for the first time in the same country, for we play two friendlies, against Kaiserslautern and Hamburg, at the end of July. The course is really something. There is plenty of practical work, tactics and injury remedies to learn and, at night, the coaches get together to share ideas.'

On arriving back in Scotland, Wallace trained on his own at Ibrox for a week, running up and down the concrete steps of the enclosure several times a day while lugging a heavy medicine ball. With big Jock it was never a case of 'do as I say, not as I do'. He wasn't nicknamed the 'Commander-in-Chief' for nothing.

He had his training schedule typed out and on the manager's desk a fortnight before the players were due back from their holidays. And after two weeks of sunshine, they had a rude awakening. They were told to pile into a minibus – destination unknown. The bus was bound for the east coast of Scotland, Gullane to be more specific, a town known as the home of British Open course, Muirfield. It would soon become infamous as the home of 'Murder Hill'!

When the players arrived at the imposing dunes, they could hardly believe their eyes as someone had preceded them and staked out a huge section of beach with little marker poles. Running up and down the dunes was probably the toughest conditioning work the players had ever encountered, although it was this type of work that made Herb Elliott the greatest ever miler.

The players soon realised that thigh muscles were more resilient and better developed and that there were smaller waist sizes in trousers all round.

One player who missed out on this brutal coaching regime was Davie Smith. The elegant sweeper had broken his leg in a league match at Kilmarnock in April and was touch and go for the start of the new season.

No rest for the remainder, though, and in mid-July, the new management team placed each player under strict medical supervision. A team of doctors and medical experts ran the rule over the squad during a visit to the Albion and returned once a week until the start of the new season.

It was all part of the grand plan to have a standard of fitness never before seen at the club. The programme involved a complete investigation of the past medical history of each player as well as a check on blood pressure, pulse rate and other physical factors. What is a common feature of pre-season nowadays was as common then as goal-line technology. But at Ibrox, times were changing.

Waddell's efforts to restore Rangers' flagging prestige were developing along clear-cut and well-defined lines. First, every player was given a chance to prove himself. Next, the manager experimented with the younger players, before a clearout saw the likes of Baxter and others leave the club. Waddell and his trusted lieutenant were raising the bar and throwing down the gauntlet to rivals Celtic, who had dominated the Scottish game for far too long.

The players breathed a huge sigh of relief, if they had any puff left, when the time came for training to stop and the football to start. First up for the new management team was a match against Hamburg, the opening game on their two-match tour of West Germany – but it proved disastrous for striker Colin Stein, who was sent off for the sixth time in his career. The dismissal was a complete mystery, but referee Klaus Wolf later accused Stein of punching a Hamburg player. Rangers lost 3-1.

There was further controversy in the second match, against Kaiserslautern, when 18-year-old Kenny Watson was sent packing in a real roughhouse match at the Betzenberg Stadium. Watson had only been on the field nine minutes when he tackled fiery Yugoslavian Hosic, who went to ground as if shot by a sniper. Sending Watson off was the only piece of decisive action taken by ref Herr Ditmer on an evening full of rash challenges.

Andy Penman was on target for Gers in a 1-1 draw in a match watched by a large and noisy Armed Forces contingent. Henderson, Johnston and Penman returned to Scotland with injuries sustained in the match.

En route to Glasgow, Rangers stopped off in London for a friendly with Tottenham. Greig returned to the starting line-up but even the skipper's drive and determination couldn't prevent Rangers losing 2-0. There was a touch of good news after the game for Sandy Jardine, when he learned that wife Shona had given birth to a healthy girl, Nicola Jane, in Edinburgh's Simpson Memorial Hospital.

A week after the Spurs game, Rangers played Celtic in the Glasgow Cup Final at Hampden. Celtic had dominated the domestic game and Waddell was keen to draw the first blood of the new campaign. He turned out his first XI, while counterpart Jock Stein played several youngsters. Sadly, it was another demoralising night for the Ibrox side as a double by Tommy Gemmell helped Celtic win 3-1.

After four matches, Rangers were still searching for their first win, and Waddell and Wallace were facing a real test of their credentials, just months into their Ibrox reign.

But there was no need to panic and after Colin Stein scored the first goal of the new domestic season – after just two minutes in a 4-1 League Cup rout of Dunfermline at Ibrox – Rangers dropped just a single point in qualifying for the quarter-finals, which included a 6-0 romp at East End Park.

The Light Blues opened their league campaign at St Mirren, and there were few winners in a no-score draw. Waddell and Wallace had flown to Germany to watch Fairs Cup first round opponents Bayern Munich in action against Borussia Dortmund. They missed the match due to travel snags and touched down at Glasgow Airport just 45 minutes before the match with Saints. With Love Street less than a mile from the airport, they made it to the ground in time for the kick-off.

The first Old Firm league game of the campaign, at Parkhead in front of 73,000, was won by Celtic, but there was scant consolation in the reserve fixture at Ibrox as goals by youngsters Derek Parlane and Derek Johnstone secured a narrow victory.

The following midweek, Rangers were unfortunate to lose narrowly to Bayern in Germany despite having four Euro debutants in McCloy, Miller, Fyfe and Conn. Gerd Muller rattled the normally mild-mannered Ronnie McKinnon before the match when he said, 'McKinnon is my lucky mascot. I'd rather play against him every night of the week than against Billy McNeill.' But Muller was hardly given a kick of the ball against McKinnon and Colin Jackson, who were outstanding in Munich.

Stein, who had been substituted in Germany for 'not sticking to his job', was still in the bad books when Rangers hosted Cowdenbeath in a league match a couple of days later. Waddell promoted 16-year-old Derek Johnstone to the first team and he responded by scoring a debut double.

Unfortunately, the Light Blues could only manage a 1-1 draw at home to Bayern, with back-in-favour Stein scoring, and crashed out on a 2-1 aggregate, but there were no scapegoats sought and Waddell, who knew his team was in a period of transition, praised his players for their effort. Contrast that to the German attitude when Bayern threatened to pull out of the competition as they felt it was hampering their chances of winning the West German championship.

Rangers were massive underdogs before the 1970 League Cup Final at Hampden. Celtic were top of the league, on course for another title, and everyone expected Rangers' four and a half year trophy drought to continue. But this Gers side hadn't read the form book. Celtic won the toss – and precious little after it. McKinnon and Jackson were outstanding and one nod of the head from young Johnstone took the trophy to Govan. Celtic's best player on the day was keeper Evan Williams.

After the game, and with the Rangers party heading for the team bus, Wallace carefully shepherded Johnstone away from the press, but the teenager said, 'I felt great when that ball hit the net. It was brilliant.' Wallace chipped in, 'Aye, but what about the ones you missed?'

Jock Wallace would coach and manage many talented players over a long period of time but when interviewed at length many years later, he revealed that arguably the best player he had ever worked with was Johnstone. In true Wallace style, though, after building up the versatile player, he gently let him down again, by saying, 'He could only play in two positions, centre-forward and centre-half, as he didn't have the pace to play anywhere else!'

Wallace had first set eyes on the player at a youth tournament in Amsterdam and from the moment Johnstone threw himself in front of a defender's boot to get in a header, he had scored a winner with his boss. Here was a player that knew no fear.

When Wallace suggested to manager Waddell that Johnstone should play against Celtic in the League Cup Final, Waddell looked hard at him before replying, 'But he's only a kid.' Wallace said, 'That's right, but he's the only player we've got who will beat McNeill in the air.'

When Johnstone scored the only goal of the match with a fantastic header from a Willie Johnston cross, and squeezed between McNeill and Jim Craig to do so, Wallace's brave decision was vindicated. DJ would go on to score more than 230 goals for Rangers – the highest since the war – and only Ally McCoist has beaten that total to date.

However, after scoring the winning goal in the 1970 final, his career didn't so much go downhill, than down south. The player failed to turn up for the Gers' pre-season tour of Sweden. He had gone AWOL. Wallace and Waddell had a pow-wow on how best to handle the situation and on their return from Scandinavia, a few phone calls revealed that Johnstone had gone to London.

Wallace headed south, and said, 'When I got to the address I had been given I was told the young Scots lad would be across the road in the pub. The first person I saw at the bar was our stay-away striker. He was ordering drinks and when he saw me he almost collapsed. He stuttered, "What are you doing here?" I blasted back, "What in the hell are you doing here?" He was the colour of a laundered sheet by this time. I said, "If you're buying drinks, you can buy me a pint." He managed to blurt out, "But you don't drink pints. It's whisky, isn't it?" "Then you'd better make it a whisky," I said.'

Johnstone did as he was told and player and assistant manager talked into the wee small hours. Wallace became a guest in Johnstone's temporary lodgings and it soon became clear that the young goal machine was struggling to cope with his immediate thrust into the limelight. Becoming a well-known player so quickly with such a big club had proved difficult.

Wallace said, 'I told him we wanted him back at Ibrox and that if he had any problems he should tell me first. Johnstone returned to Ibrox and I suppose I was like a father to him in the years that followed. As a coach at that time I had to be close to the kids and that's why I recommended Derek to play against Celtic because I knew what he could do. Johnstone had a great career as a Rangers player and won every domestic honour. He was at centre-half in our European success in Barcelona and played and scored for his country. I was delighted when he was named Scotland's Player of the Year in 1978.'

Just weeks after the final, though, the only celebrations around were for the tenth anniversary of ITV soap *Coronation Street*. There was certainly nothing of the sort at Ibrox, where Rangers struggled to keep pace with league leaders Celtic and Aberdeen, who were in second place. The Light Blues were far too inconsistent to mount a serious challenge but despite that, crowds were well up on the previous season, with an average of more than 42,000 visiting Ibrox every other Saturday. Another pleasing statistic was that 9,000 were using the boys' gate regularly, which augured well for the future.

But the whole dynamic of Rangers Football Club changed at around 5pm on Saturday 2 January 1971, when instead of talking over the pros and cons of a 1-1 draw with Celtic at Ibrox, Wallace was helping the emergency services tend to scores of dead and injured Gers fans.

Just moments after the final whistle, the scene on stairway 13 was one of total carnage. Rangers had scored a late equaliser and one theory was that fans leaving the stadium had clambered back up the staircase to join in the celebrations and had met with a wall of supporters heading for the exit. That was dispelled as a myth at the fatal accident inquiry, which concluded, 'The downward pressure of the crowd above, forced other persons to fall or collapse on those who had fallen first and as the downward pressure continued, more and more persons were heaped upon those who had fallen or were pressed hard against them.'

Regardless of cause, 66 supporters lost their lives and the football world, and wider community, mourned this awful tragedy. Match statistics would forever show that both Jimmy Johnstone and Colin Stein had scored in the 89th minute, Johnstone first, but these paltry facts were lost in a sea of casualties that stretched medics and police to the absolute limit.

Moments after the tragic crush it was all hands on deck and everyone from experienced doctors to members of the public rolled up their sleeves to do what they could to help the injured. Wallace, Waddell and Celtic boss Jock Stein were among them and were seen tending to the wounded, acting as stretcher bearer or speaking to relatives looking for lost loved ones. It was undoubtedly the blackest day in Rangers' history and one that will never be forgotten.

Rangers had been due to fly to Spain for a friendly with Valencia straight after the Old Firm fixture, but the game was cancelled and the Spaniards immediately offered to play a benefit match at Ibrox.

The club had a 14-day break from football with the next match, at home to Dundee United, attracting just over 27,000. Wallace had taken the players to Gullane for a tough work-out in preparation for a match that saw Walter Smith play for United. After an immaculately-observed two-minute silence, Greig scored early for the Light Blues and the match finished 1-1. Plans were immediately drawn up for a Rangers/Celtic Select to play Scotland at Hampden to aid the Ibrox Disaster Fund.

At the beginning of April, Rangers and Hibs fought out a goalless draw at Hampden in the first of the two Scottish Cup semi-finals, a result and performance which led to Easter Road manager Dave Ewing describing Rangers as 'rubbish'. This less than complimentary remark could have been reserved for Ewing himself, after he signed his team sheet containing a player, Eric Stevenson, who wasn't even on the pitch. The discrepancy was noticed by eagle-eyed Wallace before manager Waddell brought it to the attention of referee Bill Mullen. The SFA called it a 'breach of competition rules', but Rangers did their talking on the park and won the replay 2-1.

In the league, Rangers gave up their struggle for third spot when they lost 2-0 to St Johnstone at Ibrox to fall four points behind the Perth side with just a solitary game to play. Saints' lethal partnership of Henry Hall and John Connolly did the damage.

To the season's finale and the sight of more than 100 injured fans at the showpiece Scottish Cup Final must have brought back awful memories for those involved in the Ibrox Disaster just a few months previous. There was terrible crushing in the Rangers end and the casualty department at the nearby Victoria Infirmary was hit by a stream of injured adults and children ferried there in a procession of ambulances. Two hundred people were also arrested as Johnstone earned Rangers a replay with a goal just minutes from time in front of more than 120,000 spectators.

Just over 100,000 turned up for the midweek replay and saw goals by Harry Hood and Lou Macari help Celtic lift the cup. One month after the match, Wallace still had the players in for training three times a week. It was all part of his master plan to ensure they would hit the ground running at the start of the following campaign. He said, 'It means that when we resume our training for the new season we won't be playing catch-up.'

6

Wallace And Vomit!

LOOK up the term Gullane sands in any football thesaurus and the list of alternatives is sure to include torture, suffering, anguish and pain, although perhaps cruelty is taking it just a bit too far! The sands are just 20 minutes from Wallace's home town of Wallyford but it wasn't until reading of the exploits of a certain Herb Elliott that he began to take more than a passing interest. An Australian runner, Elliott broke the world record for the 1,500 metres before going on to secure gold at the 1960 Olympic Games in Rome.

His Australian coach, Percy Cerutty, had devised a training regime to build up strength of leg, lung and character, so much so that it soon became the accepted training model for Aussie and New Zealand middle-distance runners. Wallace reasoned that what was good enough for an Olympic gold medallist was good enough for his players. Elliott had become a true champion by running up and down sand dunes.

Wallace had known all about Gullane, but not as a tool capable of transforming men into athletes. When he arrived in the Borders town of Berwick for his second stint with the Wee Gers, he decided to take the players to the seaside – although buckets and spades were left at home.

His players headed to Gullane for extra training in the lead-up to Berwick's famous win over Rangers in 1967, and when he moved on to Hearts, Gullane was the pre-season haunt of choice. So by the time he arrived at Ibrox, the former jungle fighter knew these dunes like the back of his hand.

The players who suffered – and threw up – called it 'Murder Hill'. They will never forget the ridiculous 65-degree sandy mounds where big Jock turned his Gers stars into machines. Wallace said, 'It was sheer torture to those attempting the run for the first time but it got players to a peak of fitness that I wanted, and the fittest player on the dunes was Willie Johnston.'

Johnston, known as 'Bud' to his team-mates, admitted that while 'enjoying' them would be the wrong way to describe his relationship with the sands, he wasn't in the slightest intimidated. He said, 'Big Jock was a great man, a good coach and an absolute fitness fanatic. He introduced us to the Gullane sands – and I loved it. It was easy. For me, Gullane was only about running up and down a hill, and I found that simple enough. It was the long stuff I didn't like. I didn't believe in running six 220s or three 400s. I wanted the short sharp stuff, and I revelled in it.'

The test piece of the dune was a sprint. The players had to run as fast as they could from top to bottom, back up to the top, then halfway down and back up again. Johnston's all-time record was 13 seconds, and while Henderson, Jackson, Greig and Smith weren't far behind, the talented winger was the undisputed king of the hill.

Jackson shouldn't have been the type to revel on the Gullane sands. As a centre-half of some note, his strengths lay in the air and on the ground in the tackle, but he said, 'I knew Jock had a bit of a reputation and was something of a hard character with an army background, but from day one he wanted everyone to be fitter than the opposition, and I think he more or less gained respect for that.

'We ended up the fittest team in Scotland by a mile. Don't get me wrong, at the time it was murder. It was hard going and if people were sick they were told to keep going. Being sick was no excuse to stop because you didn't get much sympathy from Jock. But I was glad of it at the end of the day.

'You benefitted when it came to the winter months, because in those days the parks were really heavy at that time of year. We were ploughing through teams because it was just like running about in the sand, and we were used to that. You could forget the technicalities of the game, because just the sheer physical fitness inspired us and gave us a real confidence. We believed we were the fittest team around and that was enough to make us believe we were also the best.'

Alex MacDonald was another of Wallace's former players who admitted he didn't mind heading east in search of ultimate fitness, but insisted there was far more to the big man than running up and down hills. He said, 'First and foremost I liked going through to Gullane because we would stop off at Jock's mum and dad's house, and it gave us a wee break before hitting Murder Hill. Seriously though, Gullane was just something that had to be done.

'When Willie Waddell came to Ibrox he was on my back at training for about a month. Push and run, push and run. Maybe I'd been trying to be too much like Jim Baxter, and he noticed that. I would knock the ball long and stand back and admire it – or nutmeg somebody – so there is no question that between the two of them, they shaped me into what I eventually became – a real nuisance! It soon became part of my game to get into the opposition box and thankfully I managed to get a number of important goals that way.'

Willie Mathieson was a regular at left-back during Jock's first spell at Ibrox, and will never forget Wallace's strict training regimes. He said, 'I'm not surprised in the slightest at the success Jock achieved during his career. When he came in at first you just knew he was going to be a winner. He was very thorough and the training stepped up something terrible, if you pardon the pun.

'Murder Hill was aptly named. It wasn't about being quick. I mean, it was a hill, and not only did you have to run up it, but you often had to carry someone on your back. And if you started being sick he would give you a row and say, "Come on, no feeding the seagulls here!" And off you went again. He would tell you that your heart would give in before your legs, and just to keep going.'

But Alfie Conn recalled Wallace leading by example. He insisted it wasn't simply a case of 'do as I say, not as I do'. Conn said, 'At the start of the session, Jock would run the course to show that if he could do it, anyone could.

'I wasn't too bad with Gullane, because coming from Prestonpans it was my type of terrain, and I was never off the sand as a kid. But Jock used to take us to the wee dunes in the morning and then it was on to the "monsters" in the afternoon. And when you had finished for the day, it was a struggle getting your trousers back on, because your muscles had swollen up so much. But it certainly didn't do us any harm.

'I reckon we were definitely the fittest team in the league under Jock. When others were starting to get a wee bit tired you could see that we were still able to keep going. Maybe it was just that Jock wouldn't let anybody stop!'

Following eight eventful years at Ibrox, Wallace left for Leicester, a landlocked city in the English East Midlands. Many thought the move would signal the end of his love affair with sand, but they were mistaken.

At the beginning of June 1978, Wallace told his players, 'For the next three weeks you will be here on Tuesdays and Thursdays to get a feel for my sort of training. My methods can be pretty rugged so I want you to be ready.'

The players were given a couple of weeks off before reporting back for another 'pre-season' in mid-July. They got the shock of their lives on walking back through the front door as the manager had converted a section of the Filbert Street stadium into an athletics track, complete with high hurdles, for a fierce work-out.

He had also set aside a section of the ground for something else; something quite different. Many of the players stood open mouthed as a procession of lorries filtered in and out of Filbert Street, and it soon became clear that they were carrying sand. Wallace was re-creating the dunes of Gullane slap bang in the middle of the football ground. He said, 'I want the fittest side in the English Second Division. Physical condition was the basis of my success at Rangers.' He wasn't kidding and the Leicester players were in for the time of their lives.

Thankfully when he took over at Seville in 1986, locating dunes for his players wouldn't prove so troublesome!

7

The European Dream

I T was a defiant Willie Waddell who declared on the eve of the 1971/72 campaign, 'We will not give up on a single competition this season. Some of our players may have given up on the league title last year but that attitude will not be tolerated from now on.'

It was day one of pre-season and Waddell watched his right-hand man put the players, including previously injured stars Alfie Conn and Dave Smith, through their paces at the Albion training ground. The squad had just returned from a training camp in Gothenburg, Sweden, and were in great shape.

Rangers started with a 2-1 win over Everton at Ibrox, which saw new safety measures put in place for crowd control, seven months after the stadium disaster. On the field, Derek Johnstone's double did the trick, and 48 hours later a Willie Johnston goal was enough to beat Tottenham Hotspur.

Soon after, Rangers – complete with new signing Tommy McLean from Kilmarnock – were paired with French side Rennes in the European Cup Winners' Cup first round. Logistically, northwest France was a breeze, and Waddell immediately made plans to watch Rennes in action on the opening day of the French season against Bastia – before jetting back for the weekend clash with Celtic.

While in France, Waddell stumbled upon a 'top-secret' double signing by the reigning French Cup holders. Yugoslav duo Kobechack and Mojsov sat two rows behind Waddell in the stand and looked on as Rennes won 1-0, but Waddell only had eyes for 22-year-old Raymond Keruzore, who bossed the midfield.

Rangers received a boost ahead of the tie when the Yugoslavs were banned from playing after the necessary paperwork failed to arrive in time from their national FA. But if Rennes coach Jean Prouff had his worries over a duo that wouldn't take part, he admitted to being concerned about a pairing that would. Colin Stein and Derek Johnstone had started the season well and in Stein, a £100,000 buy from Hibs, they had a proven goalscorer.

But Rangers' form was patchy, and back-to-back League Cup defeats against Celtic saw them exit the competition. An opening-day league defeat at Partick Thistle followed, before the French FA announced that registration documents for the Yugoslav players HAD arrived in time.

Rangers boarded their flight for France with yet another Old Firm defeat – this time in the league – as excess baggage. On arrival at Rennes Airport, Waddell demanded an inquiry into the shambolic registration of the Yugoslavs, just as UEFA was announcing that international striker Mojsov was due to play, but that Kobechack was ineligible.

So while a confused Waddell was busy dealing with UEFA, Wallace had the players out on the lush grass adjacent to the hotel for a light training session. Afterwards, Waddell said, 'This is the kind of game where Dave Smith's ability and experience can help us.' But there was no room in the pool for Willie Henderson, who was struggling with stomach muscle issues. Rennes, on the other hand, took a leaf out of the Wallace training manual and went for a session on the beach at nearby St Malo.

When the teams faced one another at the Parc Des Sports, Smith was absent, but the 11 chosen by Waddell were more than capable, despite still being pointless back home, and Rennes occupying the rather lofty position of third in the French League.

Rangers survived a ferocious onslaught in the opening half but grew in confidence after the break – and should have won the game. The Light Blues forged ahead in 68 minutes. McLean took a corner kick, Stein raced to meet it with his head, but missed, and Johnston was perfectly placed behind him to score from close range.

But 12 minutes from time Rangers were denied victory when, from a Betta cross, Redon slid in at the back post to usher the ball over the line. Still, a draw with an away European goal, which would count double in the event of an aggregate tie, was an excellent result against a good French side.

A war of words erupted soon after the match, and began with a bad tempered volley from Prouff, who said, 'Rangers did not play any football. They came only to defend, and took the spectacle out of the game. My fans were furious.'

Waddell countered, 'If Mr Prouff is as naive as to think that teams come away from home in Europe and play attacking football then he has less experience than I first believed. It is not the responsibility of Rangers to please the Rennes fans – that's Mr Prouff's responsibility. But should he want to see attacking football, he will see plenty of it when he comes to Ibrox!'

In fact, the only thing to concern Waddell, and his coach, was a fitness doubt over Stein, who returned from France with a niggling thigh strain.

The cocky French flew in to Glasgow for the second leg and big-mouth Prouff was at it again, suggesting that the most important thing for his players wasn't to win the tie, but to play the game in the right manner. Of course, he insisted that Rangers' reputation – beaten finalists on two occasions – meant little. He added, 'I know Rangers are capable of attack, because I saw that against Celtic, but they have no individuals who worry me – we are not frightened, and playing in front of a big crowd won't be a problem. If any team has problems it's Rangers, after losing against Aberdeen.'

Waddell said, 'At the moment we have the advantage so we won't go charging forward in a senseless manner – we must keep it tight at the back.' That they did, although at times their caution frustrated the home fans, who slow-clapped and jeered.

But one moment of magic by Johnston was enough to send Rangers through to the second round. As the first half wore on he cut between two labouring French defenders and shot for goal. Aubour, the French international keeper, could only push it out into the path of the lurking MacDonald, who hammered the ball high into the net. Johnston, as well as the returning Henderson, was Rangers' best man, while Stein rattled the bar after the break. In the end, one goal, in front of 42,000, was enough to see Rangers through.

After the game Prouff, said, 'We have no complaints. We lost the game and I congratulate Rangers for their play. Henderson and Johnston were outstanding.'

As Rangers awaited the draw for the second round – which was due to take place in Yugoslavia – the club was praised for successfully adopting the 'European way' in the tie against Rennes. No gung-ho tactics from the shrewd Waddell.

As well as Rangers, Celtic, Dundee, St Johnstone and Aberdeen made it safely over the opening hurdle and were desperate to avoid a trip behind the Iron Curtain as Eastern Europe was largely inaccessible in the early 1970s. All got their wish apart from St Johnstone, who drew the Hungarian side Vasas Budapest.

For Rangers, though, it was a tie with one of the favourites, Sporting Lisbon. The former winners were one of the strongest teams in the competition, and their star player was new signing Hector Yazalde, the 25-times capped Argentine international.

But as the Light Blues looked forward to the second instalment of their European adventure, things weren't improving much on the home front. The day after the draw, they lost 2-1 at Tynecastle to slump to second bottom of the First Division. With chairman John Lawrence on holiday, talk of a crisis meeting at boardroom level was put on hold. Wallace worked the players even harder on the training ground while Waddell put in extra hours on the tactical front.

With Celtic due to play host to Maltese side Sliema Wanderers on the same night Rangers were down to face Sporting in Glasgow, Waddell applied to UEFA to switch the first leg to Lisbon to avoid two big matches taking place in the city on the same night, but the Portuguese were having none of it.

Prior to the first leg, Rangers scored five against Dundee United at Tannadice and the confidence was back – although Waddell returned from a spying sortie in Portugal to declare, 'Sporting are a better side than Rennes – it will be tough.'

A crowd of 50,000 visited Ibrox to see Rangers roar into a three-goal lead, courtesy of a Stein double and a goal by Henderson. A first-half display of relentless attacking football was among their finest ever in the European arena, and for the first 20 minutes of the second half, they treated Sporting not as kings of their own country but as a second-rate side.

But when Stein, Jardine and young Conn ran out of puff, the Portuguese, sensing a late reprieve, stepped on the gas. Chico fired home after McCloy had parried a Yazalde drive. Dinis then evaded not one but two Greig tackles before Pedro Gomes lashed the ball into the net. Cheers turned to jeers as the Rangers players trudged off the field. The second leg in Lisbon would be a nervy affair.

Forty-eight hours after the narrow win, Waddell insisted his men could still progress – if they could repeat the dizzy heights of that stunning first-half performance.

In fact, Sporting coach Vaz said, 'If Rangers were playing regularly in Portugal they would top the First Division – that is how well they played.'

Ten days before the second leg, Rangers hosted Motherwell in a league match – but the real action was taking place a few miles east, at Hampden Park, where Partick Thistle were causing one of the biggest upsets of all time in the League Cup Final against Celtic. If Rangers fans had been blown away by their first-half showing against Sporting, then Thistle fans were disbelieving as their team raced into a 4-0 half-time lead, and it was reported that Rangers supporters left Ibrox to head for Hampden to see their rivals suffer. The match eventually finished 4-1 to the Jags.

Rangers had injury doubts ahead of the second leg, over Mathieson (chest knock) and McKinnon (nose injury), but both travelled and looked certain to play. Fast forward a day or two and McKinnon would have wished he had missed the plane.

The big defender had dislocated his nose and lost a lot of blood in a match against Kilmarnock, but played on as Jardine had been sent off. But that was the least of manager Waddell's problems, as the players were stranded in London on route to the Portuguese capital. A chartered flight was cancelled by operators after being stranded in Munich due to awful weather conditions, and with a strike grounding 90 per cent of flights out of Heathrow, there were no guarantees that the Rangers party would get to Lisbon on time.

A full day of travelling, hanging around airports and snatching meals whenever they could was anything but ideal preparation for an important European tie, and the party had no option but to book in at a hotel near Stansted Airport and leave for Lisbon the following day.

Skipper Greig ensured the party was kept in good spirits throughout the airport wait and took a fair bit of ribbing for his goatee beard, which was grown to hide a nasty chin injury received in the first leg at Ibrox, and flew in the face of authority as Rangers chiefs had banned facial hair at that time.

It was a weary Rangers squad that arrived in Lisbon just three hours ahead of the UEFA deadline. A rule stated that teams must arrive in the host city 24 hours before kick-off. Rangers arrived in Lisbon at 6.30pm, and the kick-off was scheduled for 9.45pm the following night.

But there was no rest for the tired players as Wallace took them straight out for a light training session. He said, 'We will not hide behind these delays. They have given us problems but won't be used as an excuse. The players are fit enough to withstand a day's travelling. We enjoyed a training session and tomorrow we will go to the stadium for a light work-out. We are facing a difficult kick-off time and starting at a time when we would normally be finishing back home.'

Sporting skipper Jose Carlos was struggling with an injury, and boss Vaz said, 'We need Carlos in this game because we fear Colin Stein.' And Vaz was right to fear Stein. The blond centre-forward scored twice as Rangers turned in another terrific performance, but were only confirmed as winners of the tie hours after the referee had declared that Sporting would go through. The sensational decision to reverse the result ended one of the biggest European football rows of all time.

The trouble began when Sporting won the match 4-3 after extra time, which meant an aggregate score of 6-6. Rangers, ahead 3-2 from the first leg, should automatically have qualified with their three away goals counting double, but to the astonishment of all, Dutch referee Laurens van Raavens decided the tie would be won or lost on penalty kicks.

Waddell ran on to the pitch brandishing a rule book, but arrogant van Raavens waved him away. In the hush of the stadium, Rangers failed with four of their penalties – and Sporting scored with two. As the dejected Light Blues trudged off the pitch, convinced they had lost, Waddell angrily demanded that officials study the rules. Meanwhile, the jubilant Sporting players were taking the applause of the home supporters in the partisan 60,000 crowd. Finally, club managers, chairmen and official UEFA observer Andros Vardinas attempted to sort out the shambolic situation.

While they were busy talking, UEFA secretary Hans Bangerter told a *Daily Record* reporter, 'Rangers are through. Our rules previously stated that goals scored in extra time didn't count double, but this was changed and I can only assume this is where the confusion has arisen.'

Following 70 minutes of talks, a UEFA official said, 'In my opinion Rangers have qualified, but I will have to refer this to

UEFA headquarters.' Finally, at 2am, officials reversed the referee's decision – and Rangers were through. Stein's double and a single from Henderson might have mattered on the park but off it, it was the tenacity of Waddell and Wallace which ensured Rangers marched on to the last eight.

However, there was a distressing aside as McKinnon, a dad-to-be, suffered a double leg break following a second-half challenge. After a night in a Lisbon hospital, McKinnon was stretchered on to Rangers' charter flight to be met at Glasgow Airport by expectant wife Valerie and taken to hospital. The injury was expected to keep him out for six months. It was a bitter blow for both player and club.

But the day after the Rangers party arrived home, word filtered through that Sporting were set to appeal. They sent delegates to Switzerland to meet with UEFA. SFA secretary Willie Allan and Waddell also flew out to Zurich to put Rangers' case forward and after a few hours' wrangling, Rangers were declared the winners.

At the beginning of December, Rangers jetted into sunny Tel Aviv for a winter break and the players enjoyed a bus tour of Jerusalem and Bethlehem. There was far more excitement on the tour than at the Tel Aviv stadium as Rangers and a Hapoel Select fought out a goalless draw.

With the draw for the quarter-finals due to be made in Zurich in mid-January, Rangers received a boost when Uli Hoeness, Bayern Munich's 20-year-old striker, said, 'We hope to avoid Rangers. The final will be soon enough to meet them. We would rather go even to Russia than to Scotland.' Bayern were red-hot favourites to win the competition, while Rangers were ranked outsiders by bookmakers.

Sandy Jardine said, 'I'd like to avoid Torino. The Italians are difficult to play against, what with feigning injuries and all the usual kinds of gamesmanship.' But when the ties were pulled from the hat, the Light Blues were paired with the Serie A side. Waddell was delighted with the draw and said, 'We've avoided a travel nightmare – and there is also a touch of glamour associated with Italian football.'

On the eve of the first-leg clash in Turin, Rangers were rocked by an injury blow to Johnstone, who had damaged a thigh in the 2-1 league win over Kilmarnock. And skipper Greig warned, 'The match in Turin will be one of the toughest we have ever faced. The Italians have hit top form at precisely the right moment, and having played an Italian side before I know they will give nothing away. But if we get a result at their place, we must have an outstanding chance of winning the competition.'

Rangers did get a result in Italy – an incredible one against a very good Torino side. Wing king Johnston gave the Light Blues the lead as early as the 12th minute – a goal which silenced the flag-waving, cheering Italians. Overlapping full-back Mathieson sent a low cross into the area which Castellini, the Torino keeper, missed and the ever-alert Johnston thumped it into the net. Pulici grabbed an equaliser on the hour mark and while the hosts piled forward, Rangers were resolute in defence.

Afterwards, Waddell said, 'It was a tremendous result against a team I think will win the Italian title. And the home fans must have been impressed with Derek Johnstone, a player who can be the new John Charles.' Torino coach Gustavo Giagnoni said, 'Rangers put on a magnificent display of defensive football, and it will now be hard for us to win the tie.'

Keeper McCloy was a major doubt for the second leg after a grazed knee became infected. He was on a course of antibiotics, which gave Waddell sleepless nights, as reserve keeper Gerry Neef was injured, and back-up Bobby Watson ill. Regardless, Rangers prepared at Largs for their most important European tie in a decade.

Some 75,000 fans were relieved to see McCloy between the sticks, and McLean out on the wing, particularly as it was a moment of magic from the right-sided midfielder that won the tie. The second half was less than a minute old when he gathered the ball just inside his own half. He left full-back Fossati trailing in his wake before despatching a beautifully flighted ball into the box, which found MacDonald at the far post, and ready to bundle the ball over the line. It was an undignified end to such a glorious move – but no one cared as Rangers were in the last four.

After the final whistle, Waddell said, 'It was a magnificent performance by the players. They were up against a fine team and responded with confidence and ability.' Italian coach Giagnoni said, 'Rangers are a very good team. I don't consider we were unlucky.'

The draw for the last four gave Rangers the opportunity for a little revenge. The Light Blues were paired with Bayern Munich, which brought memories flooding back of that fateful night in Nuremberg in 1967, when Bayern edged Rangers 1-0 after extra time.

Waddell called it 'the final before the final'. Bayern were 5/4 favourites to win the cup – Rangers 4/1 outsiders. The other semi-final was between Moscow Dynamo and Dynamo East Berlin. Waddell said, 'This is a fabulous tie for us. We have a score to settle – although it will be difficult.' Bayern, meanwhile, contained many players who would help West Germany win the World Cup in 1974.

One man who came in for special praise ahead of the semi-final was Wallace. He was championed as one of the main reasons behind Rangers' progression in the competition, and for the 'incredible fitness shown by the players late on in games as they faced an onslaught from desperate opponents'.

Bayern coach Udo Lattek watched Rangers show grit and determination to beat Motherwell 4-2 in a Scottish Cup replay, and said, 'I have never seen a team fight like Rangers. Certainly no team in Germany can battle back like them. They were tremendous – and so were the Ibrox crowd.'

But it was a battle-scarred Gers who headed for the Bavarian capital, unsure of whether Greig or McLean – or both – would be fit for the first leg. The duo had received treatment at Ibrox before the two-hour flight to Munich.

Rangers had done their homework, with Waddell watching Bayern easily dispose of Stuttgart in a league match before Wallace took in a West German Cup tie against Cologne, in which Gerd

Muller scored twice. The Rangers coach bumped into England's World Cup-winning manager Sir Alf Ramsey, who described Muller as 'one of the world's great players'.

On arrival at the Grunwalder Stadium in Munich, Waddell decided on a training session to 'help acclimatise his players to the warm and muggy conditions', far different from the weather they had left behind in Glasgow. The Bayern propaganda machine was also in full swing and, at the airport, Greig was presented with a framed picture of Franz Roth scoring the only goal of the 1967 European Cup Winners' Cup Final, but the Rangers skipper said, 'Pictures of the past mean nothing – it's what happens this week that counts.'

Then the Bayern players had their turn. Captain Franz Beckenbauer said, 'Rangers are a better team now than in 1967 and to win the tie we will have to beat them by three goals in the first leg – and that is not possible.' Muller added, 'Rangers will win this cup. We may beat them by a single goal here but that won't be enough to progress to the final. To beat Turin (sic) as they did frightens us a little.'

The match itself was a titanic struggle but Rangers hit back to grab a 1-1 draw with a precious away goal by Stein, although it would go down in the record books as an own goal by Zobel. After the match, Waddell was astonished to learn that Bayern manager Lattek had labelled the Light Blues 'rough'. He said, 'Rangers' rough play was too much for us.'

The statement came as a shock because most of the evening's foul play had been perpetrated by Bayern's outside-right Krauthausen, who had been involved in several unsavoury incidents, including one in particular on the stroke of half-time when he fouled Greig. As he walked off at the break, Conn made for him, but was punched in the face by Muller.

A score draw in Munich represented a fantastic result, because it hadn't been achieved simply by shutting up shop. It was a night when the Light Blues added courage to caution, and played with a refreshing honesty that caught the stars of Munich on the hop. Sure, they had been on the wrong end of a first-half battering but lived to tell the tale, before growing in stature after the break. Johnstone, still a teenager, was a star in midfield and marked Hoeness out the game.

But Rangers had EIGHT players doubtful for the second leg. A mystery bug swept through Ibrox and Stein joined Jardine, Conn, MacDonald and McLean in quarantine. Greig, Johnston and McCloy were also nursing injuries.

One by one, the players began to recover, and Conn was put on standby to replace Greig, who failed to make the game. However it wasn't Conn but 'unknown' 18-year-old Derek Parlane who took Greig's place – and scored the vital goal in a well-deserved 2-0 victory. Parlane was told just 45 minutes before kick-off that he was in, and no doubt spent that period pondering the biggest match of his life.

Many in the 80,000 crowd were still taking their places on the terracing when Jardine scored the first goal with a 20-yard drive, after just 60 seconds, which deceived a surprised Sepp Maier. With 23 minutes on the clock, Parlane fired home the second, while virtually on his backside, and the mighty Germans crumbled. Johnston ran Munich ragged, while Jackson ensured Muller didn't have a single shot on target, and Smith proved the equal of Beckenbauer. Rangers were going to Barcelona.

The Light Blues' last league game before the final was played in front of just 3,000 keen supporters. Rangers beat Ayr United 4-2 to end the campaign in third place, behind Celtic and Aberdeen, while 28-year-old Smith had another reason to celebrate when he was crowned Scotland's Player of the Year on the day of the game. Meanwhile, Henderson received a free transfer after 13 years with the club and was immediately linked with a move to South Africa.

It was all systems go for Rangers as they prepared for their date with destiny on 24 May. While Waddell was finally granted a visa to go to Russia to watch opponents Moscow Dynamo in action,

Wallace was given 'complete control' of the players and put them through their paces at Ibrox. They lapped the track incessantly and worked hard in the gym.

The week before heading out to Moscow, Waddell was in Barcelona on a fact-finding mission, and did a deal with Espanyol to use their ground as a training centre. He also organised a friendly match against Inverness Clach in the Highlands. Greig was suffering from an ankle injury, but came on as a substitute in a 5-2 win. The following day, he said, 'My ankle feels fine. I felt great in Inverness and I'll be okay for Barcelona.' It was the news every Rangers fan wanted to hear.

When Waddell flew into Moscow for Dynamo's First Division match with Kairat, he encountered every possible hurdle along the way. He was given the run-around at the airport, and again at his hotel, just a stone's throw from Red Square and the Kremlin. He was told that he might just be lucky enough to be given a special ticket for the match – which would get him to the front of the queue to BUY a match ticket!

He arranged a meeting with goalkeeping legend Lev Yashin and Dynamo manager Konstantin Beskov, friends from a previous match at Ibrox, and was given a ticket for the match. He said, 'This has been the most difficult spy trip I have ever known – difficult to get here and even more difficult when I arrived. It was even hard to find out who Moscow were playing, but I made it and that's all that matters.'

Alfie Conn put himself in the frame for a Barca berth when he notched a hat-trick in the final preparation match against St Mirren. The players were given a rousing send-off by Gers fans in the 8,000 crowd.

In marked contrast, Waddell watched Dynamo booed from the field after a draw with Kairat. But the Gers boss said, 'It is going to be as hard as I thought it would be. It will be tough physically too.'

The time for talking was over and Rangers headed for the tiny village of Castelldefels, on the outskirts of the Catalan city, where they stayed at a hotel on a secluded hilltop, with the Mediterranean providing the perfect backdrop. Rangers would also have the backing of 25,000 fans – Dynamo would have none.

When the players arrived at their hotel, and with the sun splitting the sky, they were immediately warned against sunbathing. Everything seemed quite relaxed, until Waddell dropped the bombshell that Greig had gone over on his ankle in training and was a doubt for the match. The gaffer also offered an insight into how he coped with big matches, and said, 'I smoke a lot. I won't tell you how many, but it's a lot. We haven't a smoker in the team, which is good. Andy Penman used to smoke, but doesn't now!'

On the day of the game, Jackson was ruled out through injury, and said, 'In training, I pulled back going into a tackle with Tommy McLean. It's heartbreaking.' Johnstone switched to centre-half, which meant a call-up for either Penman, Parlane or Conn. The latter got the nod and played well in a match that is still etched in the minds of Gers fans. Greig led Rangers to a 3-2 win, courtesy of a Johnston double and another from Stein.

In a sparkling first half, Rangers scored twice, and when Johnston added a third, just three minutes after the break, it was all over. The fans partied like never before, and despite goals by Estrokov and Makovikov making for a nervy ending, when Jose Ortiz de Mendibil sounded the final whistle, thousands of Rangers fans, nails bitten to the quick, flooded on to the field.

Cue an incredible over-reaction from the Spanish cops and we had the infamous 'Battle of Barcelona'. Supporters were battered senseless, but while the blood and tears merged with the sweat left on the famous Nou Camp pitch by the victorious Gers players, the devastated Light Blues were denied their moment of glory when UEFA refused to allow the cup presentation to take place out on the pitch. Skipper Greig received the trophy in what resembled a broom cupboard, deep within the bowels of the stadium. It was a great shame and an anti-climax to a stunning run in one of Europe's elite competitions.

The following day, Beskov demanded a replay – as his players had felt intimidated by the threatening manner of the Rangers fans. It was the actions of a desperate man, and thankfully the European football authorities agreed. Rangers would subsequently be banned from all European competition for two years, cut to 12 months on appeal.

All that was left was for thousands of supporters to welcome back their heroes to Ibrox, trophy and all, on a wet and windy evening. Who could ever forget the players travelling round the track on an open-top lorry smoking cigars and showing off the silverware? It was a magical moment.

8

In Charge

WILLIE Waddell had been manager of Rangers for a little over two years when he passed the baton to Jock Wallace. The duo had formed a potent partnership but in June of 1972 Waddell moved upstairs insisting that his former right-hand man would have a free rein in picking the team. As general manager, he would see to everything else.

Waddell said, 'When I hung up my boots I didn't tell the player who replaced me how to do his job. I had done mine, I was finished and it was up to him. It is exactly the same with Jock Wallace. He will coach the players and pick them – with no interference from me.'

Wallace had shown that he was capable of being his own man and had never at any time asked Waddell what he should or shouldn't be doing on the training field. He got on with his job and a bond of trust quickly formed between the two. On being given the keys to the office at the top of the marble staircase, Wallace said, 'If I didn't think I was good enough for the job I wouldn't have taken it.'

And he picked his first team as manager in the relative calm of Gothenburg with Rangers tackling IFK Trollhatten as part of their pre-season build-up. The squad stayed at the exclusive Hindos training camp and as they arrived at the ground, were met by a billposter proclaiming them 'Champions of Europe'. McCloy, Jardine, Miller, Conn, Jackson, Smith, McLean, Fyfe,

Stein, Penman and MacDonald beat the Swedes 5-2 with Stein scoring a hat-trick.

Wallace, and the majority of the 5,000 crowd, were particularly impressed with the work rate of Stein, and in sweltering conditions. The new boss said, 'It was a good exercise. We came over here to work hard and find out one or two things, and everything turned out right in that respect.'

Following a tough pre-season and schedule of friendly games, Stein got Rangers' Drybrough Cup campaign off to the best possible start – with a goal in just 30 seconds in the opening match against Stirling Albion. The match saw the trial introduction of a new offside line, which ran straight across the 18-yard box. Stein said, 'I think it's all a bit of a flop. The goals a lot of people expected simply didn't materialise.' Rangers lost to Hibs in the semi-finals of a competition won by the Easter Road side, who beat Celtic in the final.

Rangers started their League Cup campaign with a 2-0 win over Clydebank – but there was a tongue-lashing for the fans from Waddell. Following the violence in Barcelona, which had led to a one-year European ban, many supporters were also involved in ugly scenes during their Drybrough Cup loss at Easter Road. Waddell's message was addressed to 'the tykes, hooligans, louts and drunkards who have no respect for society'.

He added, 'The name of Rangers has been smeared all over the world by an unruly mob who spread destruction and terror. Unfortunately the stain sticks to every decent Rangers fan. We want no part of those who cause destruction to public property, throw bottles, fight and spread viciousness with party songs and foul and obscene language. It is because of your gutter behaviour that we are publicly tarred and feathered.'

When Rangers beat St Mirren in the League Cup, former Manchester United and Scotland star Ian Ure, now a Buddy, said, 'Rangers are a much better footballing side than I was led to believe. I understood them to be just hard and physical, but they were much more. They play modern football, and moved like the top English clubs.'

Despite romping to victory in their League Cup section, Rangers' league campaign got off to a stuttering start with a 2-1 defeat at Somerset Park, Ayr. Right away, they were behind the eight ball in the race to prevent Celtic, who played their home games at Hampden that season, winning an eighth successive title.

On the day Celtic won the first Old Firm clash of the campaign, Newcastle boss Joe Harvey was at Hampden to run the rule over Stein and Johnston, both of whom had reportedly asked for a transfer. Stein, asked to play in an unfamiliar outside-right berth, wasn't at his best.

Rangers got back to winning ways the following Saturday at Ibrox against Falkirk, but required a penalty from McLean to secure a 1-0 win, which hardly had the 12,000 crowd in raptures, and when Wallace signed Quinton Young from Coventry, Stein headed in the opposite direction. A dour 1-1 draw against bottom side Morton at Ibrox meant Wallace was facing a real struggle to win over the boo boys. The expected pay-off from the recent European success had failed to materialise.

Wallace showed his mettle though one day after training. A journalist was waiting to interview a player and followed him into the dressing room. The player took off his shirt, shorts and socks and threw them on the floor, while all others added to three separate piles. Big Jock walked in, looked at him and said, 'What's that?' and pointed to the mess. He said, 'Och, the cleaner will get it.' Within seconds, Wallace had him pinned up against a wall. 'We will only be successful by sticking together, and that means everyone from the cleaners to the board of directors. If you ever disrespect anyone at this club again you will be out on your arse. Understand me?' The player got the message.

The manager was desperate for a goalscorer and tried to sign Eric Carruthers from Hearts, and Dunfermline striker Ken Mackie. Both rejected the chance of a move to Ibrox, which was almost unheard of, but Wallace quickly realised that the problem could be solved from within – in the shape of 18-year-old Derek Parlane. And the gaffer's faith was repaid when the hit-kid scored in three successive league matches in October – the latter a double against St Johnstone – to help Rangers win all three and move up the table to joint fourth.

After three months in charge, Wallace admitted he hadn't been surprised by the post-Euro slump, and added, 'We've had a hectic spell since the start of the season but I predicted it would be difficult. The players had given so much to win in Barcelona that there was bound to be a reaction. But I haven't lost any sleep nor weight. Things are picking up and I'm now getting the team together that I always wanted. I don't want any stars or prima donnas – just a team.' In his first 21 games he had used 23 players and a staggering 17 different formations.

One of Wallace's early success stories was the redeployment of Derek Johnstone to centre-half. The 19-year-old Dundonian had been outstanding in the position after a run of games in defence, and said, 'This is where my future lies. It wouldn't worry me a great deal if I was asked to play elsewhere, so long as I play for Rangers, but I prefer centre-half. I'm enjoying my football more than ever because of the tremendous team spirit we have. The manager has been hammering home the need to play as a unit and it's paying off.'

Nearing the end of November, Rangers knocked a dent in the title hopes of Hibs – and gave rivals Celtic a boost – when they travelled to Easter Road and won 2-1. Peter McCloy, it was said, had his best ever game in a Rangers jersey. The win put Rangers just a point behind second-top Hibs, and five adrift of leaders Celtic, although the improvement in the Gers since the start of the season was there for all to see.

And as pitches all over the country became heavy with the fruits of winter, Wallace's boys came into their own. The gruelling pre-season training started to pay off, especially during a home win over Dumbarton, less than four weeks before Christmas. With the scores tied at 1-1, and the match – in front of just 12,000 – pretty even, the stamina and running power of Rangers kicked in and they appeared to glide over the glue-pot Ibrox surface in the closing 20 minutes. Goals by Conn and Parlane confirmed their superiority. Just two points dropped in October and November spoke volumes.

Parlane maintained his impressive scoring run with a double at Tannadice, as the Light Blues gave their supporters an early Christmas present – a 4-1 win on a heavily sanded pitch! Hibs were the team of the moment, though, and followed up their League Cup win over Celtic by rattling eight past Ayr United. Just a fortnight later, and with the Honest Men one up at Ibrox, Wallace gave the players both barrels, and those who witnessed the half-time tirade, reckoned it was more hair-raising than hairdryer. The verbal volley had the desired effect and two second-half goals put the Gers just three points behind Celtic, although the Parkhead side had two games in hand.

New Year, new Rangers, and first up was an Old Firm encounter of the close kind, with Conn popping up in the dying seconds to fire home a winner that wouldn't have looked out of place in the Maracana. It was Pele v Gordon Banks, minus the save. The Ranger got on the end of a sumptuous Young cross to bullet a header past the despairing Evan Williams. Parlane had given Rangers the lead, while Celtic's equaliser was an own goal by Dave Smith. It was the first time Rangers had beaten Celtic in over a year and the home supporters in the 67,000 crowd partied long into the night.

And even as the snow appeared, still Rangers roared on, with a four-goal drubbing of Kilmarnock at Ibrox testament to the new-found confidence seeping through the team. When Morton fell at Cappielow, and Airdrie beat Celtic 2-1 at Broomfield, the positive amongst us dared to believe. Would this be the year the Celtic juggernaut ground to a halt? Rangers were three points clear, but Celtic had three games in hand – and it was still just two points for a win. It was the first time in five years that Rangers had topped the league in February.

Then disaster struck. As 36,000 watched Rangers beat Dundee United 1-0 in a Scottish Cup clash at Ibrox, Johnstone was rushed to the Victoria Infirmary for a head scan after being knocked unconscious during a collision. It was a tousy game and Parlane required three stitches in a head wound after clashing with Andy Rolland.

Johnstone was missing the following weekend, but Jardine scored the winner in a 2-1 victory over Motherwell and Celtic were held to a 1-1 against Partick Thistle. Two points in front, two games more played.

Both Dereks were playing well and scoring goals, Quinton 'Cutty' Young was setting them up and others were also contributing, although Wallace had words of praise for one of the unsung heroes of the defence. 'Willie Mathieson is without doubt the best left-back in Scotland. No one works harder or gives more to their team. He has had an outstanding season.' And while Wallace was extolling the virtues of the talented Fifer, Celtic were slipping up yet again. This time they could only draw with East Fife at Bayview which meant they were a point behind with a game in hand.

But Mathieson didn't escape the gaffer's wrath completely. The left-back and Tom Forsyth were the only two top-team Gers who hadn't found the net, and Wallace said, 'They have been bursting the net in practice and I've been encouraging them to get forward in games. I want us to be a goal threat all over the park.'

But one thing that did put a smile back on Wallace's face was the return to Ibrox of thousands of stay-away fans. After a slow start to the season, and home crowds dipping as low as 12,000, the Light Blues passed through the million-mark for the season in a league match against St Johnstone on the first Saturday in March. The average home crowd was now 26,000 – a ringing endorsement of both results and performance.

Saturday 10 March brought the Old Firm level at the top of the league after stuttering Celtic slipped up again. A title that had looked sewn up by Christmas was once again in the melting pot. Celtic drew 2-2 at Tannadice while a Parlane double helped the Light

Blues beat Dundee 3-1 in Glasgow. There were seven games left to play and both sides had 43 points.

Rangers had won their last 11 league games and were the form team. The mood in the camp was first class and skipper Greig told of how players were turning up for extra helpings of big Jock's punishing training routines. He said, 'It's like the start of the season and the boys are just bursting for Saturdays to come round. They are early at training every day and there are more volunteers for afternoon sessions than I've known for a while.' Greig was the only player in the squad with a league winners' medal, and said, 'We can win the title, no doubt about it.'

After two wins each, and victories in the Scottish Cup semi-finals, to set up the tenth Old Firm final, Rangers grabbed the advantage in the race for the championship as a Greig goal dumped Hearts at Tynecastle. Rangers were two points in front – Celtic had a game in hand, and the better goal difference.

One of the 'men' who had helped Rangers get a foot in the championship door was teenager Parlane, who had fired 27 goals in 38 games, and was being hailed as the first of 'Wallace's Babes' to come off the conveyor belt. When asked if Parlane was exceeding expectations, Wallace said, 'Not a bit. He is doing what he is supposed to do because he has come through the system. It's paying off for him and Rangers – but it has taken three years to reach this level. Three years from now, when he is just 22, he could be a great player and able to go anywhere in the world.'

Greig was again Rangers' hero when he scored twice against Dundee United in a 2-1 win. Celtic beat St Johnstone at Muirton. Forsyth was outstanding for the Light Blues, a performance which was hailed by manager Wallace, who said 'Tom struggled at first and people told me he was a waste of £45,000, but he has gone on to form a great partnership with Derek Johnstone in the heart of the defence – and no one mentions that 'waste of money' anymore!'

But the penultimate week of the league season proved disastrous for Rangers. They fought with everything they had against Aberdeen at Pittodrie but were forced to settle for a 2-2 draw after a stunning last-minute equaliser by Conn. Meanwhile, Celtic beat Arbroath 4-0 at home.

It was testimony to the hard work put in by Wallace and his coaching team that Rangers had managed to take the race down to the wire, although there would be no happy ending. Rangers beat East Fife 2-0 at Ibrox, but Celtic won 3-0 at Easter Road to clinch their eighth successive title. It was a bitter blow – but there was still the Scottish Cup to play for.

Having hailed the performances of Forsyth just a week previous, while bemoaning his lack of goals, it was ironic that the rugged defender should clinch the cup for his manager. Some 123,000 watched a cracking Hampden encounter and saw Kenny Dalglish give Celtic the lead after 24 minutes. Birthday boy Parlane, 20 that day, equalised before half-time. Whatever Wallace said to his players at the break had the desired effect, as Conn scored within 17 seconds of the re-start. Back came Celtic, and when Greig pulled off a tremendous 'save' from Dixie Deans, an offence which would have brought a red card today, George Connelly tucked away the resultant spot kick.

Cometh the hour, cometh the man, and Forsyth picked the perfect moment to score his first Rangers goal. McLean floated in a free kick, Johnstone nodded past Celtic keeper Ally Hunter, and the ball came back off the post and ran agonisingly along the line. Worry not, though, because Forsyth was in the right place at the right time to bullet it home – with his studs! The 23-year-old defender said, 'I was up for the free kick and thought the ball was going in after it came back off the post. When I saw it wasn't, I was so excited and almost missed it before prodding it over the line.' Forsyth was Gers' lucky charm. After 30 competitive matches for his new team, he had still to play on a losing side.

It was Wallace's first trophy as manager of Rangers – but it certainly wouldn't be the last.

9

The Cupboard Is Bare

W HILE the previous campaign had finished on a high, there was an early-season blow for Wallace when new signing Doug Houston, from Dundee United, 'came into contact' with Tom 'Jaws' Forsyth on the first day of training. As a result, he missed the opening game of the new term – a 3-0 Drybrough Cup win over Montrose – in which Parlane picked up where he had left off by scoring twice.

The Light Blues then lost a tousy semi-final to Hibs, but the last weekend in August brought a precious League Cup win at Celtic Park. Bobby Lennox had given the hosts a half-time lead but second-half goals from MacDonald, Parlane and Conn put Rangers on easy street – and top of the section.

However, the league campaign didn't quite get off to the same start and a stuttering 0-0 draw at home to Ayr United was followed up with a 1-0 win over Partick at Firhill, courtesy of a last-minute Ally Scot winner.

Across the city, Celtic were unfurling the league flag and, to mark the occasion, all home players wore number eight on their shorts. Jock Wallace was determined to make sure there would be no number nine.

On day three of the campaign, though, Jimmy Johnstone – the smallest player on the park – headed the only goal of the game to settle the first Old Firm league clash of the season, and the majority of the 60,000 Ibrox crowd went home disappointed.

Off the field, general manager Willie Waddell pressed ahead with his plans to make Ibrox the most modern stadium in Europe. With the 9,000-seater Centenary Stand complete at a cost of £70,000, Waddell sanctioned a £30,000 outlay on state-of-the-art floodlights. But still the limelight shone, for all the wrong reasons, on the team, as they crashed to a 3-0 defeat at home to Hearts. They were just a point off bottom and it was crystal clear where the problems lay. Rangers were the lowest-scoring team in the league with just one goal from their four matches – and none in three home games.

And with a European tie against Bundesliga leaders Borussia Moenchengladbach looming, the last thing they needed was to go a goal down to Arbroath in the mist at Gayfield. Thankfully, teenager Alex O'Hara was on hand to score either side of the break to ensure both points.

But when Jim Hamilton headed the only goal of the game for bottom-of-the-table East Fife at Ibrox, the home players were jeered from the field. It was the Fifers' first ever league win at Ibrox, but for Rangers, they were still searching for a home league goal – and it was the middle of October.

Wallace declared, 'This is a time for patience, not panic. The only change I will consider is bringing back goalkeeper Peter McCloy – if he's fit enough. Nobody knows better than me what the fans want, but the players are trying their guts out.'

The manager shrugged off the disappointment and flew to Germany with Waddell to spy on Moenchengladbach, who were aiming to regain top spot in the Bundesliga with victory over Kaiserslautern. A 2-2 draw ensued, but Wallace said, 'Borussia are a typical example of all that is good in German football. They had so many first-class men it was hard to pick out their star turn.'

Back on the home front, Wallace knew Rangers had to defeat Dundee United at Tannadice – and get themselves up the league table in the process. Anything other than a win would all but signal defeat in the race for the title. And it was one of the 'fringe' players, Alfie Conn, who ensured the two-hour trip down the road was a happy one as he fired a second-half double to clinch a 3-1 win, and a confidence boost ahead of Gers' European tie.

Next up was a date with the likes of Berti Vogts, Rainer Bonhof and Jupp Heynckes, the top scorer in the Bundesliga with 11 goals. But Borussia's preparations couldn't have been worse as they crashed 6-1 to Stuttgart just days before Rangers were due in north Germany.

On their arrival in Monchengladbach, teenager Alex O'Hara created quite a stir, as local journalists and photographers asked if one who looked so young could possibly play in such a big match. With his usual panache, Wallace said, 'Mind your own business!' It was game on.

The gruff Scotsman was then criticised by certain sections of the press for refusing to name his starting 11 until just a few hours before kick-off. One reporter said, 'Frankly I find this amazing. More successful clubs than Rangers give their teams in advance. Deliberately holding up selections is unfair to the customers.'

But Wallace was more interested in maintaining harmony than playing to the masses. He explained, 'There is no way anybody will know the team before the players. When we played Ankaragucu in Glasgow, I announced our team the night before the game and it caused arguments among the players, and I'm not having that again.'

Wallace pinpointed teenage full-back Klinkhammer as a potential weak link, while breathing a sigh of relief that Gunter Netzer wouldn't be playing after clinching a move to Real Madrid. But a double by Heynckes and one from Rupp left Rangers with a second-leg mountain to climb. McCloy prevented Heynckes from grabbing a hat-trick when he saved a penalty from the German international.

As soon as the Rangers players touched down at Glasgow Airport, they were whisked straight to Ibrox by Wallace to talk over exactly what had gone wrong in Germany. Wallace said, 'There are things we have to put right. There is no question of me digging up individuals. We are a team and besides me having my say first, the others can give constructive opinions as well. It is a long time since we were well beaten on the continent and it's hard to accept.'

All eyes switched to Ibrox, and what would surely be a tough battle with a Hibs side on top of the world after an impressive UEFA Cup win over Leeds United at Elland Road. But when the chips are down… at a quarter to five on the Saturday evening, the majority of fans were in fine voice as they wandered happily down Copland Road towards the subway station, fresh from watching their favourites win 4-0.

The victory proved Rangers were far from lacking in character and determination. Despite an awful start to the season, the Light Blues were just four points off the top of the league – and had taken a wrecking ball to their home hoodoo in the process. A 2-0 win over the same side just days later booked a League Cup semi-final berth.

On the eve of the return match with Borussia, Wallace insisted his side were capable of scoring four times against the classy Germans. 'We created more chances in Germany than they did. Our fans did us a massive favour by lifting us for the match against Hibs, now it's up to us to return the favour.'

Rangers switched on their new 'daylight' floodlights for the occasion and the team prepared for the mountainous task at a hotel in Largs, but manager Wallace was rocked by the news that both Dereks, Parlane and Johnstone, were out of the tie. And it was another night of glorious failure as the Light Blues matched the three scored by Borussia in the first leg, but lost two calamitous goals to exit the competition on a 5-3 aggregate. A crowd of 35,000 saw Conn grab the lead before Henning Jensen, with his first of a double, scored the goal that all but knocked the Gers out.

There was nothing else for it but to concentrate on the home front, although the next two league matches – at home to Morton and Falkirk – were tousy affairs, and just one man proved the difference between defeat and victory. John Greig scored the only goal of the game against the Cappielow side before notching a double in a 2-1 win over Falkirk. Maximum points kept Rangers in touch with league leaders Celtic, who demolished Partick Thistle 7-0 at Parkhead, with Dixie Deans scoring six.

Next on the agenda was a League Cup semi-final tie at Hampden – against Celtic. Up for grabs, apart from personal bragging rights, a place in the final and a massive boost for the second half of the campaign, was a place in Europe. Sadly, Harry Hood took centre stage and his hat-trick proved decisive. After the game, manager Wallace refused to comment, hurrying instead from the ground to the waiting team bus.

The Light Blues were given little opportunity to get the defeat out of their system as successive games against Motherwell and Dundee were called off due to adverse weather. The extra time off, however, was put to good use by centre-half Jackson, who opened an art gallery in Glasgow, 'to show off original works by Scottish artists'.

After the Light Blues had comfortably disposed of Dumbarton at a muddy Boghead, Wallace announced that he was to re-shape his team – with Forsyth moving into a more attacking role and Greig taking over as sweeper. Rangers beat Ayr United 1-0 at Somerset – just four days after Christmas – but there was no let-up on the other side of the city as Celtic slammed in six for the second successive week. Rangers were up to second in the table but the gap between the sides – in terms of goals and points – seemed larger than ever.

The sides clashed at Celtic Park in what was surely a last-chance saloon for the Light Blues. Rangers battled manfully for 90 minutes but lacked a killer edge and a Bobby Lennox strike all but confirmed a ninth successive title for Celtic. Wallace came out fighting after the game and slammed the match officials for failing to rule out Lennox's goal for offside. He said, 'The whole match hinged on a linesman's decision and it went against us.'

Parlane scored all four in a 4-2 win over Hearts at Tynecastle – but Celtic kept on winning. The four-goal show was significant for the 20-year-old striker, as it put the brakes on a disappointing run of form. Parlane said, 'It has been a bad time for me. Jock Wallace and I often discussed what had gone wrong, and we couldn't put a finger on it.' He then netted a hat-trick the following week in an 8-0 Scottish Cup rout of Queen's Park, in which McLean also scored three times.

At the beginning of February, Celtic threw their league title opponents a rare lifeline when they lost 3-2 at Motherwell, but Rangers – at home to tiny Arbroath – failed to take the bait and crashed 3-2 in front of 15,000 angry supporters. It was Arbroath's first ever win over Rangers and no doubt a sickener and career low for Wallace as former Gers star Andy Penman ran the show in midfield.

In the fall-out from the match, Johnstone was stripped of the Rangers captaincy. Wallace said, 'He is young and still learning. I decided it would be better to let him concentrate on his own game. Sandy Jardine was the logical replacement – he has much more experience.'

There was more internal strife for Wallace to deal with when Rangers lost heavily to Dundee at Ibrox in a Scottish Cup fourth round clash. Greig and McCloy were dropped for the following weekend's home match with Dundee United, a game the Light Blues won 3-1. But the Jekyll and Hyde form was just seven days away, and when they travelled to Easter Road – desperate for the win that would put them in the driving seat to earn a UEFA Cup place the following season – they failed miserably and lost 3-1. Yet another dismal performance was compounded by an injury to Parlane.

McCloy had been one of Rangers' longest-serving players, and said recently, 'The first time I met Jock was when he was at Berwick Rangers and I was at Motherwell. We played them in the league. We had been relegated to the Second Division but beat them 7-1 that day and he was in goals. You can bet it was something I reminded him about regularly! Motherwell were a far better side and we won the league and got back into the old first division.

'I joined Rangers on Friday 13 March 1970. Willie Waddell signed me and Jock came that summer and I'll always remember him phoning the house and saying, "Where are you?" I said, "I'm on holiday." He said, "Naw you're no', get yersel in here. I want to see you in training." And that was my introduction to goalkeeper training. I was always fit but other than shooting-in exercises I'd never done any specific goalkeeping work, so he was a really big help to me.

'Don't get me wrong, the manager can only pick 11 players and a lot of the guys were unhappy if they didn't get a game, but everyone respected Jock because he was open and spoke to you. And he stood by you when maybe things weren't going as well as you'd have liked. You're never going to play well all the time but when you had a wee rocky spell he was there for you.'

At the beginning of March, on Scottish Cup day, 7,000 Rangers fans headed down to Manchester for a 'friendly' with United at Old Trafford. Sadly, the encounter was marred by a series of running battles between supporters, and a senior police officer from the city said, 'It's about time Glasgow Rangers fans were kept in Scotland. To be absolutely fair, though, not all the trouble came from Scots.' Chief Superintendent Denis Grange added, 'Glasgow fans are the worst we have ever seen in the city.'

However, Wallace was quick to defend the club's supporters, and said, 'They taunted our fans and although I'm not excusing their running on the park, at least they went back when I asked them. The United fans had to be cleared by police.'

Rangers won the match 3-2 but a damning report by the *Sunday Mail* 'Judge' stated, 'Rangers supporters lived up to their hooligan reputation in Manchester, confirming beyond reasonable doubt that they remain the most anti-social element in modern day European football.'

Daily Record reporter Bob Patience controversially insisted the trouble was down to 'religious bigotry', and said, 'For me, that's the driving force which incites these fanatics to the extremes, and which has made them the scourge of Europe.'

But Wallace was having none of it, and replied, 'Signing a Catholic player will not suddenly make all the problems of the world go away. Hooliganism, anti-social behaviour, call it what you may, but I refuse to believe that religious bigotry was the catalyst for this outbreak of unacceptable behaviour.' Made for a better story though, I suppose.

As Celtic strolled towards yet another flag win, Rangers continued to toil, drawing 0-0 with Falkirk, thumping Motherwell and Clyde, and losing at home to Dundee in what was rapidly becoming another season to forget.

The fight was on to secure second place – and European football the following season. Rangers had failed just three times in 17 years to qualify for Europe, and Wallace said, 'Europe has its own special atmosphere. We don't want to miss out.' In the week that John Greig signed a new two-year contract, to add to the 15 already served, Rangers completed their fixtures with a 3-1 win over Dumbarton at Ibrox, but required Hibs to slip up against Dundee United at Tannadice. Hibs romped to a 4-1 success – with Joe Harper to the fore – and Rangers failed to qualify for Europe for the first time since the 1964/65 season.

That opened the door for participation in the Texaco Cup, and Willie Waddell said, 'We would be delighted to play in it.' A Texaco spokesman said, 'We are not concerned about the behaviour of some of the Rangers supporters. Theirs is not an isolated case. Rangers are welcome in the competition.'

Rangers may have just completed a dismal season, but Wallace, about to enter the final year of his three-year contract, was upbeat. He said, 'Right now I feel better about things than I did the day after we beat Celtic to win the Scottish Cup. The atmosphere is right and we now have the men who are playing for each other, and playing for Rangers.

'We will be a better team next season. We've had another year's experience and the players now know what I want. We were winning games this season but things just weren't right. Now I think I have the answers. We have five players who will be far better next season – Parlane, Johnstone, Scott, Young and Hamilton. And Johnstone now knows where he is going after being dropped from the Scotland team and getting some heavy rollickings from me.

'I'm not afraid of the new season – I feel no pressure. I have neither fear for the future of this club nor my own future. The feeling is right – and the music is good!'

10

No Ten In A Row

WALLACE was active during the close season and sold Alfie Conn to Spurs for £140,000 before making noises about bringing Colin Stein back from Coventry City. Stein was still popular with supporters who recalled him scoring over 100 goals in 171 appearances in his first spell at the club. But Sky Blues general manager Joe Mercer slammed Wallace and accused him of approaching the press about the player before making contact with the club. He immediately slapped a 'not for sale' sign on the player. Mercer said, 'There is no chance of us letting Stein go. He is the best centre-forward in England, and maybe in Britain.'

The draw for the first round of the Texaco Cup paired Rangers with Southampton; Mick Channon, Peter Osgood and all. The south-coast side also included a name known to Rangers fans – but for all the wrong reasons. Ally McLeod had scored four times against the Light Blues two seasons previous in a shock 4-1 win for St Mirren at Ibrox. Southampton manager Lawrie McMenemy said, 'It should be a magnificent tie – just like a top European match. And the Rangers fans will be welcome in Southampton. I know they've been criticised for their behaviour in the past but I never pre-judge anyone.'

During their League Cup campaign – which had started off with three wins and a loss – Wallace took his players to Barcelona, and the Nou Camp, scene of their greatest triumph in 1972. Rangers had been invited to play in a tournament against the hosts, Athletic Bilbao and Ajax. The manager wanted to use the competition to find out if Derek Johnstone and Sandy Jardine could thrive in their new midfield roles. He was also sceptical about the new offside rules, in place for the League Cup, and their impact on the game.

Wallace accepted that flying to Spain for a two-game tournament was a gamble, especially the timing of the competition, but said, 'Just playing against teams of the calibre of Bilbao, Barcelona and Ajax will be worth it for the experience alone. We could be up against players such as Johan Cruyff and Jose Iribar. What's not to like about that?'

And Wallace's decision was partly justified on day one of the competition when a Jardine goal, which left Spanish international goalkeeper Iribar floundering, was enough to beat Bilbao in front of 100,000, and set up a final against Barcelona, who thumped Ajax 3-0. Wallace said, 'It was a disciplined and courageous performance and I am delighted to get to the final. In fact, Iribar pulled off tremendous saves from Fyfe and Scott, which helped keep the score down to just 1-0.'

There was to be no fairytale finale, though, as Cruyff pulled the strings in front of another full house. Rangers had the audacity to take the lead through Fyfe, but the Dutch master equalised before Marcial scored a hat-trick in a 4-1 romp. Wallace said, 'We lost some daft goals. In fact, it took four of the daftest goals I've ever seen to beat us. Barcelona are a great side but we ran them close.'

With Rangers living the high life in Catalonia, Hibs beat Dundee 4-2 to top the League Cup section on goal difference. Rangers had become the first Scottish side to be invited to the Barcelona tournament in its nine-year history but now had a job to do at home, first against Dundee, and then with Hibs.

They completed part one of their mission, a 4-0 thumping of the Dens Park men. The final score failed to reflect Rangers' superiority, and merely underlined Wallace's prediction that the

Spanish competition would be good for his team. Hibs also won their game to set up a winner-takes-all meeting at Ibrox. A crowd of 50,000 turned up at Ibrox for the midweek clash but Alex Cropley scored with the last kick of the game to seal a Hibs win.

So to the start of the last old-style Scottish League First Division campaign, with the ten-team Premier League set to come into force at the beginning of the 1975/76 season – and Wallace was determined to prevent Celtic's ten-in-a-row bid, but the season got off to an inauspicious start when they could only draw 1-1 at Ayr, and Celtic destroyed Kilmarnock 5-0 at Parkhead. Not again, surely!

The Light Blues limbered up for their first sojourn into the Texaco Cup by winning a tight Old Firm clash at Parkhead. Dalglish scored for the home side, but Rangers took a stranglehold on the game after the break and goals from Ian McDougall – making his Old Firm debut – and Jackson won the match. Greig, returning after injury, was named man of the match and inspired his troops to a confidence-boosting victory. The result left Hibs as the only team in the division with a 100 per cent record after the first three league games. Wallace praised the Rangers supporters for playing their part in the win, and said, 'Their encouragement when we were a goal behind really lifted the players.'

Next up Southampton, and the most feared double act in the UK, Channon and Osgood, arrived at Ibrox in confident mood ahead of the first round, first leg match. And that mood was justified as a double from former Chelsea star Osgood helped Saints snatch a 3-1 victory. It was a masterful and assured performance by the English side.

Wallace signed winger Bobby McKean from St Mirren for £35,000 24 hours before Rangers' next league match, against Dumbarton at Ibrox, and he was a stand-out in a narrow home win. McKean, who was set to marry just five days later, said, 'I was sitting at home in East Kilbride on the Friday night wrapping wedding presents when St Mirren manager Willie Cunningham called and told me to get to Glasgow right away. I met him at a hotel and then went to Ibrox and signed at midnight. I was so excited, and even more so when I made my debut just 15 hours later!

'In fact, when I initially met Mr Cunningham, he pretended that I was signing for another First Division club, and it was only when we pulled up outside Ibrox – bearing in mind that it was pitch black – that I realised what was going on.'

Rangers had developed a ruthless streak, and at a good time too, as they travelled to Rugby Park, Kilmarnock, and rattled up six goals without reply. The Light Blues topped the league so early in the season for the first time in six years and, although early days, knew they were in with a real chance of grinding Celtic's record title run to a halt.

The only stumbling block came in the shape of a man who had been given a racehorse, a £3,000 car and a 'staggering' wage of £300 a week to remain at Southampton. Mick Channon was a wonderful player and put Rangers to the sword in the second leg of their Texaco Cup tie. Channon failed to score in the 2-0 second-leg win, but ran the show and earned the applause of Wallace, who said, 'He is the only real world-class player in England – no one in Scotland could afford him.'

Rangers moved on and scored another six on their travels – this time at Dunfermline – and Parlane netted five, including two inside the first seven minutes to effectively kill off the Pars. He had another two in the net, although both were ruled out for offside. Wallace said, 'I am delighted for the boy. We have had to coax him back into scoring mode.'

Rangers were in a rich vein of form and one man earning his share of the limelight was goalkeeper Stewart Kennedy, the one-time keeper of Linlithgow Rose. By the middle of November, Kennedy had played 25 times and Wallace labelled him 'the most consistent keeper in the country'.

Rangers took their unbeaten run to 11 with a narrow win over Dundee and Scottish football soon had its first genuine title fight in a number of years. The very prospect of a flag race going down to the wire brought supporters flooding back and Rangers were now playing to average home gates in excess of 20,000, a marked increase in the 12,000-to-15,000 crowds of the previous season.

Celtic thumped Airdrie 6-0 at Parkhead, and Rangers put five past Motherwell at Fir Park, to remain the only unbeaten team in Britain. But suddenly the wheels came off the wagon, or at least one did. Hibs, for a long period the third force in the Scottish game, came to Ibrox and won by the only goal. Johnstone suffered a knee injury and on rushed trainer Tommy Craig. As the duo left the field, referee Bobby Davidson flashed the yellow card at Craig for entering the field of play without an invite!

It was a temporary blip, and normal service resumed with wins over Dundee United and Aberdeen, at Pittodrie. Celtic also continued to win, but Rangers had the better goal difference and remained top of the pile.

The lead soon changed hands and Celtic were top for Christmas, and the traditional Ne'erday clash took on extra significance. A win for Celtic at Ibrox would see them stretch their lead to four points, while victory for the Light Blues and they would be back on top.

The match turned into the 'Tommy McLean show', as the pint-sized winger teased and tormented the Celtic defence all afternoon and had a hand in all three goals in front of 70,000 fervent supporters. Rangers were so dominant that Celtic were left picking up the scraps. McLean set up Johnstone for the opener in just six minutes, scored the second and then made the last of the day for Parlane to put the seal on a comprehensive victory.

And while Rangers were registering another five goals on their travels, sorry Celtic were slumping to a 3-2 loss at home to Motherwell. Rangers were marvellous in the Boghead mud and little McLean – this time with a hat-trick – was again the star of the show. The show of strength at Dumbarton had the bookies flapping around to change their title odds, and they made Rangers hot favourites at 4/6 to win the league.

The Scottish Cup was a different matter. After drawing at Pittodrie, Rangers lost the replay to an extra-time goal by Duncan Davidson. It was a bitter blow but they received a pick-me-up the following night when Celtic drew 2-2 with Dumbarton at Parkhead. Rangers were a point ahead with a game in hand.

Meanwhile, the Ibrox club had shot to the top of Britain's off-pitch money-earning table with an annual income of more than £400,000, through their successful lottery and *Rangers News*, which was selling around 25,000 copies per week.

Saturday 23 February 1975 was the pivotal day in Rangers' attempts to halt Celtic's charge for ten successive titles. While the Light Blues made the short trip to Shawfield, to face Clyde, Celtic headed through to Edinburgh for a showdown with third-top Hibs. McKean and O'Hara secured a Rangers win, but a double from Arthur Duncan put Celtic to the sword in a 2-1 win. Peter Latchford made his debut for Celtic in goals and was anything but a success. The opening paragraph in one national newspaper's match report suggested, 'Celtic just don't have it any more'. The tide wasn't just turning, it had turned.

The following Saturday it took a last-gasp McLean winner against Hearts to keep the gap at four points, and with seven games left, Rangers re-signed Colin Stein from Coventry for £80,000 to help them over the line. The Stein transfer included a special clause. The striker had been suffering from an ankle injury and Rangers signed him on the premise that he wouldn't break down in training or while playing. They had a month's grace before the transfer fully kicked in, but supporters needn't have had any fears on that front.

Stein said, 'I'm a bit nervous about coming back although I don't know why as the fans have always been great to me. I enjoyed my time down south but Rangers always had a special place with me. It was a wrench to leave but all I want to do now is stay and score goals.'

Stein played his part in Rangers' win over St Johnstone but his next game – at Dundee – was anything but a happy affair. 30,000 packed into Dens Park but violence erupted on the terracing when the striker was sent off for arguing with referee George Smith, after a tussle with Dundee's Tommy Gemmell. It was alleged that Stein swore at Smith. The incident proved the catalyst for fans to hurl cans and bottles, before invading the pitch and fighting with opposition supporters.

Police with dogs moved in to quell the unrest and several Rangers players – including skipper Greig – appealed to supporters for calm. Order was restored after five minutes and Rangers, one down from the first minute, refused to surrender. They equalised through McLean six minutes after the break and Parlane scored a late winner to ensure another two vital points in the title race.

And with Dundee United winning 1-0 at Parkhead, Rangers suddenly found themselves eight points ahead with six games left to play – and Celtic boss Jock Stein conceded the title. He insisted Celtic couldn't win a world record tenth successive title. It may have been music to the ears of the massive Rangers support – but Wallace was having none of it, and said, 'It was a great victory, given we were down to ten men. All we won, though, was another two points.'

The following Saturday, Gers fans taunted their rivals with 'Hello! Hello! It's three in a row' as Celtic slumped to yet another defeat, this time at Airdrie. A returning Johnstone scored twice as the Light Blues brushed Motherwell aside to go nine points clear with five games left – and remember, it was only two points for a win. But Wallace refused to accept the title was won, although that great day was just one week away, and when Rangers travelled to Easter Road, all they needed was a point – which is exactly what they got.

Stein was the hero of the hour when he threw himself at a McKean cross to bullet home the header that cancelled out Ally McLeod's opener. The ground was packed. The majority of the 38,585 crowd were decked out in red, white and blue and when the final whistle blew, 29 minutes after Stein's goal, the stadium erupted. The home fans quickly made their exit, leaving the vast terracing to resemble a blue sea of Ibrox, and the Rangers players received a rapturous welcome when they re-emerged from the tunnel to take the traditional lap of honour.

However, the biggest cheer was reserved for Wallace, the man who had reclaimed the championship after an 11-year wait. After the final whistle he had planted a big smacker on the forehead of his goal hero, but this time he simply lapped up the adulation of the supporters. Wallace, renowned for his hard-man image, had earlier shown his softer side when he sent on Greig with just two minutes remaining to replace Jardine. The Rangers skipper said, 'I just want to say thanks to the boss. It was a wonderful gesture and I was thrilled to be allowed to share in what was a great moment.'

Wallace said, 'This is the greatest moment of my life. I'm proud of each and every one of my players. Now it's Europe, and the big one. A few years ago I left Hearts because I wanted to be a part of the biggest competition in Europe – and now we're in it. Working for Rangers is the best job in the world. If I won the pools tomorrow I'd pay to work for them.'

It was Stein's first goal since rejoining the club and he said, 'I wasn't particularly worried about not scoring before today. I knew the first goal would come – but, boy, what a time to get it. It will live with me forever.'

The title may have been in the bag, but Wallace demanded his players reach the 55-point mark, and a draw at Tannadice and wins over Aberdeen and Arbroath put them over the threshold – with a game to spare. As Celtic lost their eighth game of the season, Hibs moved above them to finish runners-up.

A last-day defeat to Airdrie at Ibrox in front of 60,000 failed to take the gloss off Rangers' title win, especially as they had ended the campaign 11 points clear of their biggest rivals, and supporters lapped up the sight of warrior Greig parading the league trophy round the track while riding a chariot!

In 1875, Rangers had shared the inaugural First Division championship with Dumbarton. Now, 100 years on, the last ever old-style title was theirs, and theirs alone.

11

Three 'n' Easy For Gers

FOR Rangers, the long road to retaining their mantle as top team in the country started in the quiet Norwegian seaport town of Stavanger. There, the newly-crowned Scottish champions met Viking, who had also qualified for the European Cup, in a challenge match. With several players on international duty with Scotland, Wallace used the friendly to give squad members their opportunity, although it was a seasoned campaigner who showed the way. Not even the bands, parades, smoke bombs and fireworks, as the Norwegians celebrated a national holiday, could shift the spotlight from Alex MacDonald, who notched a hat-trick in the 5-0 win.

The players enjoyed a few days' rest before jetting off on their long-awaited world tour. Canada, New Zealand and Australia were on the itinerary but Wallace would have to do without his four internationals for the first game in Vancouver. Schoolboy Alistair Dawson and 19-year-old Martin Henderson were added to the squad.

Wallace said, 'We've left a number of disappointed players behind but we're taking some youngsters because we want to push them on. We're thinking of Europe and the need to widen our resources.' Dawson made his debut in the opening game, which Rangers won 4-0 thanks, in the main, to a Graham Fyfe double.

After some excellent hospitality, the Rangers party left for New Zealand and a sell-out match in Auckland.

Meanwhile, in Bucharest, Jardine picked up a groin injury in the European Championship match, which ended 1-1, and was ordered home to Glasgow to rest up. The others, Parlane, Jackson and Kennedy, began the marathon 53-hour journey, by air, to New Zealand.

Rangers, meanwhile, beat a New Zealand Select 3-1, thanks to a Johnstone double and a goal by MacDonald. Youngsters Dawson and Henderson were rested for the next match of the tour, against Canterbury in Christchurch, and the game ended in a shock 2-2 draw. More of a worry for Wallace, though, was injuries to key players. MacDonald was carried off with a suspected broken ankle while Johnstone, Forsyth and Dawson, who had come on as a substitute, picked up knocks. Stein and Greig scored for the Gers.

When the party moved on to Oz, Sydney Airport was jam-packed with exiled Gers fans desperate for a glimpse of their heroes. Rangers were in town to play an Aussie national side, but Wallace wasn't among the advanced guard, as he had been left behind in Wellington with club officials. The party had been broken up due to fog, and the others were 'follow-following' on a later plane.

But the gaffer was delighted when he discovered that MacDonald had only dislocated his ankle, and he added, 'The fact that the Aussies have so many of their World Cup squad playing means we face a tough match. For me this is the big one of the tour. We want a win for the supporters who have given us such a fantastic reception.'

Former Celtic star Willie Wallace was refused permission to play for the Aussies as he hadn't been resident in the country for the statutory 12 months. Meanwhile, the Australian Soccer Federation confirmed it was to ask Wallace to be the national coach for the build-up to the 1978 World Cup finals in Argentina. A spokesman for the governing body, which planned to offer an annual salary of £12,500, said, 'We will approach Mr Wallace while he is in Australia.'

The Socceroos were keen to replace outgoing Yugoslav boss Rale Rasic, who managed the team at the finals in Germany. Wallace responded by saying, 'At the moment there is only one country for football, and that is Scotland. I'm a Rangers man through and through and very happy at Ibrox, where I still have a big job to do. I'm flattered by the approach, though.'

Rangers, buoyed by the inclusion of Parlane and Jackson, beat the Aussies 2-1, thanks to a double by the former – which raised Wallace's stock even higher. He said, 'It was a tremendous performance and the result was the one I was looking for. The reception we got from the 32,000 crowd made the Cricket Ground seem just like Ibrox. Nearly everyone there was a Rangers fan.'

The party moved on to Brisbane, where once again they were set to face the Aussie national squad, and 'relaxed' by watching the Wales v England rugby league match where forearm smashes were the order of the day, which prompted Wallace to say, 'If you wanted to learn the art of fighting this was the place to be. It was a real Donnybrook.'

He added, 'Beating the Aussies again would be tremendous. We have suffered from jet-lag, dateline changes and injuries, yet we have produced the results and football to match.' But the Light Blues' hopes of a Commonwealth clean-sweep ended in Brisbane, when they lost the match. Wallace said, 'It was a good, hard game and they were the better side. We were disappointed because we had set our hearts on completing the tour undefeated and I thought we could do it.'

Wallace put his players through a brief training session ahead of their match in Victoria and scowled after discovering he had been dubbed the 'Kilted Killer' by the local press, due to his penchant for training his players hard. But a smile broke through when his injury crisis started to clear up, with McKean, Forsyth, Greig and Dawson all able to take part in the session.

Prior to the game, big-mouth Aussie coach Tony Boggi boasted about what his team would do to the Light Blues. Wallace countered by telling him Rangers never lose two games in a row, and he was spot on as the Gers cruised to a 5-1 victory. Rangers were 3-0 up after 20 minutes and the game was effectively over. Boggi reacted by saying, 'Players in Melbourne are much too slow. Rangers annihilated us with their speed. I place the blame on the club coaches who do not get their players fit enough, and on the players themselves who don't want to train.'

Before the next match, against South Australia, Wallace hit out at members of the Aussie press for criticising his team, and said, 'Frankly, a lot of them don't know a thing about football – and they haven't liked it when I've told them as much. They haven't taken the trouble to understand the spate of injuries which have upset our planning and tactics.'

The Hindmarch Stadium was no place for the faint-hearted and the match with South Australia didn't materialise into the easy victory Wallace had hoped for. In fact, it took an Alex Miller penalty ten minutes from time to secure a 2-1 win. 33,000 saw Aussie World Cup star James Lean put the hosts ahead from the spot on the hour, although Parlane equalised six minutes later.

The final match of the month-long tour was against Western Australia, in Perth, and attracted a crowd of 10,000. Johnstone gave Rangers a half-time lead but they were stunned by two goals after the break which saw the tour end in defeat.

On their arrival back in Scotland, Wallace was quick to sing the praises of 17-year-old Ally Dawson, and said, 'We left with a boy and came back with a man. He is all grown up and ready for first-team action. The boy was a bit strung out because of exams when he joined us. On top of that, he didn't know the first-team players all that well. Then he caught a virus and picked up an ankle injury. But believe me – he slotted in really well.'

Colin Stein awaited the draw for the first round of the European Cup with added interest as he eyed the club's Euro goalscoring record, held jointly by the 'terrible twins', Jimmy Millar and Ralph Brand. Stein had scored ten times in Europe for Gers, just two behind Millar and Brand, and was given the opportunity to beat the record when Rangers were drawn against Bohemians of Ireland. The first leg was down for Ibrox but Bohemians manager Billy Young was keen for a switch of dates, so the Dalymount Park side could make an extra few quid.

Meanwhile, Rangers were installed as red-hot 5/4 favourites to win the first ever Premier League title, a fact that didn't interest Wallace in the slightest. He said, 'My main concern is winning games, not in what the bookies say. I can hardly wait for the new season to start. I think we are in for a terrific year with big crowds most weeks. Competition for first-team places will be keener than ever.'

Rangers opened with a challenge from top German side Hertha Berlin, who finished runners-up in the previous season's West German Super League. And they didn't disappoint. Despite Parlane giving the Light Blues an early lead, a double from Hans Weiner and a goal on the hour had Hertha on easy street before the Gers grabbed a second through MacDonald late on. Sadly, McCloy was cruelly taunted by Rangers fans after he lost the third goal, as chants for Stewart Kennedy rang round the stadium. Wallace said, 'Peter has the character to get over that kind of criticism. It won't affect him.'

Wallace stuck with McCloy for the opening League Cup match of the season and he was rewarded by an assured display in Rangers' 6-1 success over Airdrie. However, McCloy was shamefully barracked by a section of the crowd before the match, and although Wallace refused to condemn those responsible, he said, 'The big fellow was outstanding and made several terrific saves.'

The pantomime continued the following Saturday when the Ibrox tannoy announced that Kennedy was in goals despite the man sporting the number one shirt quite clearly being McCloy. And the big keeper was having a great game – even saving a penalty kick – until he goofed with ten minutes to go by allowing a Joe Wark drive to squirm under his body and into the net. The goal ensured Motherwell a share of the spoils.

McCloy made sure there would be no gaffes in his next game – a 6-0 romp over Clyde at Ibrox – to put the Light Blues in the driving seat for a quarter-final place. Scotland boss Willie Ormond was at the game but somehow managed to overlook on-form winger Tommy McLean, despite the wee man setting up five of Rangers' six goals. On the same night, Rangers reserves beat Clyde 11-1.

However, crowd violence again made the headlines when Rangers travelled to Motherwell for a League Cup tie. The players were taken off the park when fighting in the enclosure spilled on to the pitch.

And worse was to come the following weekend when Rangers hoisted the title flag before their opening league match of the season – against Celtic. The week previous, Waddell had defended the club's right to unfurl the flag on the opening day of the season, and insisted it wasn't provocative. He said, 'This is a sporting occasion and I know the Celtic supporters will treat it as such. I don't anticipate any trouble.' A Celtic supporters' chief had appealed to Rangers not to unfurl the flag.

Sadly, the match was marred by unprecedented violence in which almost 100 supporters were arrested, three stabbed and a further 77 injured. Before the match, supporters of both clubs went at each other and after the game, an 18-year-old Rangers fan was thrown over a bridge and on to the M8 motorway.

To the football, though, and Rangers had started off the new campaign in the best way possible. Wallace had stated pre-match that his team were in the best possible shape and proved it by beating Celtic 2-1. Dalglish had given Celtic the lead just before half-time but goals by Johnstone and Young ensured a real psychological feather in the cap for Wallace and his boys. McCloy was named man of the match to once again justify his inclusion.

Next up was the club's first European Cup tie in more than ten years. Bohemians visited Ibrox for the first leg and despite manager Wallace appealing for patience among the support, his side romped into a 4-1 lead in the opening half-hour. But the manager was fuming the following day when he learned that Alex MacDonald had missed the tie unnecessarily, due to a clerical blunder by UEFA. A Swiss official said, 'MacDonald should not have been banned. We're sorry.'

Rangers had withdrawn MacDonald from the squad after receiving a letter saying he was due to serve a ban for bookings collected two years previous. MacDonald had, in fact, only been booked once. An angry Wallace said, 'Though we won 4-1, the communication from UEFA denied us the use of a valuable player. It could have cost us a place in the second round.'

Rangers moved into the semi-finals of the League Cup, but only after a nerve-shredding extra-time win over Queen of the South at Dumfries. Celtic, Partick Thistle, and Montrose, who knocked out Hibs, were the other qualifiers. Meanwhile, a 1-1 draw in Dublin – after which the Gers team bus was stoned – ensured Rangers progressed to the second round of the European Cup.

French cracks St Etienne lay in wait but the preparation for the Light Blues couldn't have been worse. Thumped 3-0 by Ayr United at Somerset, they lost their place at the Premier League summit to Celtic, and a 2-1 defeat at Motherwell the following Saturday added to the woe. Celtic were the big winners that foggy afternoon, when their match with Hibs at Celtic Park was abandoned after 83 minutes – with the Easter Road side 2-0 up.

Ahead of the tie with St Etienne, Wallace admitted he had yet to find a settled side, especially with the likes of Forsyth and Jardine missing large chunks of the season through injury. Of the first leg at the Geoffroy-Guichard Stadium, the boss expected the French to carry the game to his side, especially with 40,000 screaming fans behind them. He was also aware that on one of the widest pitches in Europe, St Etienne would pin their hopes on the speed of two tricky wingers, a commodity which had more or less become extinct on the European stage.

Rangers were forced to alter their line-up before the match when McCloy suffered a suspected fractured wrist saving a Colin

Stein thunderbolt. Wallace's pre-match prediction came true in 28 minutes when lightning-quick winger Rocheteau zipped past Miller and sent in a cross for Pat Revelli to hammer into the net. Rangers had a few opportunities but were undone by a defensive error with virtually the last kick of the ball. MacDonald was lethargic with a pass to Jardine and in nipped Bathenay to whip the ball past Kennedy. Rangers had been just 30 seconds from a decent result.

But the Light Blues had the perfect opportunity to erase the memories of their French disappointment just three days later when they met Celtic in the League Cup Final at Hampden. The scriptwriters must have been hard at it the previous night as MacDonald went from zero to hero in just 72 hours. Young sent over a delightful cross and MacDonald, as he had done so often in a marvellous career, ghosted in front of a defender, this time Danny McGrain, to glance home a header for the only goal of the game.

And from the red-hot atmosphere of an Old Firm cup final to the red-hot atmosphere of an Old Firm league match. It ended honours even, with Parlane giving Rangers the lead, and Paul Wilson equalising three minutes later. It meant Celtic maintained their one-point advantage at the top of the table. Next up for Wallace was the second leg against St Etienne, but it was to be a disappointing night as the Frenchmen earned a 2-1 win to ease through to the next round.

When Rangers lost to Hearts at Ibrox, at the start of November, some hacks called it a crisis. It was the Gers' fifth defeat in seven games and, as a consequence, they dropped into the bottom half of the table. Wallace came out fighting and demanded an improvement from his players. He demanded more character – and got it. Comfortable wins over Dundee United and St Johnstone put the Gers back on top. Wallace had tinkered with his formation and it paid off. One of their main problems had been a lack of goals, but with nine in two games, it looked like a case of problem solved.

But by Christmas, Celtic had established a three-point lead in one of the closest title races in years, with the top five having lost at least four games by the turn of the year. The New Year's Day clash between the Old Firm at Ibrox was shaping up to be a cracker – and crucial.

And it was the man from Montrose who proved the difference in another enthralling contest. Kenny Watson scored the only goal of the game, before a crunch win at Tynecastle hoisted Rangers level on points with Celtic, who had the better goal difference. It was perhaps credit to Celtic caretaker boss Sean Fallon that he had kept his side in front for so long given that manager Jock Stein had suffered serious injury in a horrendous car crash on the main England to Scotland trunk road.

One of the main reasons for the Rangers revival was the return to form of Jackson and Forsyth. Wallace had the pair in for extra training sessions, but while one Colin was enjoying an Indian summer, another was at his lowest ebb. Stein had featured in just 12 of the 38 games that season and was being kept out the team by Henderson and Parlane. Wallace said, 'He has lost confidence and only he can fix it. You have to work hard to get a first-team jersey at Rangers and everyone knows that.'

By the end of January, Rangers led the title race, and their next four fixtures – Dundee, Ayr and Motherwell away from home, and Aberdeen at Ibrox – were crucial. But they slipped up in the first of the four, registering a draw at Dens Park.

Rangers beat Aberdeen at Ibrox, and Wallace sang the praises of Derek Johnstone. 'Pound for pound,' he insisted, 'he is the best player in Britain. Derek is big, strong and has great stamina. He heads the ball better than most others and I can play him as a sweeper, centre-half, midfielder or centre-forward and he will do a terrific job in each position.'

After the game against the Dons, which Rangers won 2-1, Pittodrie boss Ally MacLeod said, 'It will be a different story next week when we play Rangers in the Scottish Cup.' He was right as rampant Rangers posted a 4-1 success. It was a St Valentine's Day massacre and for once, MacLeod was speechless.

Ayr United and Motherwell were duly despatched in the Premier League but Celtic still topped the table by a point. The flag race was heating up as the season entered March, although a break for a Scottish Cup quarter-final tie against Queen of the South at Palmerston proved one-sided as Rangers won 5-0. Suddenly, there was talk of Rangers winning an astonishing treble of Premier League, Scottish Cup and League Cup, which was already in the bag.

Saturday 13 March was the day the Old Firm were supposed to meet at Ibrox, but flu in both camps put paid to the fixture. It was cancelled 48 hours before the scheduled kick-off as eight Rangers players were confined to bed. But the postponement brought an amazing outburst by Hibs managing director Tom Hart, who claimed there was NO flu at Ibrox and that both halves of the Old Firm were scared to play in case they got beat. Immediately after the Hearts v Hibs match, he said, 'I'm disgusted at the action Celtic and Rangers took to get their game postponed. They were afraid to meet each other. They are cowards and I'm disappointed in them.'

Rangers chairman Rae Simpson hit back, 'Tom is wide of the mark. He has put a lot into the game and I respect him for that but he must not think he can get away with making such rash statements.'

Wallace's squad was just about back to full fitness on the eve of their home league clash with Hearts, with one reporter suggesting the manager had Rangers playing 'magnificent football'. Hearts were the only team to win in the Premier League at Ibrox that season, but goals by Johnstone, Greig and McLean ensured no repeat and the Light Blues remained tucked in behind Celtic, just one point adrift.

After the win over Hearts, Wallace was asked if his side could win the treble, 'If there were ten competitions in Scotland I'd want Rangers to win every one. I would like to win the treble this season, if not the next, but you can take it that at some point I will. Or, more correctly, Rangers will. Okay, I'm a big hard man. Every boss has to be tough, but I've got men under me, not wee boys. They win the matches, not me.'

And he had special praise for his skipper. 'What a great player John Greig is, has been, and in my view will be for some time to come. The team is loaded with talent but not one is a big-head. The treble is there for the taking but I won't be celebrating while we haven't won anything. But I'll sure as hell tell you this, nobody ever wanted to win anything more than me. Maybe Willie Waddell, but I'll go for a dead-heat on that. We are a team. That's what Rangers is all about.'

A 3-0 win at Easter Road proved the Light Blues were genuine Premier League contenders, but Celtic continued to grind out results, such as a 1-0 home win over St Johnstone in front of just 16,000. Celtic still led the league table by a point – with just seven games to go. The following Saturday, Celtic lost at Tannadice as Rangers cruised to another 3-0 victory, this time at home to Dundee. Greig was again among the scorers.

Meanwhile, Hibs' big-mouth MD Tom Hart was ordered to apologise to both Rangers and Celtic for his 'coward' outburst, but for once he seemed lost for words. A fortnight's silence prompted the League Management Committee to discuss his fate. Forty-eight hours later, Hart offered a grovelling apology and insisted the use of the word 'coward' hadn't been meant to reflect on any individuals.

Regardless, Rangers had bigger fish to fry but on the eve of the home match against Ayr United, winger Quinton Young was sensationally told to leave the club. 'Cutty' was given a free transfer by Wallace and told, 'Don't come back!'

At the time, Young said, 'I have been a Rangers fan all my life so when I was told by the manager that the club no longer wanted me I was shattered. I was unhappy at not getting first-team football so I asked the boss for a meeting. When I confronted him I was shocked to hear him say, "If you want a transfer you can have a free right now – and don't come back."'

Rangers had enough in the tank to edge home against Ayr, but Celtic slipped up again in a 1-1 draw at home to Aberdeen. The following Saturday, Rangers clinched the inaugural Premier League title. It took Derek Johnstone just 22 seconds to fire the only goal of the game – and before a Dundee United player had even touched the ball.

And guess who missed the goal? Wallace was just emerging from the tunnel when he heard the roars of the fans, and admitted that all he saw was big DJ standing with his arms in the air. 'That'll do me,' was all he said.

Meanwhile, Ayr United boosted their survival hopes with a 2-1 win at Celtic Park. The championship was now the property of Rangers Football Club and Jock Wallace. The boss said, 'I never had any doubts we would not win the championship. We had a poorish spell in the early part of the season but we found ourselves again.'

Rangers were gunning for the Scottish Cup – and the treble – and only Hearts stood in their way. As 75,000 fans filed into Hampden, once again Johnstone scored inside a minute to get the champions off to a flying start. In fact, as the game had started a minute or so early, Johnstone had in effect scored before kick-off! MacDonald scored on the stroke of half-time and big DJ wrapped it up with a sweet shot from close range.

The traditional lap of honour had been banned at cup finals, but a defiant Wallace led his players round the edge of the Hampden turf with the cheers of supporters ringing in their ears. One reporter heaped praise on the gaffer's undoubted management skills, but Wallace growled, 'Shut up about me and give my boys the credit.' Wallace was, however, due credit, especially for the way he had galvanised the squad during an early-season loss of form.

And the campaign was brought to a satisfactory conclusion when Greig was named Scottish Football Writers' Player of the Year at the age of 33 – the first man to win the honour twice.

But there was still time for Wallace to become embroiled in a war of words with Manchester United manager Tommy Docherty after the latter had likened Tom Forsyth to a Clydesdale horse. Docherty reckoned his sweeper Martin Buchan should be included in the Scotland side for the final Home International match against

England at the expense of Forsyth. He said, 'When you talk about Buchan and Forsyth, it's like comparing a thoroughbred with a Clydesdale, or a Rolls-Royce with a van. Forsyth is a big strong, hard fellow, but as regards finesse, class and speed, Buchan has it every time.'

Wallace responded by saying, 'I bitterly resent Mr Docherty's allegations about Tom Forsyth. In his time with Rangers he has won two league, Scottish Cup and League Cup medals. He has represented Scotland at various levels and never let his country or club down. I am resentful that Docherty has chosen to call two fine players into dispute. It is Willie Ormond's job to pick the Scotland team. Docherty should keep quiet and I'll be telling him this to his face.' Forsyth had played in wins over Wales and Northern Ireland, and Ormond waded into the debate by saying, 'I select the teams, not Tommy Docherty.'

Scotland beat England 2-1, Forsyth was exceptional and Docherty apologised. One story with a happy ending.

12

Turbulent Tour

THE flames of Tommy Docherty's savage attack on Tom Forsyth were dying down when Rangers arrived in British Columbia at the start of their tour of the USA and Canada. At a press conference, the Ibrox party were given a pre-match handout in which Eckhard Krautzen, coach of Vancouver Whitecaps, described Rangers as 'aggressive', and Manchester United, due in Canada the following week, as 'a side of high skill'.

Jock Wallace was fuming and said, 'You don't sweep the board in Scotland with a team that has nothing to offer in football ability. We will show the Whitecaps that even with a "Clydesdale" in the team, we can turn on the style and entertain the public. This fellow Krautzen used to be a friend of mine. He was my interpreter at a coaching school in Bayreuth after Rangers had beaten Moscow Dynamo in Barcelona. He has visited me at Ibrox but the last time he saw Rangers play was three years ago, and we have changed a bit in style since then, and I intend to ensure he discovers that.'

Wallace took a squad of 17 across the pond but the party didn't include Sandy Jardine, who had been troubled by a heel injury for most of the season. Wallace worked closely with the Rangers medical staff to draw up a training programme for the international defender.

Five games were scheduled for the treble winners, with three in the northern states of America and a couple in Canada. Wallace said, 'The tour is preparation for our assault on Europe, hence the reason we've brought Kenny Watson, Alex O'Hara and Iain Munro.'

It was a weary Rangers party that had arrived in Vancouver after a marathon 17-hour journey from Glasgow – and they flew straight into a scare. Yes, another one! The city had just been shaken by a tremor, but the players were reassured by supporters at the airport that it was 'pretty normal'. One fan added, 'There was a tremor, a quite distinct one, but there was no real damage done in the city. We suffered some power cuts and that was about it. It was a little frightening, mind you.'

And things hadn't gone too well back home either. Derek Johnstone had overslept and by the time he reached Glasgow Airport from his home in Dundee, the flight to Heathrow had left. Thankfully, though, the connecting flight to Vancouver was delayed an hour and DJ made it with a little to spare.

The players were wanted men by the media, and were forced to cancel their day off to satisfy demand for local television and radio interviews. Advanced sales for the match against the Whitecaps were the best ever seen for a touring match, and a local official said, 'Rangers are a big attraction because of their great success in Scotland – but they were also impressive when they won here last year.'

The Whitecaps were backed by millionaire Wendy McDonald, president of her own engineering firm. She had pumped $100,000 into Canadian soccer and the glamorous grandmother – who had ten children and 18 grandchildren – was a director of the club.

Wallace decided to field his Scottish Cup Final-winning team and the opening game proved a real razzmatazz affair watched by more than 13,000 – double the Whitecaps' normal gate. The match was played on tartan turf but Rangers found it hard going and were twice forced to come from behind before eventually snatching a 2-2 draw.

The following day, Rangers received two requests from North American soccer clubs – and not your average requests either. Krautzen had the audacity to ask Wallace if he could sign Greig and Johnstone for the following season, which was the Scottish close season, before millionaire businessman Bill Cox, owner of the Hartford club in New England, invited Willie Waddell to fill the general manager's role at his club. On the move for Greig and Johnstone, Wallace said, 'It's something for us to think about. Mind you, it's a wee bit of a turnaround from a man who was criticising us for a lack of skill recently. It's unlikely we will let them go but it's an honour for the club that the West German has realised their true value.'

Krautzen was so determined to land the players that he offered to pay for them out of his own pocket, after the club refused to foot any more transfer bills!

Cox wanted Waddell to stay on for a month at the end of Rangers' tour to offer his expertise. He turned down the request because it had come too late. When in charge of Kilmarnock in the 1960s, Waddell had met Cox at an invitational tournament in New York, and jetted out to St Louis to help a team he was involved with.

Rangers' next tour match was against Seattle Sounders, who included former Ibrox favourite Dave Smith in their ranks. The Sounders also had Geoff Hurst, England's World Cup Final hat-trick hero of 1966. The game was to be played in the Kingdome Stadium, an arena that made the best European stadiums look like relics from the dark ages. The $60m super stadium towered 350 feet in the air and was one of the city's main tourist attractions. It had seats for 65,000 people and as well as soccer, it staged basketball, baseball, religious crusades and even symphony concerts.

The stadium had a giant cinema screen which flashed action replays to supporters, but the seats in front of the screen were the cheapest in the house at just $2.50, because the people sitting there couldn't see action replays. There were also 45 smaller monitors all over the ground. The one drawback was the synthetic turf, although it was expected to be of a better quality than the surface at Vancouver, where Tommy McLean and Johnny Hamilton had picked up blisters.

MacDonald scored the only goal of the game, and it was well worth watching again on the big screen. While the Seattle defence kept an eye on the two Dereks, wee Doddie stole in to plant a header out of the reach of the goalkeeper. Just over 11,000 fans watched the action in the Pacific port and saw Rangers turn in an outstanding performance. They hit the woodwork three times and Parlane had a header cleared off the line.

The Light Blues were then sleepless in Seattle as they played their next game just 24 hours later in neighbouring Portland, where they faced the Timbers in the Civic Stadium. The Yanks were in the middle of their Presidential race and with candidates Gerald Ford and Jimmy Carter in town, both were invited to attend the match, but Wallace refused to get too excited, and said, 'It would be fine – but we have other things to think about!'

Chris Dangerfield gave the Americans the lead midway through the first half but McLean equalised just four minutes later with a 30-yard shot that skidded all the way across the synthetic surface and into the net. The game then became a dour struggle until a horrific tackle on MacDonald by Neil Rioch, brother of Scotland star Bruce, prompted a touchline rammy. Pursued by angry Gers players Forsyth and Miller, Rioch ran off the field and only an intervention by Wallace took the heat out of a tricky situation. Rioch was booked for the challenge and Rangers had the last laugh when O'Hara popped up in the last minute to score the winner.

After the game, the Rangers party were guests of honour at a presentation dinner, and Timbers gaffer Vic Crowe – a former manager of Aston Villa – apologised to Wallace for the conduct of Rioch. The challenge had left Doddie with stud marks on his CHEST, but asides from MacDonald, McCloy, Greig, Miller, Jackson and Hamilton were also carrying injuries and left Wallace with a selection headache for the next game in Minneapolis.

With McCloy the only goalkeeper in the party, Wallace contemplated using Derek Johnstone between the sticks. The 'Girvan Lighthouse' was having round-the-clock treatment on a damaged ankle and was rated just 50-50 to make the game against Minnesota Kicks. He said, 'I can hardly get a shoe on at the moment but we're hoping the regular ice packs will help.'

Wallace spoke about his selection problems, and said, 'We may have to use big Derek. I've looked at other possibilities, such as flying Stewart Kennedy out, or borrowing a keeper from one of the teams here, or even playing myself, but big Derek has played in goals in practice games and I wouldn't be too worried about using him. Let's face it, he could head most of the shots away!'

McCloy passed a late fitness test which allowed DJ to play at centre-half, but it was the forgotten man of Ibrox, Colin Stein, who bagged the opening goal of the game, although the Kicks scored twice in three minutes to take the lead. Henderson levelled on the hour, and Greig missed a late chance to win the match.

Fans from the Toronto Rangers Supporters' Club turned up at the airport to welcome the Light Blues back to Canada – and the players were told that they would be facing the great Eusebio, one of the finest players in the world, in the game against Metros Croatia.

Wallace was desperate to end the tour unbeaten, and as the party relaxed at Niagara Falls, the gaffer took Kenny Watson aside and told him he would have a special role in the CNE Stadium – he would be marking Eusebio. The Canadian side had the best defensive record in the North American League and Wallace knew his team would need to play well to win.

And play well they did, but the match – which ended in a 2-1 win to Rangers – descended into a riot when Johnstone was hacked down by Yugoslav hard-man Mladen Cukon, and then headbutted by the thug, who was sent off for his outrageous behaviour. And that was the cue for Metros' Yugoslav coach Ivan Markovic – known locally as 'Ivan the Terrible' – to race on to the pitch and lunge at the official. Three times Eusebio tried to stop him – and three times

Markovic tried to punch the Portuguese star. It was an incredible sight and Markovic was eventually led from the field of play.

At half-time, the crackpot Yugoslav went to the Rangers dressing room to apologise to Wallace, and the gesture helped restore calm among the 20,000 crowd. And how the crowd had roared after just 40 seconds of the first half when a Forsyth cross was headed home by Henderson. Midway through the second half Eusebio equalised, but walked straight off the park as he was still 'traumatised' by the madcap antics of his coach. With nine minutes to play, Johnstone was brought down in the box and Miller despatched the penalty kick.

The following day, Eusebio described his manager as a 'crazy man', and vowed never to play for him again. However, Markovic – who clearly hadn't learned his lesson – said, 'Eusebio is paid to play, not to think. I am paid to think. He is only a player, the same as the others. I will deal with him in due course.'

The incident in Toronto left a sour taste in the mouth, but if Wallace thought the drama was over, he was badly mistaken. On the eve of their departure, he received not one but two offers to remain in Canada as a coach. He was offered £20,000 a year to manage Vancouver Whitecaps, while Toronto Metros revealed they were 'monitoring the situation'.

Wallace refused to discuss the move and insisted he was just looking forward to getting home, although he was scheduled to head to Croix, in France, almost straight away to accompany the Rangers youth team to a prestigious tournament.

13

The Viking Warrior

THE Ibrox trophy cabinet was bulging and the new season offered the prospect of even more silverware. The squad was largely the same and with a domestic treble behind them, the manager saw no reason to tinker too much.

But a whistlestop tour of West Germany brought defeats against Werder Bremen and St Pauli, before Rangers hosted the first ever Tennent's Caledonian Cup. They invited FA Cup holders Southampton and Manchester City, winners of the English League Cup, to take part, with Bertie Auld's Partick Thistle making up the numbers. After seeing off the Jags, Rangers faced Southampton in the final but lost 2-1 in front of 40,000.

When it really mattered, Rangers demolished St Johnstone 5-0 in the League Cup opener. Normal service had been resumed, although Wallace confirmed he had been to watch Clydebank's talented winger Davie Cooper. He wasn't alone, as Scotland boss Willie Ormond was also in the stand.

Celtic salvaged a draw in the first Old Firm game of the season after being two down and Rangers' miserable run continued when FC Zurich came to Ibrox for a European Cup tie and left with a draw. It didn't get any better and when Clydebank visited Govan for the first leg of the League Cup quarter-finals, Cooper inspired his side to a 3-3 draw. The Bankies wide boy was in demand, and turned down an approach by Arsenal. West Ham, Liverpool, West Brom, Derby County and Aston Villa had also made enquiries about Coop.

On the Saturday before the return match in Zurich, Rangers thumped Hearts 4-2 in a victory inspired by iron man skipper John Greig. The players and management then turned their attention to achieving Mission Impossible, and doing what no Rangers side had ever done before – qualifying after failing to win the home leg.

There was much talk before the match about Rangers' tired and old-fashioned approach to European matches, and how they would eventually have to change their style to the 'Bayern Munich way', a nod to the German club who had completely reinvented themselves in the European arena.

Once again, though, they were killed off by an early goal. The Light Blues pounded their opponents but just couldn't score. They had five players booked, and Johnstone sent off, but at the end of the night, honest endeavour proved insufficient. Moments after the final whistle, the post-mortem began. 'The Rangers players – Tommy McLean apart – lacked class. We just don't have it in Scotland anymore,' was the opinion of a leading Scottish hack. 'In our desperation to find new idols to replace immortals like Morton, Baxter and Meiklejohn, we glorify players who wouldn't have been allowed to carry a hamper into Ibrox 20 years ago.'

There was no disputing the gulf in quality between Rangers and the leading lights of Europe, but the defeat to Zurich had been Rangers' first of the season and perhaps the team would be judged more on how they performed on the domestic front. The manager was determined to repeat his incredible success of the season before – but it would be a big ask.

First up, though, was the 'banana skin' tie against First Division leaders Clydebank. The first leg had ended 3-3 but Greig handed Rangers an aggregate lead by scoring first at Kilbowie – until Cooper once again grabbed centre stage. He hammered in the equaliser on the hour to leave Wallace sweating for the final half hour. There were no more goals and the sides also drew a blank during 30 minutes of extra time. Referee David Syme tossed a coin for choice of venue for the third match and Greig called it right.

Before that, Wallace took his side down to Birmingham for a friendly match against Aston Villa – and promptly wished he hadn't bothered. Rioting broke out in the crowd after Frank Carrodus scored a second for Villa and the day ended with scores of supporters and policemen suffering awful injuries in some of the worst scenes of violence witnessed in the UK. The match was immediately abandoned and Willie Waddell admitted he didn't know where to turn. He added, 'These louts are killing us, it's a bloody disgrace. The best thing for clubs to do is not to ask us to face them in a challenge match, which is a tragedy. We are crucified within Britain.'

Clydebank proved a stubborn old mule and a third game failed to separate the sides. A crowd of 15,000 watched a 0-0 draw at Ibrox, and the League Cup quarter-final roadshow rolled on to Firhill. Parlane put Rangers ahead after just seven minutes, and Cooper levelled 60 seconds later. But a McKean goal on the hour was enough to finally settle the tie after more than seven hours of football.

The semi-final was a disaster. Rangers and Aberdeen clashed at Hampden Park and just one team turned up. The final result of 5-1 to Aberdeen was every bit as embarrassing as it sounds, and Wallace responded by trying to sign Cooper. Clydebank owner Jack Steedman insisted Coop was happy and would see out the season with the Bankies.

Rangers were in turmoil. Big characters were needed, not only in the dug-out but on the park as well. The next match was against league leaders Dundee United at Ibrox, and the players had to stand up and be counted – and did just that. Goals by Jackson, McKean and Parlane secured a 3-0 win, and Rangers were equally as ruthless in their next game, a 4-0 success at Kilmarnock where once again centre-half Jackson was the man with the goal-den touch. The win powered the Light Blues back up the table into third spot, just behind the 'New Firm' of Dundee United and Aberdeen.

The Light Blues started 1977 with a 3-0 home win over Kilmarnock in which Parlane and Johnstone were head and shoulders above the rest. Next up was the rearranged Old Firm clash and Rangers entered the game joint third top with Dundee United, two points behind leaders Aberdeen and one adrift of Celtic. The match appeared to be heading for stalemate until Jackson headed an Andy Lynch cross past a despairing Kennedy and into his own net.

Wallace said, 'We lost at Parkhead, but we haven't lost our championship. We are three points behind with 19 games to go, so the race is far from over. It's worth pointing out that we won the title by six points last season, and seven the season before – and you've still to see the best of Rangers.'

There was little love around on Valentine's Day when Rangers lost 3-2 at home to Dundee United and with that defeat, many insisted, had gone their chances of retaining the championship. It was all the more galling considering goals by Jackson and MacDonald had Rangers two up, and apparently cruising to victory. Celtic beat Partick Thistle 2-0 to increase their lead at the summit.

On top of Rangers' on-field woes came a transfer request from Parlane. The 23-year-old striker said, 'I want to leave Ibrox. I've been thinking about my future for some time and feel I must get away. I had a meeting with Mr Wallace to talk over my position and the answers I got weren't convincing enough. I asked him for a transfer and offered to give him it in writing but he told me not to bother.'

However, Wallace said, 'Parlane is a player expected to do his job here. If he wants to talk about a transfer then let him get on with it. I don't want to talk about it.' Keeper McCloy also reportedly asked for a move but his request was turned down.

The following week, Parlane helped Rangers to a 1-0 win over Aberdeen to go second. In the wake of the defeat, Dons boss Ally MacLeod, who never had any problem bigging up his own teams, said, 'We would be the most worthy champions – and Dundee United would be the next most worthy. We are playing the kind of football that Scotland taught the continentals in the 1920s and 1930s. We are attractive and entertaining. We might not win the title – but we deserve to.'

Wallace insisted there was far more to winning a title than attractive football, and added, 'You have to have a team of winners for a start. Players must be willing to fight when the cause seems lost – that's what we did at Pittodrie.'

Rangers were second, five points behind Celtic, and with only an outside chance of rescuing their title, but when they edged Motherwell and Aberdeen beat Celtic at Pittodrie, a chink of light appeared. A midweek draw at Tannadice helped only one team, though – Celtic.

It was all eyes on the Scottish Cup and a 2-0 win over Motherwell offered access to the last four. Wallace said, 'This was our best performance of the season and everyone contributed to the win.'

Just moments after the quarter-final ties had ended, police announced they were to launch a probe into three Aberdeen players for allegedly betting on their own team to lose a fourth round replay against Dundee – which the Dens Park men won 2-1 at Pittodrie. It was a real shock scoreline at the time.

The following weekend, Alfie Conn made his debut for Celtic against Rangers at Ibrox in a real must-win match for the Light Blues. He was the sixth player to have turned out for both halves of the Old Firm, and when Parlane scored his second of the match in 79 minutes to put Rangers 2-1 ahead, it was bedlam inside Ibrox, but Roy Aitken grabbed his second with six minutes to go and the match ended all-square.

There was anything but bedlam inside Ibrox for the next match. A tedious 1-1 draw with Ayr United was watched by just 7,000, and Wallace said, 'Obviously I am concerned about the gates. The supporters are not turning out because of our league position – it's as simple as that.'

And Rangers' title hopes were finally extinguished when they lost 1-0 to the already-doomed Kilmarnock. But Wallace wasn't the only Old Firm manager under pressure, and after Celtic had edged Dundee United that day, Jock Stein accused Radio Clyde of being biased towards Rangers. When asked by Bob Crampsey if the league title was sewn up, he replied, 'The league is far from over,' before changing tack and saying, 'Your programme hasn't said one good word about Celtic this season. You have failed to recognise any of our good points. Of course, your DJ Richard Park makes it quite clear where his allegiances lie.' Was it pressure or classic Stein tactics aimed at taking the heat off his players?

The following midweek, 23,000 turned up at Hampden for the Scottish Cup semi-final tie against Hearts, and were forced to endure one of the most boring matches ever witnessed at the national stadium – but Rangers won 2-0 thanks to goals by Jackson and Jardine.

The league was finally lost – officially – when Celtic won by a single goal at Easter Road. Despite Rangers mauling Ayr United 5-1, it was mathematically impossible to catch the other half of the Old Firm and the Light Blues looked ahead to the Scottish Cup Final.

For manager Wallace though, it was time for the post-mortem, and he said, 'Three injuries cost me the championship. We missed Jackson, Forsyth and Johnstone for large chunks of the season and it proved too much for us. No team can lose three players of that class and hope to continue without losing their edge.

'I have no fears about the future of Rangers. I have a good team and they can play at any level and I'm certainly not worried about competing in Europe next season. Scottish and European football is completely different and will remain so while we allow tackling from behind. Our front players aren't allowed to stop a ball, control it and turn. They are hit from behind, so this discourages attackers from holding it up.'

But despite clinching the runners-up spot in the league, the season ended in abject disappointment for Rangers fans when a controversial goal took the Scottish Cup to Parkhead. Kennedy parried a Roddy MacDonald header and Johannes Edvaldsson followed up with a shot from close range which appeared to strike Derek Johnstone on the knee. Referee Bob Valentine pointed to the spot and Lynch scored. Wallace said, 'The players didn't think it was a penalty. The decision upset the team.'

Rangers left for Sweden almost immediately after the final, although Jardine wasn't on the plane. The 28-year-old had refused re-signing terms and Wallace said, 'There is little point in having an unhappy player on a trip like this.'

Skipper John Greig was down in the dumps and admitted that if he lost his place in the team the following season, he would hang up his boots. 'If that happens then I'm out. I've told Rangers I won't hang around and accept charity. If I don't do a job for them in the first team, then I'll go. Reserve football is not for me.'

The Rangers party headed to Sweden and a surprise lay in store for Greig and his manager. High in the wooded hills of Hunneborg, six miles from Trollhattan, Greig and Wallace were inducted as Vikings at a late-night ceremony watched by Rangers chairman Rae Simpson and the players.

Wallace was to be known as 'Battstag', while Greig's new Viking moniker was 'Bowelk'. They were presented with documents to prove that they had earned the names of those legendary Viking warriors. Both wore helmets and capes during the traditional banquet that followed, and the main dish – prime roast rib of elk – was eaten with bare hands. The Rangers players paid tribute to their skipper by singing 'Bowelk, Bowelk, Born is the King of Ibrox Park' (to the tune of 'Noel').

Rangers then destroyed Trollhattan 7-2, with warrior Greig leading from the front and scoring the sixth in front of over 5,000 appreciative fans. It was the perfect way for the players to relax and unwind after a disappointing season.

But on Wednesday 8 June 1977, Rangers fans received a glimpse into the future when Davie Cooper signed for the Light Blues in a deal worth £100,000 to Clydebank. Cooper said, 'When I turned Jock Wallace down last season it was because I didn't think I was good enough to play for a club the size of Rangers. Now, eight months later, I reckon I'm a better player and ready. I'm from Hillhouse, in Hamilton, and a Rangers supporters' bus leaves from just across the road. When I was younger, I was on that bus every week, but I never dared to dream that one day I would play for Rangers. Now I have the chance and I'm determined to grab it with both hands.'

Wallace added, 'Cooper is the most exciting prospect in Scottish football.'

14

Trophies Galore

COOPER was the buzz word around Ibrox as the start of the 1977/78 season edged closer, although another youngster, 19-year-old Bobby Russell, signed from junior club Shettleston, had slipped into Ibrox almost unnoticed. But while the former was set to light up Scottish football, over at Kilbowie, Clydebank used a chunk of his transfer fee to install state-of-the-art floodlights.

Davie Cooper made his Rangers debut in the Scottish Highlands against Ross County in a pre-season friendly and Wallace declared himself satisfied with his big-money purchase. Coop was at the heart of everything good about the Light Blues and his new gaffer said, 'Davie seemed to be getting the feel of it and looked better as the game progressed.' Coop enjoyed his debut and said, 'I'm happy that I've got a game behind me. I honestly thought I'd scored with a shot late on but when the keeper touched it over the bar it almost broke my heart.' Russell made his debut against Nairn County a couple of days later.

In a pre-season interview, Wallace revealed he was putting his faith in youth to help push the first-team players to greater things. He said, 'Players such as Cooper, Russell, Billy McKay and Kenny Watson can help us achieve success, as we now have great strength in depth. But our experienced players also have a role to play. I rate

Tom Forsyth among the best defenders in Europe, while John Greig still has much to offer.'

At the beginning of August, Wallace flew out to Switzerland to watch Rangers' European Cup Winners' Cup opponents Young Boys of Berne in action, but his problems lay nearer to home, as the Light Blues lost the opening match of the Premier League season at Aberdeen. Goalscorer Russell, and Cooper, were outstanding but the Dons, managed by Billy McNeill, had too much in the tank. After the match, an agreement to sign Kilmarnock's Gordon Smith broke down when one of the two makeweight players in the deal refused to move to Rugby Park. Wallace vowed to do all he could to land the promising front man.

A 1-0 win over Young Boys was followed by a home defeat to Hibs, and Rangers found themselves at the foot of the table after the first two matches. When Wallace was leaving the stadium he was subjected to chants of 'What a load of rubbish', and 'Wallace must go'. Most players also ran the gauntlet of abuse. It was early days but fans feared another season of disappointment, and with the trophy cabinet bare, the pressure was firmly on the broad shoulders of the boss.

As manager of Rangers, Wallace knew what was expected of him, and on his appointment five years previous he had said, 'I know what I'm taking on. If I don't have success then I must expect the sack.'

The spectre of Scot Symon still hung in the cold Ibrox air. A man who was ruthlessly axed despite winning 17 major trophies in 13 years, Symon said, 'Unfortunately the boo boys make themselves heard and people listen to them. I feel that the real Rangers fan is prepared to take setbacks.'

A crowd of 18,500 turned up at Firhill for Rangers' next league game, most expecting the Light Blues to continue their dismal run, but ruthless Rangers set about their hosts with gusto and victory was achieved by means of finesse, skill and rhythm – and not the long punt or muscle. New signing Gordon Smith scored twice and Russell got the last of the four as Jock's babes ushered in the dawning of a new era.

It was a high-spirited Rangers party that flew out to Berne for the second leg of their preliminary round tie with Young Boys, and when Johnstone gave Rangers the lead just minutes before the break, there was a real sense of optimism in the air. But Young Boys scored twice in the first 15 minutes of the second half to tie the aggregate score at 2-2. Up popped Smith, though, to send Rangers through on an aggregate of 3-2 and even a late red card for Johnstone couldn't dampen the enthusiasm. Rangers would face Twente Enschede in the first round.

Spitz Kohn, boss of the Dutch side, immediately identified Cooper as the danger man, saying, 'He has excellent ball control and great pace. I was also impressed by the substitute McKean. The wing play of Rangers was excellent.'

But Rangers looked down and out at the break in the first Old Firm game of the season – until boss Wallace got his claws into his misfiring team. A double by Edvaldsson had Celtic on Easy Street, but two goals by Smith and one from Johnstone gave the Light Blues two points and a massive psychological boost. Now it was Celtic, with just a single point, propping up the rest.

The wheels came off a bit the following midweek when Rangers drew a blank in the first leg against Twente at Ibrox, and a comprehensive 3-0 defeat in Holland ended all hopes of a gleeful reunion with the trophy won just five years previous.

The real focus for the Light Blues was now the home front and Wallace galvanised his troops for a long and arduous campaign, battling for silverware on three fronts. He was determined to give supporters something tangible to cheer.

And the gruff boss proved once again that he was the Patron Saint of Lost Causes when Rangers roared back from the dead to grab a vital point in Paisley thanks to a gutsy 3-3 draw, before successive league wins took them up to third, behind Dundee United and Aberdeen.

Rangers' renaissance was spotted across the pond and Tampa Bay Rowdies publicly courted Wallace as a replacement for Eddie Firmani, who had left to manage New York Cosmos. The Rowdies, with Rodney Marsh and former Aberdeen star Davie Robb on their 'roster', were impressed by the manner in which Wallace seemed to coax the best from his players, but the big man turned the job down.

Rangers proved themselves genuine title contenders when they travelled up to Dundee and promptly knocked United off the top of the table. Russell was outstanding, but a Johnstone hat-trick in just nine minutes at Motherwell eased the Light Blues into second place, just a point behind Aberdeen, whom they met in a top-of-the-table clash at Ibrox the following Saturday. And what a match. Five booked, one sent off, three penalties – it had everything but, most importantly, Rangers won 3-1 to top the league for the first time that season, and boy how they looked like staying there.

The only thing that looked likely to derail Rangers' flag charge was an electricity crisis. With the country in the grip of a power workers' dispute, Rangers general manager Waddell asked for permission to play a home league game against St Mirren on a Sunday – and was told to clear it with the people at Littlewoods Pools. The game went ahead on the Saturday and the Gers edged it 2-1.

Johnstone was again on the goal trail, this time at Somerset Park, when his treble helped Rangers to a 5-0 win. Their lead at the top of the league remained at three points – but only because there was a new contender in town. Partick Thistle beat Aberdeen at Firhill to move up to second spot, thanks to an unbeaten run of eight games.

Christmas came and went and presents were exchanged but on Saturday 7 January, Rangers all but ended Celtic's title hopes. A 3-1 victory in the Old Firm match at Ibrox left the Parkhead club fourth bottom of the league. But it was the manner of the victory which pleased the majority of the 51,000 crowd, as dominant Rangers bossed the contest from start to finish.

A series of blizzards then caught Scots on the hop and there was little football played after the turn of the year, with Rangers next playing at the end of February. Wallace was still on course to turn around the situation at Ibrox in sensational style, and a 5-3 win at Motherwell ensured Rangers kept a vice-like grip on their Premier League lead.

Wallace won the Manager of the Month title for February thanks to three straight league wins, progress in the Scottish Cup and bagging a League Cup Final place. Typically, the award came with a curse as they lost their next match 3-0 at home to Aberdeen when 21-year-old Steve Archibald, playing in only his third Premier League game since a £20,000 move from Clyde, scored twice.

The Gers got back on track with a 4-1 win over Kilmarnock in the Scottish Cup quarter-finals – and it turned into the perfect dress rehearsal for the following week's League Cup Final against Celtic at Hampden. Cooper and Smith may have been rookie Gers, but they teamed up to claim the first trophy of the season, with Smith's goal in extra time proving the winner. Miller swung in a cross from the right, Peter Latchford parried MacDonald's header and the ball broke to Smith, who stooped to head home – before being submerged under a sea of blue.

Just three days before the final, though, the Rangers family were rocked by the death of winger Bobby McKean. The man signed by Jock Wallace in 1974 from St Mirren had been found dead in his car outside his house in Barrhead. The word 'tragic' didn't come close to describing the enormity of the situation. Bobby was married with a two-year-old daughter.

Rangers and Aberdeen were locked on 44 points at the start of April but the Light Blues had a game in hand. With just six games left, though, there was no margin for error.

Next up was a Scottish Cup semi-final against Dundee United. For 70 minutes, supporters craved something, anything to break the monotony – and Johnstone provided it with a trademark header that went in off the post. Skipper Greig clinched a place in the final by controlling a pass from McLean and smacking it past Hamish McAlpine.

But a setback arrived in the form of a recommendation from the SFA that the 5-3 win over Motherwell be replayed due to crowd trouble. The news saw Waddell take to the field at Ibrox and blast out a defiant message to beaks at Park Gardens, when he said, 'As you know, we are having a few problems with the SFA. On behalf of the board I would like to say that we will back to the hilt, the performances and results of the team. We will also back to the hilt the good supporters of Rangers. We will abide by the decisions of the SFA, but no way will we accept that they will crucify the club for the actions of five per cent or less of our support.'

Rangers thumped Ayr United 5-2 at Somerset, but were left walking a title tightrope when all they could muster against the Honest Men at home was a 1-1 draw. Aberdeen led the table by a point, but had played a game more.

The following Saturday, Rangers won 2-0 at Clydebank, and the Dons thumped Motherwell 5-0. The status quo prevailed, but Rangers' game in hand was at Tannadice, and the match was played just 72 hours after Rangers humbled the Scotland national team 5-0 at Ibrox in the John Greig testimonial match.

Before the game with United, Wallace said, 'If we win our three remaining games, we are champions. The players know exactly what is required but there is still work to do.' A Johnstone goal in 16 minutes at Tannadice was the only one of the game, and part one of the mission had been accomplished. The same sides met at Ibrox a few days later and this time it was a stroll in the park as Rangers cruised to a 3-0 win – the title was within touching distance. The Light Blues were top by a point and victory over Motherwell at Ibrox seven days later would secure the title.

Wallace said, 'It has been a good championship, but we can only lose it. We have no injuries and will have a break before facing Motherwell.' Meanwhile, Aberdeen boss Billy McNeill insisted all his side could do was concentrate on beating Hibs. The Dons could only manage a draw but it mattered not as early goals by Jackson and Smith settled the nerves and ensured that Wallace clinched a third championship in just four years.

Some 47,000 fans were at Ibrox and when referee Tom Muirhead blew the final whistle, the manager raced on to the pitch and threw his arms around skipper Greig, with Cliff Richard's 'Congratulations' booming out of every loudspeaker in the stadium. It was a moment of unbridled passion. Wallace said, 'I never had any doubt that we would do it. Though this is the second time we have won the Premier League title in three years, I think I've had more satisfaction out of this one. No one at Ibrox can remember the last time we clinched a championship at home. When you win it before your own fans it is special. I'm delighted – a happy man, but now we must prepare for the Scottish Cup Final.'

Rangers won the league by two points from Aberdeen, with Dundee United 13 points adrift in third place. Celtic finished a distant fifth – a staggering 19 points behind Rangers – and missed out on Europe.

The following weekend, Greig capped an incredible season – his testimonial year – by leading Rangers to a 2-1 win over Aberdeen to clinch a second domestic treble in just three years. But while goals by MacDonald and Johnstone – his 39th of the season – were lauded by more than 60,000 supporters, the man of the match, by some distance, was Russell. Johnstone and Russell were the chief architects of MacDonald's opener, before the latter used the lofty stage of a Hampden cup final to display his superb range of passes. Russell was simply the best and fully deserved the £100 cheque from sponsors Younger's Tartan Special.

After the match, Wallace said, 'Our players were magnificent. We took them away to Largs to relax, and told them to play their football that way at Hampden. They played the game the way the script was written. I'm especially delighted for young Russell, because he missed the League Cup Final due to injury. Sandy Jardine gave him his medal on that occasion, but now he has one of his own.'

As a result of the Hampden win, Wallace became the first Rangers manager to win a second modern-day treble. Skipper Greig said, 'I'll be back at Ibrox next season and looking for more medals. I've signed a new contract, but I'm not saying how long for.'

Just days after the final, Johnstone, Jardine and Partick Thistle keeper Alan Rough were in the firing line as they travelled to Argentina with Scotland's World Cup squad. The three players had gone out for a walk and jumped a fence to get back into their hotel complex. And that's when armed guards forced them to stand with their hands in the air – with automatic rifles pointing directly at them. What the players didn't realise was that the perimeter fence was electrified, and had been switched on before they had returned from their visit to a local town. Jardine said, 'It was the most frightening experience of my life.'

Back home in Scotland, Wallace insisted that a treble was to be repeated, not savoured for the rest of your life. He agreed that young talent such as Cooper, Russell and Smith had been the catalyst for the second treble, but added, 'I have a lot of respect for my players but I'm not too sentimental about them. I've seen too many managers run into problems because they have stood by players when they knew in their heart they should have made changes.'

Wallace had vowed never to be caught out that way and said, 'I've had three teams since I came to Ibrox. One when I was coach and the team won the Cup Winners' Cup and then I became manager and knew we had to change things. The second one came when we won the treble and then lost out the next season and I knew that further changes had to be made. The third team is the one that has just won all three competitions. It's the sweetest moving of them all.'

Speaking of the pressure at a club like Rangers, he said, 'We are Rangers and have to win, whether that's the first team or reserves. The reserve coach Joe Mason once went to bed at five o'clock in the evening because his team lost. They were still top of the league and had won the league the previous four years but he felt that way because they lost. That's the way we live. It can't be any other way with Rangers, yet I enjoy it.'

Respected journalist Ken Gallacher said, 'Jock Wallace wasn't a Struth, a Symon, nor even a Waddell. He was his own man. What he shared with the others was a capacity for winning honours. That, after all, was the most important thing.'

15

Jock Wallace: The Silver Fox

IT was enough to make those watching the news perform a double take: perhaps not quite a JFK moment, but a bolt from the blue nevertheless. On the evening of Tuesday 23 May 1978, Jock Wallace quit as manager of Rangers. Just a fortnight previous, he had led his side to their second treble in three seasons by beating Aberdeen 2-1 in the Scottish Cup Final at Hampden.

Straight away the jungle drums suggested a move to Leicester City and Filbert Street secretary John Smith did nothing to kill off the rumours when he said, 'I cannot confirm that Jock Wallace is joining us as manager – but I can't deny it either!'

Rangers supporters were in shock. There was nothing to suggest Wallace had been unhappy at Ibrox and if anything, the season just ended had offered a new dawn to those who had watched the club yo-yo between success and failure in recent years. In Cooper, Russell and Smith, Wallace had the bones of a successful side for many years to come, but had taken the decision after a 'crisis' board meeting at Ibrox.

He said, 'I have quit Rangers and am now looking for a job. I have been unsettled and unhappy at Ibrox for some time and have informed the directors of my feelings. I resigned and they accepted my resignation.' It looked suspiciously like the manager had known for some time that he was leaving, and that a deal had already been struck with the Foxes.

Within 24 hours, Rangers had appointed John Greig as manager, and Wallace announced that he would never reveal the reasons behind his decision to quit the hot seat. He said, tersely, 'What happened at the meeting is a secret between me and the club. I will never discuss it.' He would take his secret to the grave.

Leicester were favourites to sign the manager with arguably the hottest CV in the country, although US side Tampa Bay Rowdies tried to hijack any done deal and offered Wallace the chance to manage across the pond, although he politely declined.

Were Jock to take the Leicester job, not only would his estimated annual salary of £12,000 double instantly, but so would the status of his club car. At Ibrox, he drove a modest Hillman Hunter, while vice-chairman Willie Waddell cruised around in a luxury Mercedes.

Meanwhile, outgoing Leicester manager Frank McLintock, the former Arsenal captain, insisted that Wallace would get it tough, unless the Filbert Street board gave him money to spend. He added, 'I could hardly believe it when I heard that big Jock would be getting more than £25,000 a year. When I took the job for £14,000 I was perhaps too keen to get into management.'

Wallace duly signed a three-year deal with Leicester to confirm football's worst-kept secret. As Scotland began their ill-fated World Cup campaign in Argentina, Wallace began the task of helping Leicester bounce straight back up to the English top flight – and it would be quite a campaign for the Foxes' sixth Scottish manager. He laid down an instant marker by promising adventurous football.

Peter McCloy said, 'I'm sure Jock had his own reasons for leaving Rangers, but he certainly never divulged them to anyone else. We all followed his career at Leicester with interest, and looked out for their results. But he always kept in touch, which was good.'

Journalist Graham Clark wrote *Football is the Wallace Religion*, Jock's 1984 biography. He first met Wallace while working with

Rangers News, before heading south to work at Aston Villa and then Ipswich Town. When Wallace took over the reins at Leicester, he invited Clark to be the club's public relations officer. It was a position he accepted with relish.

Clark said, 'When Jock went to Filbert Street I think he wanted a friendly face around. I had also worked with the City general secretary Alan Bennett at Villa, so between them they took me to Leicester as PRO – and Jock's interpreter! When I came back to Glasgow it was to the *Evening Times*, where I worked with Jock on a daily basis.

'When he was at Rangers and I was at the Times, I recall on a number of occasions "interviewing" him when we were in the Ibrox sauna before jumping into the big old bath – which was like a swimming pool – and it was ice cold. Jock was fantastic but the one thing I simply can't divulge is why he left Rangers in 1978. That must forever remain a secret.'

Before settling in behind his Filbert Street desk, Wallace headed to Majorca on holiday – and who should be resident in a hotel just along the front in Palma Nova but Greig. On his return from the Balearics, Wallace was forced to split his time between Leicester and Glasgow, where his family still lived. His wife, Daphne, had been taken into Knightswood Hospital for tests on a chest complaint. And just a month into the new season, Wallace received the sad news that his father had died at the age of 68 in his home village of Wallyford. It was a poignant trip north for the funeral of the dad he had doted on.

Wallace had only been in the Leicester job a matter of months when speculation was rife that he was ready to return to Scotland. Former Rangers player Roger Hynd had quit as manager of Motherwell to become a physical education teacher and the Fir Park side wanted Wallace to replace him. The new Leicester boss insisted he was flattered, but growled, 'No way, I have still to prove myself at City. I'm only interested in one job apart from the one I have and that's the Scotland job. The English Second Division is a good league and compares favourably with our Premier League, but there are more clubs with ambition. They are all full-time and want to get into the top bracket. It won't be long till we join them.'

At the beginning of 1979, Wallace showed English football what his young Leicester side were capable of when they knocked First Division Norwich City out of the FA Cup. When the final whistle sounded, Wallace leapt from the dug-out, fist pumping the air and trademark scowl etched across his face. More than half the side which beat the Canaries 3-0 were under the age of 21. Two of them, Andy Peake and David Buchanan, were 16-year-old apprentice professionals, and the type Wallace viewed as key in his rebuilding job.

He said, 'I know the kind of team I want and we are heading in the right direction. When I took the job I knew there was a lot of work to be done. I wanted players with the right attitude, who wanted to play for the club and wanted to win. There is no other way as far as I'm concerned. We have good youngsters coming through and they showed that against Norwich.'

Wallace and his assistant, fellow Scot Ian McFarlane, looked capable of guiding Leicester towards the First Division. They had completely outplayed Norwich and it was Wallace's first taste of the special FA Cup atmosphere since his move south the previous summer.

He said, 'It's a big change for me going into a cup tournament down here with a Second Division team after being involved in so many finals with Rangers. But I have no regrets. Don't get me wrong, I still love Rangers and look for their results, but it was time to move on. There are things to do here, another team to build, challenges which are different from any I faced at Ibrox.

'When you see young players pushing through the way these lads are you feel a sense of accomplishment. Martin Henderson scored a fantastic third against Norwich. How many would have squeezed the shot in from that angle? He did it because he has been brought up my way since he was a youngster at Ibrox. For me, he was just about the best player we had over the 90 minutes. I bought him from Philadelphia Fury for £20,000 and wouldn't sell him for five times that now!'

Henderson said, 'I have found it more difficult playing in England because the defences are better organised than they are in Scotland. But the boss has worked with me and there has been an improvement in my play. I enjoyed that goal.'

Wallace added, 'I'm ambitious for Leicester and for myself. There are things to prove, more mountains to climb, if you like, and I'm going to climb them.' And the popular boss made new friends when he released Peake for the England youth team, on the eve of an important FA Cup replay at Oldham. Wallace insisted the World Cup qualifying game in Italy was too good an opportunity for the player to miss.

A matter of weeks after pulling off the FA Cup shock, one newspaper suggested that Barcelona, the UEFA Cup semi-finalists, wanted Wallace to spearhead their £5m drive for Euro honours. The Catalans were reportedly ready to offer the 43-year-old a three-year contract worth a staggering £450,000 after failing to lure Ipswich boss Bobby Robson, a former team-mate of Wallace's at West Brom. The Spaniards were said to be impressed by his remarkable record at Rangers, and by the manner in which he had re-shaped Leicester – and produced a £340,000 trading profit in the transfer market.

He made it clear that he was ready to meet the Spanish club, and said, 'I hope this story is correct. I have had no direct contact with Barcelona so far, but they obviously realise I possess more experience of European competition than most people.' Barcelona, it was thought, could buy out the remaining two years of his Leicester contract for around £50,000.

Just a fortnight after the Barca story, Wallace turned down an approach from an unnamed English First Division club. As Leicester prepared for a home game against third-top Crystal Palace he insisted he was going nowhere, but swooped to sign Gregor Stevens from Motherwell. The 24-year-old defender had a look at the Leicester set-up, spoke to Wallace and agreed a £150,000 transfer. Rangers had been on the trail of Stevens before he moved south and the player only turned out a handful of times before moving on again – to Rangers in a £150,000 deal. There was the inevitable talk that Wallace had acted as 'middle-man' in a bid to get the player for the Light Blues.

Wallace had 18 young Scots at Leicester – his 'hungry bairns', as he called them – and enjoyed the role of father figure. The nerve centre of Filbert Street was the manager's office, where two colour photographs of Rangers and a portrait of the Queen hung proudly on a wall. It was also rumoured that Wallace kept a musical box which played the tune of 'Follow Follow'.

He said, 'Some people think we have too many Scots. They've nicknamed it Little Scotland but it will stay that way as long as they keep winning. I've had as many as eight Scots in my first team. I sign them because I know their temperament and moods. They have aggression and are hungry to get on. It stems from their background. In Scotland success in football is still a big thing for youngsters.'

Tough but paternal, Wallace made no bones about his goal. 'I want to make my team a family. The discipline is fierce but so is the respect they get from me in return. Some of these youngsters are getting into the big team while still in their teens. We pay higher wages than any club in the Scottish Premier League, but I make sure my youngsters don't squander their money and insist on seeing their bank books regularly to check on how much they are saving.

'Until they are 19 all players stay in a lodge house which the club owns near the ground. I know the temptations which youngsters face while away from home but we employ a landlady to keep an eye on them and the place is run like a hotel. If there is any trouble I go up and read the riot act. But the bairns are good lads who know that success in football depends on discipline on and off the park.'

Wallace brought in an education officer and investment expert to look after the interests of the players. He was on top of everything, from making sure meals were served on time to the players' boots being in perfect condition.

He said, 'Education is as important for my young players as for my own kids. As soon as they arrive here, arrangements are made for them to attend further education classes. Some go on day release – others to night school.'

The senior players were encouraged to take business management or accountancy courses to prepare them for the day the last ball was kicked. One of Jock's players graduated with a university honours degree. He said, 'I look upon Leicester as a British club. We've got Cockneys, Irishmen, four or five coloured boys and of course the bairns. There's no bigotry down here.'

One of his young signings, Paul Friar, had played for Celtic Boys Club, and the talented midfielder still talks highly of his 'boss' to this day. He said, 'I was still at school when I was "recommended" to Leicester. I had been offered S form contracts with Celtic and Partick Thistle but was invited down to Filbert Street and was in awe of the facilities, which were magnificent. I had been in at Celtic but when you compared Barrowfield with Leicester it was night and day.

'I came back up the road and had a meeting at Parkhead with manager Billy McNeill. He wanted me to sign but my dad and I decided to think it over. We went out to the car and he produced a letter from Leicester, with a contract offer in it. I signed it there and then – in the Celtic car park!

'I had many one-to-one dealings with Jock. On one occasion, I needed a new pair of boots, and they were kept in his office. I was about 17 and had 15 or 20 first-team games under my belt. I said to him, "I need a new pair of boots, boss." "What's up with your old ones?" "They've got holes in them." Eventually, he said, "Okay, what size?" "Eh, a seven, boss." Then he would sidetrack you, and say, "How you enjoying it here? How's the digs? How's the landlady?"

'On his right hand side, he had the best boots, like Adidas World Cup, top of the range, and on his left, Adidas El Crappo, the pits of the boot world. We were still chatting, and he reached over to his left and grabbed a pair of crap boots. "Try them on, son. Aye, they look okay, how are they?" and he'd have you walking up and down his office. It was like being in Clark's.

'I said, "They're actually a bit tight, can I not try on those ones," and pointed to the good boots. He wasn't happy and smacked me with a crap boot before saying, "These boots, son, are for the first team." He was making sure I knew my place. He didn't like his 17-year-olds getting too cocky, but I was quite proud of the fact I'd gone into his office in the first place.

'Once a week he would have a meeting with all the players and staff in the dressing room. They could sometimes last two hours and we called them a "Jock-anory", after the kids' programme about storytelling. But looking back, it was fantastic that he involved everybody, from the first team down to the kids.

'I've never been into the whole Old Firm thing but when we were being interviewed for the Leicester programme, we would all say that our favourite team was Celtic just to wind the big man up. He was very popular despite working us hard at training, and I think the world would be a far better place now if we had more people like Jock around. He inspired and taught good habits.

'He simplified things. After leaving Leicester I found it difficult cutting through all the bullshit and double-speak from managers and coaches. Jock preached hard work and effort and his motivational skills were second to none. But he was also very honest and you knew where you stood with him. He was a really nice man. I played under a lot of managers but he was the only one to leave a lasting impression.'

Meanwhile, Wallace was enjoying his time south of the border and admitted that the only thing he missed about Scotland was not getting to see his mother regularly. But his time was at a premium and was as far removed from your typical nine-to-five man as it got. He lamented the fact that the fans weren't as passionate in Leicester as they were in Glasgow, but balanced that out by trying to make the Filbert Street experience a real family affair.

He started a family club and within a month or two had more than 1,500 members. A section of the ground was reserved for parents with children and he arranged regular social nights with players in attendance. The Foxes were also ahead of their time when it came to corporate hospitality, which brought in extra revenue.

His players were handsomely rewarded for their efforts and guys such as Alan Young, a striker from Kirkcaldy, and full-back Bobby Smith, once of Hibs, were reportedly earning in excess of £15,000 a year. Wallace admitted the Leicester wage structure had initially given him cause for concern, but once he had put a system in place, which rewarded first-team players for positive results, he was far happier. At that time, only a handful of players in Scotland's Premier League were in the same wage bracket as the Leicester players.

There was to be no bonus at the start of 1980, however, when Leicester were sensationally knocked out the FA Cup by non-league Harlow Town. For the Second Division leaders it was a no-win situation, simply a hurdle they were expected to clear. The Foxes led 1-0 at Filbert Street but conceded in the last minute. In front of a record 9,723 at Harlow's Sportscentre ground, Leicester lost 1-0. It was a major source of embarrassment to manager and players.

But that didn't prevent Wallace being linked with the vacant job at Hearts, after Willie Ormond was sacked. He shrugged it off and by the start of February, a 1-0 win over Newcastle had cemented Leicester's place at the top of the Second Division, albeit on goal difference. He said, 'On top, that is the only place to be. Anybody who doesn't agree, or who pussyfoots about by saying it's maybe better to be third or fourth at this stage, has probably never known what it's like to be at the top, and probably never will.

'I know the feeling and I love it. Going to the top in this tough league has made me feel as proud as I did when I was at Ibrox. For half an hour we were magic – then Newcastle gave us a real going over. But if you can fight against all the odds for an hour and still come out winners then there can't be much wrong.

'We have the guts, fitness and hunger to go all the way. That is the attitude I have always demanded and now that we have it I am proud again. These players deserve to be top of the league. I want them to get to know the feeling well, to taste it, to love it as much as I do. We have had our knocks, like the terrible defeat by Harlow, but you are often the better for a shock like that. You realise that if you want the prizes you have to fight damn hard for them, and to never stop fighting to keep them.'

The win over Newcastle proved pivotal as Leicester went on to secure the title for the sixth time in their history. As a result, Wallace was offered a new contract despite still having over a year of his initial three-year deal left to run. He had turned the club around in just 21 months and Denis Sharp invited him to pledge his future to the Foxes for another five years. He told supporters, 'I can assure you that Jock will be with us for a long time.'

Seven days later, Wallace agreed to the five-year deal – despite interest from other teams in England – and capped a fine season by winning the English Second Division Manager of the Month award, for which he was given a gallon bottle of Bell's whisky.

But the following season was one long struggle against relegation and it was a battle they were forced to succumb to when, along with Norwich and Crystal Palace, they dropped back down to the Second Division. Their worst run came in November, when they lost four games in succession to plummet to the foot of the table.

Just before Christmas 1980, Wallace was invited up to the Albany Hotel in Glasgow for the annual Sports Photographers' Lunch. He was the principal guest, but the show was forced to go on without him when he failed to turn up. Winner Allan Wells was presented with his Sportsman of the Year trophy and the party vacated the premises around 5pm.

Just over an hour later, there was a phone call to the home of organiser Dave McNeil, of the *Sunday Mail*. 'Hello, Jock Wallace here. I'm at the Albany. Where are all these photographers? When does the dinner start?' Mrs McNeil explained that it had been a lunchtime affair. A stunned Wallace then had to embarrassingly explain to his accompanying Leicester director that they had made the journey for nothing!

Wallace's mind had obviously been on Leicester's relegation struggle, and he received support from an unexpected source after the Foxes beat Manchester United 1-0. Reds manager Dave Sexton said, 'This was our hardest match of the season in a physical sense. If Leicester can retain such spirit, they might yet force an escape route.'

It was Leicester's second high-profile win after victory over Liverpool, which put the pressure on fellow strugglers Norwich and Brighton. Wallace declared, 'We have the ability required to stay up. They proved it during the first 45 minutes with the best sustained spell of attack since I arrived here.' Jim Melrose, Wallace's £250,000 buy from Partick Thistle, scored the winner.

At the end of January 1981, there was further anguish for Wallace when Leicester were again the subject of a giant-killing act in the FA Cup. This time it was Third Division Exeter City who slayed the dragon 3-1 in a fourth round replay in Devon.

Wallace still had one eye trained on Scotland, and was disappointed to see Rangers struggling badly. He said, 'Look at that attendance at Ibrox on Wednesday – under 5,000. I can't believe it. It's difficult for me to see past Rangers as an ex-manager and I'll certainly not criticise them. I wish my pal John Greig nothing but the best.'

Leicester were in dire straits and required seven points from a possible ten to survive. Only a blind optimist could see them achieving it. Wallace retained that optimism but rued the fact that his team only seemed capable of playing for half an hour each game. He needed to get them going for 90 minutes.

Despite their predicament, there was no doubt Wallace had transformed Leicester City in his three years in the East Midlands. He had raised attendances to an average 25,000 and was revered in the town. On one occasion, while driving through the centre of town, he stopped the traffic to challenge a motorist wearing a

Baby Jock with his father, also Jock

Toddler Jock – 'X' marks the spot

Jock with his sister Eleanor in the back garden at Wallyford

Corporal Jock Wallace, KOSB, in Malaya

Another trophy - The KOSB team emerge victorious ... again

Perfect match - Jock and Daphne on their wedding day, April 14, 1960

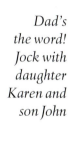

Dad's the word! Jock with daughter Karen and son John

Diamond geezer … Jock in action for Airdrie

Past and present … Jock played for both Hereford and Bedford Town

Jock the giant killer … In goal for Berwick against Rangers in 1967

Heroes … Jock's 1967 Berwick team

*Berwick
Rangers
1968*

*Keep on running …
Training with Hearts*

*Stretcher bearer …
Ibrox Disaster 1971*

Jock's best signing … Derek Johnstone

Through their paces … Rangers train at Espanyol ahead of the final in Barcelona

Murder Hill … Kick up the backside for Alex O'Hara at Gullane

Glasgow Rangers … 1970s style

Proud … From left, Jock Wallace, John Greig, Stewart Kennedy, Sandy Jardine and Colin Jackson

High jinks … Alex MacDonald and Willie Johnston playing it for laughs

Cheers … The Rangers players enjoy their Scottish Cup celebrations

Trailblazers … John Greig and Jock Wallace celebrate the first Treble

Flying out … From left, Alex MacDonald, Eric Morris, Stewart Kennedy, Bobby McKean, Derek Johnstone and Jock Wallace heading abroad in 1976

All smiles …
Celebrating a
League Cup win
with chairman
Rae Simpson

That's my boy …
Jock with Martin
Henderson after
the Scottish Cup
success of 1976

Namesake … With legendary Celtic boss Jock Stein

Measuring up … Jock and Andy Ritchie at Fir Park

Looking S-Well … The Motherwell team group

Jock along Paseo Maritimo, Fuengirola, Spain, enjoying retirement

Proud Scot … Jock shows off his legs

Dream team … In the dug-out with Alex Totten

Sup for the cup … With Celtic boss Davie Hay

Second time round … With the Scottish League Cup

Back home ... With Rangers in the 80s

Best buds ... Jock and goalkeeper Nicky Walker

Spanish culture … Jock enjoyed his time in Seville

Jock's rock … With wife Daphne

We are going up … Celebrating promotion at Leicester

Shaken, not stirred … With 007 Sean Connery

Miracle worker … Jock at Colchester

Pulling no punches … Jock and wing king Willie Henderson

*Paying in …
Jock is just
a face in the
crowd*

*Mark of
respect …
A minute's
silence
before
Rangers play
in Denmark*

Respects … The likes of Sandy Jardine, Colin Jackson and Walter Smith at Jock's funeral

Tears … Jock's Ibrox shrine

Rangers scarf. As horns hooted, the surprised driver explained it had been given to him by his dad. Wallace wanted the people of Leicester to follow the Foxes.

He said, 'I'm a much better manager now than I was at Ibrox. At first, I was demoted from king to jester, and English managers wanted to have a go. Well, I won the Second Division championship and will do it again if we go down.

'I have had to learn the hard way, to fight for every crumb. I like to balance the books and oversee everything – secretary, hospitality, groundsman, the lot. When I was at Ibrox I had very little to do in the afternoons. Sometimes I'd stare at a picture of Tom Forsyth and think, "How can I make you an even better player?"

'I believe football should be about honesty and fun. The other week one of our crisp sellers turned up in Manchester United colours. I kicked his backside round the track and the crowd loved it. Next week he chose Leicester's colours.

'I look at Scottish football now from the outside and worry about it. Look what we've got at Filbert Street – restaurants, bars, and special boxes and we're not even reckoned a big team in England. Bet your boots we will be big if we can stay in the First Division.'

Leicester lost their survival battle, with a defeat to fellow strugglers Brighton the final nail in the coffin. Red cards for Alan Young and Kevin MacDonald left the team with a mountain to climb but, if truth be told, relegation had been 'secured' long before the Brighton game. Goals were the problem with Leicester the lowest scorers in the division.

Wallace was still in place the following season and relegation didn't seem to have lowered his standing with the passionate Foxes support, who hailed him as the new Shankly. He was still revelling in being his own man at Filbert Street rather than simply team manager, and said, 'At Rangers, I was team manager. Here at Leicester, I'm involved in everything and that suits me fine. That's one of the reasons I left Ibrox. Having said that, I'm still a Rangers supporter. It's the first result I look for every Saturday night.'

Wallace, who was 46, admitted that his lifestyle had changed since he quit Ibrox, and said, 'I did take time out to wind down. That's something I seldom did at Ibrox, which was my fault.' He was playing more golf, with wife Daphne, and received lessons from son John, who played off a handicap of six. Perhaps the family had taken on Jock's penchant for fitness as Daphne also played squash, while daughter Karen was keen on jogging and squash.

Daphne admitted she enjoyed the freedom that the 360-mile switch from Glasgow to Leicester had allowed. She said, 'Because of John's position, people tended to stand off you a wee bit. In fact, more people spoke to us after he decided to leave Rangers.'

Jock said, 'While I still get regular invitations from Scotland, they all tend to revolve around football. Down here the people are more recreation-conscious, and with Leicester being the only team in the county, Daph and I get asked to everything from rugby and cricket dos to butchers' and plumbers' functions.'

Leicester had a decent season back in the Second Division and narrowly missed out on promotion, as Luton Town clinched the title. They enjoyed a successful FA Cup run and reached the semi-finals, where they lost 2-0 to Tottenham Hotspur at Villa Park. The match was reportedly marred by Foxes fans jeering Spurs' Argentinian midfielder Ossie Ardiles over his country's participation in the Falklands War. Spurs retained the FA Cup with a replay win over QPR, but did so without Ardiles and compatriot Ricardo Villa, who had withdrawn from first-team duties over the South Atlantic conflict.

There was a remarkable incident in an earlier round when Leicester used THREE goalkeepers in a tie against Shrewsbury Town. The match itself was an incredible affair, with the Foxes winning 5-2 and, at one point, Wallace insisted he was almost tempted to pull on the gloves himself.

City lost two goals after Mark Wallington was injured and Alan Young took over between the sticks. He took a knock and had to be replaced by another outfield player, Steve Lynex. Wallace said,

'When Steve took over in goal from Alan, after Youngy had replaced Mark, I handed him my specs and told him to go out and do us a turn. Seriously, I've never been prouder of a team – they were magnificent.'

It was Leicester's seventh home win on the trot, and one with *Roy of the Rovers* qualities. Having taken the lead, goalkeeper and skipper, Wallington, playing his 333rd consecutive match, was injured. Wallace admitted, 'I took a chance and put Alan in goal. When he took a knock, I sent in young Lynex, but I was afraid Shrewsbury would start pumping in high balls at him – as he's only 5ft 7in – so when Young was fit, I changed it back again.'

Ever keen to try his hand at something new, Wallace started his own business, but insisted it wouldn't affect his job at Leicester. He said, 'My loyalty to this club is first, last and always.' He launched the firm in Glasgow and cemented his reputation as a big hard man by getting into the building trade and concrete mixers. He laughed, 'You know me, if I'm not mixing it one way then I'm mixing it the other!' Jock Wallace Agencies (Plant) Ltd, was born.

The whole idea began in Leicester when a small firm, Wallace Plant and Engineering, offered him some promotional work. The company had produced a concrete mixer called 'Wee Wallace'. Phone calls started arriving at Jock's home and office, with people asking about his connection with the building trade, which gave him ideas about developing his own business. He said, 'It's being launched quite deliberately in Glasgow because there's a big demand in the city for building equipment.'

Building blocks were put in place for the 1982/83 season but before he had even started to prepare in earnest for promotion back to the top flight, a spanner was thrown in the works. David Hay left Motherwell and the Steel Men wanted Wallace as their new boss. It would be an interesting close season.

16

Jock's 'Boy'

STRIKER Alan Young was born in Kirkcaldy but managed just a single reserve game for home-town team Raith Rovers. It was while playing for Scotland schoolboys against England and Wales that he impressed Oldham Athletic, and had been at Boundary Park for five years when the Latics were drawn against Leicester City in the cup.

He recalled, 'The match was cancelled seven or eight times due to the weather. When it was eventually played I was up against one of my best mates, Martin Henderson. We grew up together and he was best man at my wedding. Anyway, we won 3-1 and I scored a hat-trick.

'Next day I got a call from Martin, who said, "The gaffer fancies you! Can you give him a ring?" I told him I couldn't because I was contracted to Oldham. Next day, the phone rang and I knew right away it was Jock Wallace. He said, "How long you got left on your contract?" I told him it was up in the summer and he told me to get my arse down to Filbert Street. Freedom of contract was just coming in, and I almost became the first player to move under the new rules, but Gerry Gow beat me to it by a couple of hours.

'Anyway, I met Jock and Alan Bennett, the Leicester secretary, in a bedroom at the Four Seasons Hotel, as it was all very hush-hush. Jock asked how much I was on a week. "£100," I said. He promised to double it, and give me a good signing-on fee, and said, "Right, sign it," and he thrust a pen into my hand.

'I recall him saying, "The Leicester City bandwagon is on the move and if I were you I'd get on. I've got this young lad, Gary Lineker, he's gonna be a cracker and I need someone to look after him, and that's you."

'I signed the contract but to be honest I really didn't know the exact terms. I then received a copy and it was all just as Jock had promised. I was on £200 a week, got a great signing-on fee and a three-year deal. The first thing I did was head off to Sweden with the squad for pre-season. We played nine games in three weeks and I scored 18 goals, so that set me up nicely for the new season.'

Young loved working with Wallace, and not only did he rate the gaffer as an excellent football manager, but never tires of singing the big man's praises in his role as an after-dinner speaker, as he helped him both on and off the football park.

He said, 'Jock would always say that he could "smell things". He would come into the dressing room before a game and say, "I've just walked up the tunnel and their players are fuckin' shitting themselves. I can smell their fear."

'But on one occasion, when my marriage wasn't in the best of places, he came up to me at training and asked me several times what was wrong. I pretended that everything was great, but he wasn't daft and I eventually spilled the beans. He said, "I knew it, I could smell something wasn't right." He told me I hadn't smiled for three weeks, and reminded me where his office was if I ever wanted to talk.

'Get this, next morning my door goes at seven o'clock. It was a big bang, and it was big Jock. In he comes and says, "Right, son, get the kettle on. Where's the missus?" Next minute he's off upstairs and brings the kids, Lesley, who was three, and Jordan, who was 18 months, down with him. He started talking and playing with them. He was chatting away, had his tea and then left – but warned me not to be late for training.

'It was the most bizarre thing and my wife just looked at me – shell-shocked. Later that day, he said to me, "You've got problems son, but I know you can work them out. In the meantime, when you come in here you need to forget about them. In here, you're my employee, but when you go home you need to sort things out and if you need a hand you know where I am."'

Young valued his relationship with Wallace and a healthy respect soon developed between both men, although the prolific striker knew exactly where to draw the line. He recalled, 'I like to think that Jock and I had a special relationship. If he needed to get a message across to another player he would do it through me. He would come into the dressing room, go ballistic with me, and then leave. The other players would rally round and I'd be able to talk to them. He knew that if he hammered one of the younger guys he would lose them.

'We went down to Bideford, in Devon, one year when the pitches up in Leicester were frozen, and played a local amateur team. That night he told us to go out and enjoy ourselves, and set the curfew for 1am. He warned us that if anyone was late, everyone would be fined.

'Of course, the Four Musketeers were the last back at the hotel, and that was me, Bobby Smith, Eddie Kelly and Martin Henderson. When we walked in, he said, "I might have known you lot would be last," and he bought us all a drink. Half an hour later, Eddie and Bobby went to bed, and Martin wasn't far behind. The gaffer and I stayed up knocking them back until 4am.

'The next morning, we were down on the beach running at 9.30am and I was dying. I was a good trainer and was normally at the front, but not that morning, I hid somewhere in the pack. But the gaffer, bright as a button, soon noticed and shouted, "Mr Young, get up to the front where you belong, and if you wanna drink 'til four o'clock in the morning, make sure you're okay for training." He had just gone from drinking buddy to boss. You could be his friend one minute but when the work started, you were just an employee.'

Young added, 'But I loved working with him day in, day out and when he left I was devastated. He went to Motherwell, I believe, to get closer to home. I think his dream was to manage Scotland.

'He always said you should train as you play. No tracksuits, no socks at the ankles or jerseys hanging out your shorts. If he spotted that he would shout, "Tuck that shirt in, you look like a Celtic player!"

'When Gordon Milne took over, the standards soon dropped. A couple of shirts outside the shorts, a few socks at the ankles, the discipline was gone and I knew it wouldn't ever be the same again. When Milne arrived at the club I said to him, "Welcome to the club Mr Milne, I think we can have a good season. You have a great bunch of lads here," and he replied, "Thanks, but from now on you'll call me boss."

'I thought to myself, he's not my boss. I went to see him and said, "I think we've got a problem. You're not my boss, Jock Wallace was my boss." He said, "I know more about you than you think." He knew I was one of Jock's lads, and I called the boss at Motherwell. He said, "Christ, if I could get you and Lineker up here we would skoosh this league." I said, "Gaffer, you couldn't even afford me!"'

Young admitted that when Wallace died, he cried like a baby at the funeral. He said, 'Jock's wife, Daphne, said to me, "You know something Alan, Jock thought of you like a son." It was wonderful to hear that.

'I later heard that the graveyard where Jock was buried had been vandalised. They had spray painted headstones and turned a lot of them over – but not Jock's. I like to think that the moment they went anywhere near his grave, he would've spooked them by shouting, "Don't you even think about spray painting my headstone!" Even in death he was a fearsome man.

'To this day, I still get emotional talking about Jock, and if things are getting me down, I sometimes talk to him at night. He was such a big influence not only on my career, but also on my life.'

17

Well At Home

AMBITIOUS Motherwell were back in the Premier League for the 1982/83 season and immediately on the prowl for a new manager after former Celtic player David Hay quit the hot-seat. Jock Wallace, a former steel worker, was the name on the lips of everyone associated with the Steel Men and club bosses made their initial approach during the close season. However, the Foxes boss was tipped for the top job at managerless West Brom, one of his former clubs. In turn, Bertie Auld and Benny Rooney were installed as paper favourites to succeed Hay.

Meanwhile, the big man was asked to model the Wallace tartan ahead of Scotland's participation in the 1982 World Cup in Spain. He said, 'What do you think of these legs then? If that doesn't put the fear of death into the Brazilians and Russians then I don't know what will.'

Motherwell chairman Bill Dickie made an official approach to his counterpart at Filbert Street. The salary was believed to be among the highest in the Premier League, but the former Rangers boss still had four years remaining on his Leicester contract and while he was keen on the Well job, a cross-border tug-of-war was brewing.

The major stumbling block to a swift return for Wallace appeared to be the compensation demanded by Leicester. Motherwell were worried it could be as much as £80,000 – a sum they would struggle to find on top of wages and a transfer kitty. Wallace broke his silence to say, 'It was always my intention to return to Scotland at some stage. Motherwell have a great deal of potential and I believe I could help them realise it. I've also been impressed with the board. They speak my kind of language.' Scotland manager Jock Stein had also been quoted for the job, which underlined the extent of the club's ambition.

The confusion over Wallace's future heightened when it was reported that Foxes chairman Len Shipman had given Motherwell permission to talk to the ex-Rangers boss, a claim rubbished by other board members. Vice-chairman Tom Bloor said, 'Motherwell have not been given permission to approach Jock. We received a call from them but agreed to leave the matter until our chairman is back from a holiday in America. I'm disgusted with the way they have acted. Jock has still four years of his contract to go and we expect him to stay.'

However, Dickie said, 'After speaking with Leicester I decided time was wearing on and contacted their chairman in America through an intermediary and was given the go-ahead.' Meanwhile, the in-demand boss was topping up his tan in Spain.

At the end of June, Motherwell directors flew to Spain for a meeting with Wallace and insisted that all had gone well. The club admitted they were awaiting his response but were hopeful he would be at Fir Park the following season.

But a fortnight passed, and with no signature on a contract, Motherwell extended their deadline in a last-ditch attempt to iron out potential legal problems, and to await the outcome of a meeting between Wallace and Shipman. The Leicester man had just returned from America and immediately threatened to report Motherwell to the Football League. The Steel Men admitted they had approached Wallace twice – but only with City's consent.

Reports suggesting Wallace was set to sign a ten-year deal worth anywhere between £35,000 and £50,000 on 12 July were wide of the mark as Leicester directors dug their heels in and refused to sanction any move north of the border. In the meantime, it was suggested that Aston Villa, Sunderland and West Brom were monitoring the situation.

Wallace said, 'I have enjoyed my stay at Leicester, but few managers could refuse the kind of terms Motherwell are offering. It represents security for my family and I.'

By mid-July, the long-running saga took a new twist when Leicester refused to accept Wallace's resignation. At a press conference at Filbert Street, Shipman issued a hard-hitting statement in which he criticised both Wallace and Motherwell. He said, 'We are annoyed at the way Mr Wallace was approached by Motherwell FC and have reported them to the Football League. We have asked the league to take strong action against them. Two years ago, Mr Wallace signed a long-term contract tailor-made for him, at least four years of which remain unexpired. It includes annual increases, a generous pension scheme, a very good basic salary and attractive incentives. We have denied him nothing and are staggered and disappointed by his actions, but we still hope he will reconsider.'

But while Shipman was talking to the media, Wallace was clearing out his desk at Filbert Street and heading north. City were also in the process of taking legal advice, and insisted that until the whole messy affair was resolved, Wallace would be unable to take on another job.

With the on-off deal rivalling *The Mousetrap* as the longest-running mystery of our time, Wallace was finally confirmed as the new manager in a statement by Dickie. On Friday 16 July Wallace said, 'Exactly 15 minutes ago I signed a contract as the new manager of Motherwell. The terms are confidential and as I only made my mind up today, any speculation in the press before now has been without foundation.'

With that off his chest, he agreed to answer questions pertaining only to football and as usual, stuck to his word. 'No comment' was the phrase of choice as he sat flanked by chairman Dickie and his own lawyer. He then offered, 'It's no use being second – I want

Motherwell to be on top. I haven't seen them play yet, but I have heard of most of the players at the club.

'Davie Hay did a good job and it's up to me to keep it going and help establish Motherwell in the Premier League. The whip will be out at training. I'll be telling the players I want total commitment and support, and they'll get that from me in return. It had always been my intention to return to Scotland someday, and my main reason for taking the job was to get back home.'

Football agent Bill McMurdo was involved in the deal to take Wallace to Fir Park and recalled, 'Jock and I lived near each other in Tranent, so I'd known him since the early 1970s. He was a big Rangers fan and travelled with his dad on the Tranent Loyal Rangers Supporters bus, the same one as me. But I really got to know him while he was at Leicester. I was working for Derek Johnstone and he had some trouble at Rangers so we went down to see Jock for advice, and were there for a week. We stayed in touch and when he wanted to come back up the road, he asked if I could find him a club.

'I spoke to Motherwell and they were delighted to attract such a massive name. Motherwell were great to work with. However, Jock wanted a clause in his contract that would allow him to leave should Rangers come in for him at any time. It was a long shot but he was a massive Rangers man. Motherwell agreed, and when it happened, they were as good as their word.

'But the Rangers move presented a little problem. When Jock left Motherwell, he stayed with me for a while, and one night he said to me, "Bill, I've got a wee bit of a predicament. I would love to take Frank Connor with me to Ibrox, but how do you think it'll go down with the supporters?" Now, Frank had played for Celtic and was like the Catholic version of Jock!

'I love Frank, he is a great guy, but I didn't think it was a good move. I said to Jock, "You can handle the pressure, but will Frank?" He was a strong wee guy but I didn't think he needed the hassle. I felt that Jock would get time if things didn't go according to plan, but with Frank there, I didn't think he'd get that time.

'As it turned out, he brought in Alex Totten, who is another smashing guy, and Frank went to Celtic, where he enjoyed two spells at Parkhead. You know what, though, I would love to have seen him at Ibrox, because he was a real football man and knew the game inside out.

'While Jock and Frank were at Motherwell, we'd go out for a meal and as the others tucked into their food, Frank would be showing me how he expected the team to line up – using the salt and pepper shakers, and anything else he could get his hands on!'

But while Wallace settled into the job, the backroom squabbling continued. As the Football League Management Committee looked at City's complaint regarding an illegal approach, Dickie insisted, 'We acted with absolute integrity.' Leicester chairman Shipman countered, 'That's laughable. Jock had four years remaining on his contract here, and we consistently refused Motherwell permission to open negotiations. We even sent them a recorded telegram underlining that fact. Our solicitors are also in action. We must work out whether to sue Motherwell, Jock – or both!'

Connor was Wallace's first signing, and duly arrived at Fir Park as his right-hand man. While at Parkhead, Connor, a former youth team coach, had helped develop youngsters such as Charlie Nicholas, Mark Reid and Paul McStay.

Meanwhile, the Football League announced that it would be unable to back Leicester in their fight for compensation – believed to be around £150,000 – as the matter was outside its jurisdiction.

When the fixtures were released, Motherwell were drawn to meet Rangers on the opening day of the season at Fir Park, and Wallace said, 'It couldn't be better.' As he drew up plans for pre-season training, one location featured high on the list – the terrifying sands at Gullane, and it wasn't long before the anguished cries of struggling players could be heard by dog walkers and couples strolling along the beach. Wallace, nicknamed the Sheikh of Gullane, was 'back home', and said, 'It is a great all round exercise. It stretches the hamstrings, the Achilles tendons, develops the lungs and the thighs – it's fantastic.'

Leicester decided to sue both Motherwell and Wallace. Shipman said, 'We are going for Motherwell for enticing our manager away from us and approaching him without permission. When Jock resigned we gave him seven days to reconsider his decision, but heard nothing. Consequently we are taking action against him for breaching his contract. Quite recently Mr Wallace gave me his word that he would do no such thing.'

To those who suggested Wallace was stepping down a few rungs on the career ladder, he said, 'I firmly believe I can go anywhere in the world and do a job. My record proves it and now I want to keep Motherwell in the top bracket and move upwards from there. My approach to the game has never changed. I still believe in good attacking play. That was the way my side won the treble.'

Wallace's first task was to re-sign out-of-contract players such as Brian McLaughlin, Willie Irvine and Hugh Sproat, and one man he remembered well from his time at Rangers, Alfie Conn, who recalled, 'I was already at Motherwell when Jock was announced as the new manager. He walked into the dressing room for the first time and said, "Some of you already know me, but most of you don't. By the end of next week, you will all know me very well", and he looked over at me and said, "Is that right Alf?" I said, "That's right gaffer."

'A while later, as I was recovering at home from an Achilles operation, Jock came across to the house in Coatbridge to see how I was doing. I was sitting with my wife when he walked in. "Any whisky in the house son?" I said no. "There's £20, away down to the corner shop and get two bottles son!"

'We were actually born and brought up not that far from one another. He was from Wallyford and I was just a mile and a half away at Prestonpans. Both mining communities so we had similar upbringings. I signed for Rangers in 1967 but first worked with the big man just after the European Cup Winners' Cup Final. You knew what you were getting with Jock and if you were honest with him, you wouldn't have a problem. If you tried to pull the wool over his eyes then you were in bother. I learned quickly not to even attempt it, but it wasn't through fear, really, it was more about respect.'

Wallace was also keen to implement a youth policy at Fir Park, in a bid to unearth and develop a Bobby Russell or Derek Johnstone, and Connor was the man to help do that. When asked why he had taken him on as assistant, he said, 'Simple. I took Leicester up to Berwick for their centenary match and met up with Frank. I was impressed. We are both on the same wavelength. Apart from that there was something else which worked in his favour – I'm better looking!'

With many people sounding the death knell for football in Scotland, due to falling attendances and a lack of cash, Wallace preferred to talk up the game. He said, 'Of course we have problems, and they are serious, but I believe we have a quality product, and that it's one of the cheapest forms of entertainment around. Our main priority must be to provide attractive, attacking football. But there are other important aspects which we in Scotland seem to be wakening up to rather later than England. They are very aware of the need to market the game, and now we are following fast along the same commercial lines.

'Most clubs now have some form of sponsorship, and are actively developing other ways of bringing in revenue. Then there are the facilities. For too long we've neglected them and expected fans to put up with conditions that have, quite frankly, been disgraceful. That's changing fast. In fact, side by side with establishing Motherwell in the Premier League, I'm just as concerned about improving things for supporters.'

At the start of his first season in charge, Wallace's remit was to keep the Steel Men in the Premier League, and he achieved that – but only just. Well finished third from bottom as Morton and Kilmarnock suffered the drop. Then the bombshell, as Wallace was asked to make cuts to his squad. He had brought in the likes of Ally Mauchlen and Nicky Walker from Leicester, as well as Jo

Edvaldsson and Bobby Flavell, but players had to head out in order to balance the books. Well had 18 full-time professionals and 14 part-timers, mostly kids.

But Wallace was happy with one player in particular, and said, 'Up here there is far greater tactical discipline. I found that out the hard way with a few heavy defeats early on. Only now am I getting my message across to the players, and the best example of that is youngster Brian McClair. He was totally undisciplined and really instinctive but I gave him a fair bit of stick, and his hard work has paid off with a place in Scotland's Under-21 squad.

'Since coming back to Scotland, I think my attitude to players has changed. I used to drive them hard, but now I have a softer approach. I tend to go for a bit of coaxing – and as you know, that was never my style. I still work around 80 hours a week, though!'

Wallace arrived back from holiday to discover McClair had been sold to Celtic. Connor had also moved to the Parkhead club and one can only imagine the tension during a hastily-convened board meeting. Wallace said, 'In Frank I had a diamond, and they don't grow on trees.'

Regardless, he set off for the sands of Gullane. Captain Edvaldsson led his men repeatedly up the hill and the players cooled off with a splash in the sea before tucking into a hearty three-course meal at a local hotel. It was all part of a team-building operation which Wallace hoped would push Motherwell clear of the relegation zone in the new season.

The Well boss was forced to break off from pre-season training to appear before SFA beaks to explain comments made in a newspaper the previous season. He was severely reprimanded for claiming the Old Firm gained an unfair advantage in games because they pressurised referees.

It was then back to Gullane, where he vowed to take pounds off his new signing, the enigmatic Andy Ritchie. Wallace parted with £25k to get his hands on the former Morton and Celtic star, and revealed how Ritchie was sick three times on his first visit to the beach. Wallace insisted Ritchie had been overweight and unfit but as soon as he had licked the player into shape, it was one 'weight' off his mind!

The opening match of the Premier League season saw Well travel to Tannadice to tackle league champs Dundee United, and after watching them raise the championship flag, they were forced to endure a 4-0 mauling. However, Motherwell had enough in the tank to see off Berwick Rangers in the new knock-out style League Cup second round.

The Steel Men managed just two points from their opening six league matches but held leaders Hearts at Tynecastle to leave the manager wondering if they had turned the corner. The following Saturday, though, they lost to bottom markers St Johnstone at Fir Park – the Perth side's first points of the season. After the match, a group of disgruntled fans chanted 'Wallace must go', to which the manager responded, 'The fans are entitled to shout. I do plenty of shouting myself at the players. There is nothing you can say in defence of a performance like that.'

What a difference a week makes, and when Well travelled to Ibrox and beat Rangers 2-1, the chants of irate Rangers fans could be heard above the booming noise of the PA system. 'Greig must go', but a posse of 60 policemen guarded the front door at Ibrox. The same cry was directed against the board before supporters began to shout for Wallace as their new manager. It was fully an hour before they dispersed.

Motherwell followed up their Ibrox victory with a battling draw against Dundee United at Fir Park, but by that time Greig had been sacked, and the hunt was on to find a new Rangers boss. Wallace had a job to do at Fir Park, though, and the Steel Men picked up another point at St Mirren the following week.

Seven days later, Wallace was installed as the new manager of Rangers and he left Motherwell joint second bottom of the table on seven points from 11 matches. Bobby Watson took over the Fir Park hot-seat.

18

The Second Coming

JOHN Greig was under enormous pressure and it was cash at the gate as his underperforming stars earned him a reprieve by beating Porto 2-1 at Ibrox, although a late counter by Jacques wiped the gloss from the scoreline. Peter McCloy was axed for the following game after shouldering the blame for Porto's late strike.

Seven days after losing at Dundee, 1,000 supporters staged a post-match demonstration outside Ibrox after the defeat to Motherwell. Chairman Rae Simpson released a statement saying, 'John Greig is still the manager of Rangers Football Club. The Board of Directors can't react as if there is a crisis every time the team loses a match.' But after just nine games, Rangers were seven points behind league leaders Dundee United, who had a game in hand.

The following midweek, United signed Derek Johnstone on a month's loan from Chelsea, just eight weeks after his £25,000 move from Rangers, and he scored a double in a 3-0 win over Morton. Meanwhile, Greig decided enough was enough and vowed to axe his underperforming stars. He snapped up Northern Ireland international Jimmy Nicholl from Toronto Blizzard and Rangers clinched a League Cup quarter-final place with a 2-0 win over Hearts at Ibrox – in front of just 12,000.

But just 48 hours later, Greig quit the Ibrox hot-seat, and admitted it had been one of the toughest decisions of his life. He said, 'This is obviously a very sad and emotional day for me as Rangers has been my life.' Greig informed the players of his decision before walking out the doors for the last time as manager.

Cue the speculation on who would be the next boss, although there appeared to be just two names in the frame – Alex Ferguson, a former Gers player, and Dundee United boss Jim McLean. Meanwhile, Rangers slumped to second bottom of the Premier League table after losing 3-0 to St Mirren at Love Street. The club was in an awful state and required major surgery.

Asides from looking for a new manager, there was also movement behind the scenes as John Paton was nominated for the position of chairman. But supporters were only interested in who would lead the team out of the mire and received their first big disappointment when Ferguson turned down the job. 'I'm staying at Pittodrie,' he said, after being handed a new five-year contract believed to be worth £60,000 a year. On the same day, Rangers, under the guidance of caretaker manager Tommy McLean, lost 1-0 in Porto, to exit the Cup Winners' Cup on away goals.

Tommy's brother Jim had emerged as front-runner for the post, and in a bid to lure him away from Tannadice, where he was manager and director, he was told he could sign whoever he wanted – regardless of religious denomination. On Sunday 6 November McLean held lengthy talks with the Rangers board and, it's believed, was offered an annual salary of £65,000. The following morning he decided to stay put, 'for family reasons'.

Northern Ireland boss Billy Bingham was then linked with the post, but said, 'I'm flattered to be mentioned in connection with Rangers, but I won't be pushing myself for the job, that's not my style. I've never scrambled after any manager's job – if they want me, they know where I am.'

They knew where Bingham was but chose to look closer to home. On the morning of Thursday 10 November, Jock Wallace was appointed manager. Wallace was delighted, until a compensation hitch with Motherwell threatened to derail the deal.

A settlement was finally agreed and Wallace was driven to Ibrox in the early hours of the morning for 'secret' talks, before directors Jack Gillespie and John Paton emerged at the front door at 5.20am to tell waiting reporters that there was unlikely to be any news that morning. Just after 7am, though, Paton was back at Ibrox to declare, 'We have a new manager!'

Wallace then walked out on to Edminston Drive, and said, 'This is the most marvellous moment of my life. To be back at Ibrox again is incredible. I have been told by the board that I have complete control over who I select, and I will sign players on ability. Religion will not come into it.' And with that, the new boss beat a hasty retreat.

Wallace's first game in charge was, ironically, against Ferguson's Aberdeen at Pittodrie. The new Gers boss was gushing in his praise for the Dons, but added, 'Every player at Ibrox will be given a fair chance but I know what I want. The formula must be right. I've seen the team only once through true blue eyes and I'm not going to condemn them on this. I need time to think. Bawling and shouting is not the answer – there is a great deal more to management than this.'

Wallace packed plenty into his first day back at Ibrox. After saying his goodbyes to everyone at Motherwell he held separate talks with the Rangers reserve players, then the first-team squad and coaching staff, supervised a training session and announced the team to play Aberdeen.

Before choosing the starting XI for Pittodrie, he conferred with interim boss Tommy McLean, and said, 'The two of us picked the team.' It was: McCloy, MacKinnon, Dawson, McLelland, Paterson, McPherson, Nicholl, McCoist, Mitchell, Redford and Cooper.

Rangers lost 3-0 at Pittodrie and Wallace was heavily criticised for 'rewarding' his players with a three-day break. He said, 'Morale is low, heads are down and the players have been under a lot of pressure. I want them to go away and come back with a fresh mind. I'm even going to take a day off myself.'

Bill McMurdo, whom Wallace nicknamed 'Agent Orange', recalled, 'Before the match in Aberdeen, I was invited up to the team hotel to get my tickets. Jock asked me to travel to Pittodrie on the team bus and I was delighted to accept. Once on the bus, he said to me, "Give me a Rangers tape, I want to put some music on." I passed over a cassette and the first song was "No Surrender" (which Jock sang to the tune of "Amazing Grace" as his party piece).

'Jock acted as compere and encouraged the players to sing. Those who didn't know the words were urged to learn them for the next away game. Jimmy Nicholl knew the words inside out and Jock said to him, "Brilliant, Jimmy. You know all the words, you're the captain today!" It was priceless.'

Wallace spoke frankly about Rangers' plight, joint second bottom of the Premier League with only seven points, and said, 'It's not a false position. We haven't been scoring goals. Now the players have to fight for their lives. There will be discipline, you can't achieve anything without it, and everything comes secondary to the team. No one player is more important than any other.'

The defeat at Pittodrie was Rangers' fifth successive league reverse but the supporters had faith in the 'Wallace Way' and big Jock would be given time to turn things around. He was just delighted to be back at Ibrox and said, 'Managing Rangers is my dream job, the one thing in my life I have always wanted more than any other. To me they are more than just a football club – they are a way of life.

'I've always been a Rangers fan, ever since I was a lad of nine and they came through to play near my home on the east coast. The team that made me a Rangers fan for life still trips off the tongue: Brown, Young, Shaw, McColl, Woodburn, Cox, Waddell, Gillick, Thornton, Duncanson and Caskie.

'I've served all my other clubs with complete loyalty and worked regular 18-hour days but my intense feeling for Rangers has never left me in 31 years of full-time football. I know this will bring the obvious question that if I'm so Rangers-daft then why did I leave in 1978, but I'm not prepared to rake over the ashes of that decision. I did what I thought was right at the time and have no regrets.

'But I feel I've come back a better manager. In those days I was team boss and Willie Waddell ran the club. We both did our jobs. I always knew there was more to running a club than putting a winning team on the field. I was aware the business side was very important but I should stress that the division of duties between myself and Willie was not the cause of my leaving for Leicester.

'Now I feel I'm a club manager in every sense. I want to be intimately involved in every aspect of the club, including the commercial side, the lotteries, the advertising, contracts, the whole works. That doesn't mean I'll interfere because Rangers are a well-run organisation. They have loyal people who have been working very hard in their own departments for years, and doing a fine job. But it stands to reason that Rangers will stand or fall by results on the field. It is the team which sets the keynote for everything else.'

When asked how he felt about being third choice for the job, behind Ferguson and McLean, he said, 'As far as I'm concerned, I was first choice when Rangers approached Motherwell for me – and that's all that matters. I don't mope around reading reports about how Alex Ferguson and Jim McLean were considering the job. I didn't have my fingers crossed that they would turn it down. I was too busy doing my own job at Motherwell.

'I don't know if the others really wanted the position, and I'm not interested in why they turned it down – I'm just glad they did. Of course, they both have very good teams and I appreciate how a manager builds a rapport with players but for me the pull of Rangers beats everything else in football.'

Just days into his new job, Wallace was asked when he would sign a Catholic, and replied, 'To listen to some people you'd think that all the problems of Rangers could be solved at a stroke – by signing a player who is Catholic. But for me, that's not a priority.

The chairman said that we are a non-sectarian club, and that I can sign any player I want. But that must be a means to an end – to help make Rangers great again – rather than an end in itself. I have signed many Roman Catholics – and released a few. When I was with Leicester I also signed several coloured players – and freed some of them, too.

'It's ironic that in my last spell with Rangers, when we were winning the occasional treble the subject of signing Catholics seldom came up, but now that the club is going through a difficult spell, everyone is jumping on that particular bandwagon. It has been turned into a campaign, and exploited by people who should know better. The emphasis should always be on football.'

Meanwhile, Motherwell chairman Kiddie announced that after five managers in five years, his club needed stability. Falkirk boss Alex Totten emerged as favourite for the job, although Dickie denied any approach to the Brockville gaffer. Days later, Wallace reshaped his backroom staff. Out went Tommy McLean, and in came 37-year-old Totten. McLean revealed that he had turned down the role of second-team coach.

Wallace seemed delighted to get his man and said, 'Alex is a Ranger now. He was my first choice for the job. He is a time-served manager, somebody who will do a right good job for us.'

Totten, a dad-of-two, quit his job as a sales manager with a tyre firm in Falkirk to take the job at Ibrox, and had a bit of a reputation as a salvage expert having already turned around the fortunes of both Alloa and Falkirk. His playing career had started under Bill Shankly at Liverpool, and then Bob Shankly at Dundee.

He recalled, 'The first time, in fact the only time, I ever met Jock, I was manager of Falkirk and fancied the big boy Bruce Clelland at Motherwell, so Jock said, "Come through and see me." I went through to Fir Park and was just ten minutes in his company. Then, on 11 November 1983, at 8am, the phone went and my wife answered it, but didn't recognise the voice. I took the receiver, "Jock Wallace here son, how would you like to be my assistant at Rangers?"

Right out of the blue. He told me he was going to Aberdeen the following day for his first game and that he would call me on the Monday. I was told to keep it quiet – which, as you can imagine, was tough.

'Next day we were playing Clyde. We're sitting there, I can't believe the secret I'm keeping and who comes on the television, on *Saint & Greavsie*, but big Jock, and I'm thinking, no one knows that he phoned me yesterday.

'After the game against Clyde, our chairman said to me, "Motherwell want to interview you about the vacant gaffer's job." I thought it was only manners to go through to the Coatbridge Hotel and meet their chairman, who said, "Alex, we want to offer you a five-year contract. We've had so many managers here that we're now looking for a bit of continuity."

'It was a great contract and I told them I would call them on Wednesday, which I did. I said "I really appreciate the offer but I have to turn it down and you will find out why in the next couple of days."

'I had to be at Rangers at four o'clock on the Friday and had the whole range of emotions. Joy, trepidation, pride etc. Stan the commissionaire said, "Mr Wallace is waiting up the marble staircase." Jock said to me, "Great to see you son, you're now a Ranger. Come and meet the directors." And there was Willie Waddell, Rae Simpson etc, and that was me – a Ranger!

'On one occasion Jock and I were in Switzerland, and we'd had a wee drink and I asked him, "Why did you want me?" He said, "Ten minutes was enough," and that was that day in his office at Motherwell.

'My first game in the dug-out was against Dundee United and we walked out the tunnel together. I was quite shy. The big man led the way and was punching the air, and lapping up the cheers. I was walking behind him and didn't know what to do. I met all the players for the first time before the match, Davie Cooper, Ally McCoist etc and I think we went 26 games with just one defeat, and beat Celtic 3-2 in the League Cup Final, when Ally got a hat-trick.

'It was a whole new way of life because I'd been part-time at Falkirk and so to go to a big club like Rangers was incredible. My dad was a big Rangers fan and Jock would invite him up to the office after a game, and he would say to dad, "This will be Alex's office, because one day I'll step up to be general manager." And that was the idea. Liverpool had great continuity, and that was Jock's way of thinking, but sadly it never materialised.'

By the turn of the year, the Light Blues were 13 points behind league leaders Aberdeen, but showed the pace-setters they were up to the task in a no-holds-barred match at Ibrox. Europe's team of the year arrived full of confidence but by the end of the 90 minutes, Dons boss Alex Ferguson insisted he was happy to leave with a point. For Rangers supporters, there was hope. In a match that saw Ally Dawson and Aberdeen's Eric Black red-carded, Wallace said, 'We've come a long way in two months.'

And when the Light Blues embarked on a nine-match unbeaten run, Wallace insisted he had reintroduced the 'laws of the jungle'. When he met the players for the first time in November, he had said he would take the heat off them for six weeks – and then it was up to them to win the respect of the fans.

He said, 'The response has been magnificent. What has impressed me is the way the players have responded to my training, coaching and tactical discipline. My first aim with any team has been physical and mental fitness, but the most important thing is the mental spirit of a team.

'It's something I learned as a jungle fighter in Malaya. You had to develop this mental spirit where you respected and trusted those around you. You had to help and cover each other because your life depended on it. The football field is no different. I took over a bruised and battered team going nowhere. This is not a criticism of the previous manager, but a fact.'

By the end of February, Rangers had stretched their unbeaten run and moved up to fourth in the table, but Aberdeen continued their relentless march to the title.

One player proving his worth second time around for the gaffer was Bobby Russell. The midfielder with the silky touch had cost just £365 from Shettleston seven years previous but was proving pivotal as Rangers battled to regain respectability. Russell was described by one journalist as 'an old tanner ba' player unaffected by decimalisation'.

Russell said, 'The change in training has made us stronger and fitter. After that you only worry about form. The game is all about confidence and once you've won a couple of matches, you develop a habit of winning and the boss tells us it's the best habit in the world. I think we were all sitting back waiting for someone else to make it happen. Now *we* do it. The boss has made us more competitive.'

Wallace said, 'Earlier in his career, Bobby had been freed by Sunderland. When he was first brought to my attention by our chief scout, Laurie Cumming, I urged him to keep playing junior football, and we got him a job. Other teams were after him but he gave me his word that he would sign for Rangers and he was true to it. I like players like that.

'While he was working, he would turn up at Ibrox every Tuesday night and I put him through his paces – four 40-yard sprints, a circuit and four 150s. For six months, that was all he did. He had the skills and I just needed to build him up. When we were taking him on full-time he told me he had three weeks' holiday after finishing his job. He asked what he should do. I told him to come to Ibrox to train – and he did. The first day at training I thought, "Boy, you're some player." His one-touch was different class.'

Jock's agent Bill McMurdo said, 'Jock was a football man through and through and a big honest guy. I never knew him to hold a grudge, well, apart from once and that was against the journalist Gerry McNee, whom Jock felt had given him an unfair press on many occasions. When Jock came back to Rangers he was asked by the *Scottish Daily Express* to write a weekly column. I did the deal but Jock insisted on a clause that McNee would never, under any circumstances, ghost-write the column. The boss said he couldn't put it in the contract, but gave me a cast-iron assurance that such a situation would never arise.

'Bobby Maitland wrote the column but he was off sick on one occasion and the editor called me up and said, "Can you ask Jock if it's okay for McNee to write the column just this once?" I did, and Jock, who must have been in a good mood, agreed, but when the paper came out and McNee's byline was on the story big Jock went ballistic. He called the paper and went mad at McNee, who phoned and reminded me about the "deal".

'I called Jock and told him he owed McNee an apology, and that he had okayed it. He admitted forgetting about it and asked me to get McNee up to his office after the next game. It must have been hard for Jock but he apologised, and McNee said smugly, "That's okay, just don't let it happen again." I'd never seen Jock move so quickly. He had McNee pinned up against the door within seconds, and I had to pull him off … eventually!'

A 17-match unbeaten run had helped Rangers into the final of the League Cup and the last eight of the Scottish Cup, although they would exit the latter after a replay with Dundee. They were also the best supported team in Scotland with an average of 19,483, more than 5,000 ahead of league leaders Aberdeen.

But their preparation for the League Cup Final against Celtic couldn't have been any worse. The Saturday before, Ian Redford and Robert Prytz were sent off against Dundee in a controversial Scottish Cup tie at Ibrox and banned for the match. Nicky Walker and Bobby Williamson were already out. Wallace took his team to Belfast for a preparation match against Linfield, and declared himself happy with a 4-0 win.

The squad then travelled to Turnberry to prepare for the biggest match since the gaffer's return, and 16-year-old midfield starlet Derek Ferguson had staked his claim for a final place by scoring in Belfast. 18-year-olds Robert Fleck and Hugh Burns were also added to the pool.

A dramatic Hampden final went to extra time and it was Super Ally who emerged as hero when he completed his hat-trick in the 104th minute to give Wallace the perfect homecoming present. Celtic had been overwhelming pre-match favourites, but Wallace's side were imperious in a match watched by 66,369. Russell was the undisputed man of the match, and the Parkhead side proved bad losers when they tried to harangue referee Bob Valentine just before the presentation ceremony. By that time, only one half of the ground was still populated with supporters.

The win ended two years of heartache and Wallace said, 'I've never been one for singling out players but Russell had a tremendous game. He is an outstanding player. "Rusty" is a quiet, unassuming guy. He was combing his hair after the match and I said to him, "Kid, you were brilliant." He just looked at me and said, "Thanks gaffer."

'I delayed announcing the team because I wanted to psyche up the players. We had our main tactics talk the night before the match, not that they paid much attention when they got out on to the park!'

The final Old Firm game of the season took place at Ibrox in April, and a spectacular overhead kick by Bobby Williamson sealed a 1-0 win – and ended Celtic's title hopes. It was also Jimmy Nicholl's last match before returning to parent club Toronto Blizzard. The Northern Irishman was made captain for the day – and was promptly sent off for kicking out at Brian McClair!

Rangers ended the season with three matches in four days. First, they drew 0-0 at Easter Road, before beating outgoing champions Dundee United 2-1 at Tannadice, which sealed fourth spot. Forty-eight hours later they beat Hearts 3-2 at Tynecastle in a testimonial match for Gers legend Alex MacDonald, the new boss at Hearts.

It was then off to the sunshine of Australia for a summer tour – although with Wallace in charge, there wouldn't be much time for sightseeing. However, it soon turned into an injury hell for two players, Bobby Williamson and Colin McAdam, who suffered broken legs, under different circumstances. John MacDonald and Bobby Russell were also injured and skipper John McClelland refused to accept new contract terms. Oh, and Ally McCoist didn't have his troubles to seek either!

He said, 'I'll never forget that tour as long as I live. Before leaving, I was in the shop at Glasgow Airport and when I looked around for the rest of the lads they had gone. Someone told me they were already at the departure gate and I ran there as fast as I could. Big Jock looked furious and grabbed me, before saying, "You're late – that's you on your last warning!" And we hadn't even left Glasgow!

'When we got to Heathrow, there was a bus taking us from one terminal to the next, and I got lost. I missed the bus and ended up at the wrong terminal. I couldn't even begin to give you an indication of the fear running through my body when I found the right terminal. Jock leapt from the bus and grabbed me by the scruff of the neck. He was tearing into me, saying that one more misdemeanour and I was right back up the road. Suddenly I looked over his shoulder and there was Ian Redford, Bobby Williamson and John MacDonald at the back of the bus giving me absolute pelters – and making rude gestures!

'We arrived in Melbourne at 5am and Jock said, "Right, everyone get to bed for a few hours, and be downstairs no later than 8am for a team meeting and breakfast." I'm rooming with Bobby Williamson, and we wake up at 8.10am, and I just think, "Oh my god", and started packing again, because when Jock said eight, he meant eight.

'Anyway, we went down for breakfast, and walked in quietly, just in case he hadn't picked up on our absence. We sneaked a glance at him and his head came up ever so slightly and his eyes cast a sideways glance at us, and his head went back down to his cereal. Me and Bobby sat down and I said to him, "What happened there, d'you think we got away with that?"

'Big Colin McAdam and Davie Mitchell were sitting next to us and Colin said, "You're the luckiest bastard alive Coisty," and I said, "How?" and we looked over at the door and there was Alex Totten just walking in – and he was five minutes later than us! I looked over at Totts and mouthed, "You've just saved my life!"

'It was a great tour and we played the Aussie national team in Melbourne, and again in Sydney. We went to Auckland and Davie Cooper absolutely terrorised the wee New Zealand right-back. He turned him inside out and at the end of the game, big Jock went over to the lad and patted him on the head, and said, "You know what son, I almost felt sorry for you there!" And that was big Jock!'

19

Keeping The Connection

JOCK Wallace wasn't the type to use more words than necessary. Why use a dozen when a handful will do? He chose them carefully but had a real liking for a couple in particular. 'Character' was a favourite, while 'loyalty' was also high on the list. When it came to his players, he showed them loyalty and expected nothing less in return. He got it from most, and one player in particular. Nicky Walker had a habit of working with Wallace.

In demand as a teenager while playing Highland League football with Elgin City, he was aware of interest from several clubs and had just enjoyed trials with Manchester United and Derby County when Wallace and Leicester came calling. He had a decision to make.

Walker said, 'There were a few clubs interested in me when I was 17 and still at school. Leicester had a scout in the north of Scotland called Harry Dunn and he came round to the house one night to tell me that City wanted me down for a trial. It was just the start of an incredible period in my early career.

'After a ten-day trial I went off to Sweden with the first team, which was amazing. I was like a wee boy in a sweet shop, mixing with all these English First Division players. I was scared to speak to some of them at times, but as a huge *Match of the Day* fan, I knew them all from the TV!

'I was down at Filbert Street for a few days after that and the gaffer asked me to sign. I was studying for my Highers at the time and he made it clear that he wanted me to keep them going. I'd wanted to be a PE teacher and had a conditional acceptance from Jordanhill College, which was the best in Scotland at the time, but as I was soon to be resident in Leicester, the club enrolled me in the PE College at Loughborough. Leicester offered me a four-year deal and I accepted. This little boy from the Highlands was made up but I knew there was a lot of work to do before I was ready for the first team.'

Walker left school and started training full-time at City. The regular keeper, Mark Wallington, was club captain and an iconic figure at Filbert Street, as well as an England Under-23 international, but when he was injured, it was time for the rookie keeper to get his gloves on.

He said, 'I made my debut against Chelsea at Stamford Bridge which, as you can imagine, was incredible, but the gaffer obviously had faith in me. I also played against the likes of Charlton and Sheffield Wednesday, both big clubs at the time. It was a big deal but something I still managed to enjoy.

'There was an FA Cup semi-final against Spurs looming and I felt I'd done enough to be involved but Mark was just about fit and the gaffer called me in to his office and told me he was going with experience. We lost the game and afterwards he told me he'd made a mistake.

'But I couldn't fault Jock. He was a fantastic man and just had this aura about him. He was a real man's man but he looked after the kids at the team. We had about 18 young professionals at the time and the club had a house which we all lived in. It was great having the company of people my own age and we also had a landlady to look after us. We got one good meal a day provided and the gaffer would just walk in now and again to see how we all were – although he was probably checking up on us. He was like a second father and we looked up to him.

'People really liked Jock as a person, and you always wanted to do your best for him. Don't get me wrong, if you did something wrong or stepped out of line, you got a rollicking, but I suppose you expected that if you'd messed up.

'Just before signing for Leicester I was playing for the school team in the morning, Elgin in the afternoon, and another three or four teams throughout the week. It was wall-to-wall football. I went on a tour of California with a local boys' club, and then to Holland for a youth tournament with Inverness Caley… and then Sweden with Leicester. Life just didn't get any better.'

Wallace left Leicester in 1982, but if Walker, a full Scotland international, thought he had seen the last of his old mentor, he was mistaken. He said, 'The gaffer called a couple of months after leaving Filbert Street and I signed for Motherwell in January 1983. Hugh Sproat was at Fir Park in those days and he was a big fans' favourite, so it wasn't just a case of going up there and becoming number one.

'Leicester didn't stand in my way. They had a ready-made replacement in Ian Andrews – who would one day play for Celtic against Rangers in the famous 5-1 game at Ibrox – and he was a year below me at Filbert Street. Ian played for England youths so they were happy to let me go.

'I remember signing on the Thursday night and driving up to Scotland to meet Jock and his assistant, Frank Connor. The next day was a real eye opener. I turned up at training to discover the players being put through their paces on a red ash park. I asked Jock who we were playing the next day and he said, "Celtic at home, son. Bit of a baptism of fire, eh!"

'It turned out to be a great day because we won 2-1 and I played and thoroughly enjoyed it. I played the second half of the season and loved the regular first-team football. Then came the summer and when Rangers came in for Jock, he moved to Ibrox. He told me he wanted to take me with him and just to sit tight. There was a lot of interest in me at the time but I'll always remember him saying, "I'm coming for you – don't go anywhere else." And he did.

'I started off the season with Motherwell, which I was more than happy to do, but Jock was true to his word and I joined Rangers in December 1983, which was the biggest move of my career. Playing for the gaffer was great, because I got on really well with him, and was delighted to follow him. He was always up front – what you saw was definitely what you got.

'To go to Rangers was just incredible, though. You know Rangers are a massive club, but you don't realise just how big until you actually get the chance to play for them. The whole thing about the marble staircase, etc, is awesome. It was totally different to what I'd known previously anywhere in England and simply took my breath away. Ibrox is such an iconic football stadium.

'Peter McCloy and Jim Stewart were the other goalkeepers at the club but I still managed to play eight times in my first season, although the day I signed for Rangers was a whirlwind. It was early morning and I was out walking the dog when the phone rang. I was supposed to play for Motherwell against St Johnstone that day but Jock said, "Where are you?" I told him I was out with the dog. He said, "Walking the dog? Get your arse in here. I've a contract for you to sign."

'It was crazy. I headed straight for Ibrox and was taken up to the manager's office. "Here," he said. "There's your contract." I signed it without knowing how much I was getting or how long it was for. It sounds stupid now but I just wanted to play football and, especially, for Jock. I remember Kenny Black and Kenny Lyall going to Fir Park as part of the deal. I lived in Hamilton at the time so it was an easy commute to Ibrox, although I remained there even when I moved to Hearts.

'A lot of people perhaps only saw the big, gruff, sergeant major side of Jock but he was also a really caring man. He was definitely old school. Pat on the back if you did well but a real hammering if you messed up. I was devastated when I heard he had Parkinson's disease. In fact, when his son John was up north recently we hooked up and had a good chat about the old days.

'I was around the same age as John and he used to play for a couple of teams in Leicester and was always in and around the club. He was telling me that when his dad found out he had the condition, naturally the family rallied round, but they became tighter and started to spend much more time together.

'When Jock passed away a reporter called looking for my reaction. I was completely stunned and totally lost for words. I went to the funeral in Wallyford and it was like a who's who of football, with just about every club imaginable represented.

'But that was the measure of the man – he was well loved by everyone.'

20

Trouble Across The Water

THERE were several comings and goings at Ibrox in the summer of 1984. Gregor Stevens re-joined Motherwell, while Iain Ferguson and Cammy Fraser were signed from Dundee – with the former hitting five on his debut during Rangers' tour of Switzerland and Germany.

Davie Cooper was in stunning form as the Light Blues opened their league campaign with a goalless draw at home to St Mirren, but a mixture of perspiration and desperation brought a 2-1 win at Dumbarton, and while Redford and McCoist got the goals, new signing Ferguson insisted he was settling in well.

He said, 'I must admit my legs were trembling the first time I met Jock Wallace. He said to me, "Right son, I've brought you here to score goals. Understand?" The boss made it clear what he wants from me and I'll give it my best shot for him.'

Ferguson put on five pounds during Wallace's strict training regime, and declared himself stronger for the challenge ahead. He returned to his old club at the start of September and scored the first in a 2-0 win, which pushed unbeaten Rangers up into second spot. The players limbered up for their UEFA Cup tie with Bohemians in Dublin by playing their part in a thrilling encounter at Pittodrie against the league leaders. The match ended 0-0 and Wallace fell foul of referee Hugh Young when he lambasted the match official for ignoring the injured Ally McCoist, who lay motionless in the Dons box for several minutes before the game was eventually stopped.

But that was nothing compared to what lay in store for the Light Blues when they crossed the water to Ireland and an evening of terror in Dublin. Large numbers of Rangers supporters were up in arms when around a dozen or so Bohemians fans climbed on top of a small block of flats directly behind the end that housed the 3,000 Gers fans. When they started pelting the visiting supporters with rocks and bottles, Rangers fans pleaded with the Garda to remove them, but it seemed to take an eternity for them to do so.

The away end had been largely good natured throughout the first half but that all changed at the break when a home supporter ran on to the pitch to taunt visiting fans, which was the cue for several Rangers supporters to scale a 20-foot high chicken wire fence. Wallace made his way to the away end and appealed to the large Rangers support for calm, but was shouted down by a section of the hooligans, and when one guy called him a Fenian b******, it became clear that many had travelled to Dublin just to cause trouble.

It was one of the most poisonous evenings in the history of the club and after the match, Wallace said of the 'fans' responsible for the trouble, 'They don't know how to behave. They can sing, shout and bawl all they want but they are not entitled to throw coins and break fences. I was scared of these guys. They behaved like crazy men. I was more worried about them than the game.'

Rangers were fined £2,000 by UEFA for their part in the Dalymount Park riot, but a spokesman for the governing body said, 'The commission reserves the right to take further action after completion of its enquiry,' which hinted that Rangers hadn't heard the last of the matter.

On the journey home, many Rangers supporters' buses were pelted with rocks and petrol bombs in pre-planned attacks. 'Never again', was the cry in unison when supporters eventually arrived in the relative calm of Larne.

There is an enduring image on the front page of the *Daily Record* on the day after the game, taken by snapper Eric Craig, which shows Wallace urging fans to get off the fence behind the goal – and receiving abuse. It was clear that many 'fans' didn't know who he was. It was no great surprise that Rangers lost the match 3-2.

Rangers put the tie to bed with a 2-0 second-leg win at Ibrox, before disposing of Meadowbank Thistle in the League Cup semi-final on an aggregate of 5-1 to book their place in the Hampden final. A 2-0 Premier League win at Love Street also helped the Gers maintain their place in the top three, just two points behind leaders Aberdeen.

The Light Blues were drawn against Inter Milan in the next round of the UEFA Cup and limbered up for a visit to the San Siro Stadium with a disappointing 0-0 draw at home to Dumbarton. It was a setback, but not the end of the world as far as Wallace was concerned. He had eyes on the bigger prize, and said, 'If we get through against Inter it will be a major breakthrough. We're still a bit naive tactically but are equipped to do well. The physical condition of the players is remarkable. We've done all the hard work and know we can fight for 90 minutes. Now we've got to face Inter Milan and learn from them – and maybe they will learn a wee bit from us.'

Sadly, it was the Light Blues who received a lesson in the art of finishing from the Italians, although it was a German, Karl-Heinz Rummenigge, who did the damage. He scored in the 3-0 victory, and said, 'When I scored the third goal I felt great, because it meant we will be playing in the third round. There is no way back for Rangers.'

In between the matches against the Italian giants, Rangers faced Dundee United in the League Cup Final. The Tannadice side stood between Wallace and his tenth trophy as Gers boss. And after a pulsating 90 minutes, in which John McClelland was outstanding, an Iain Ferguson goal was all that separated the sides. Rangers were kings of Hampden once again.

And Ferguson was on target twice in the return match against Inter at Ibrox. Aussie striker Davie Mitchell also scored but the Italians eased through on an aggregate of 4-3.

Rangers' title hopes were dealt a severe blow a few weeks before Christmas when they lost 2-1 at home to league leaders Aberdeen, despite Mitchell firing Rangers ahead. The defeat saw the Light Blues slip seven points behind the Granite City side.

Scoring goals was again a problem and with the festive season looming, Rangers had managed just seven in nine league matches at Ibrox. On the day they struggled to a 1-1 draw against Hearts at home, Stirling Albion were slamming in 20 without reply in a Scottish Cup tie against Selkirk – with David Thomson bagging seven.

But when the team isn't playing so well, it's always nice to have something to keep you warm. Cammy Fraser gave not one little present, but two after firing the opening goal against St Mirren the week before Christmas. The team had been plodding along, struggling to break down the Buddies, and the natives were getting restless. Cue the Fraser goal, and a little bit of unnecessary extras – the V-sign to supporters in the Govan Stand. They responded by booing the player every time he touched the ball – while fans in the Copland Road end, who perhaps hadn't seen the gesture, chanted 'There's only one Cammy Fraser!'

Afterwards, Wallace said, 'I couldn't see what kind of gesture he made, but if he made a V-sign then he must suffer the consequences. Mind you, he has my permission to give me the V-sign the next time he scores a hat-trick!' It was a sad indictment of how far Rangers had slipped that only 12,763 attended the match.

Next up was an Old Firm encounter at Parkhead, and while the league title looked a distant dream, matches between Rangers and Celtic were never in need of a sideshow. This one looked like ending in the narrowest of home wins until a moment of indecision by Celtic keeper Pat Bonner cost his side dear. Should I stay, or should I come for the ball was the big question. With just five minutes remaining, he punched the ball to the feet of Davie Cooper, and the classy winger cracked it into the empty net. In the aftermath, a Celtic ball boy was led from the field for making offensive gestures to the Rangers support.

New £100,000 winger Ted McMinn grabbed his first goal for the Gers in a 4-2 win over Dumbarton at muddy Boghead and typically it was no ordinary goal. He took a corner from the left with his right foot and the inswinger sailed over keeper Gordon Arthur and into the net. Welcome to Ted's wacky world.

Iain Ferguson proved he knew the way to goal with three in two league matches at the start of January – but Gers managed just a solitary point from the games against Dundee and Hibs. Already, the league title was a two-horse race between Aberdeen and Celtic. The final nail in the coffin arrived late in January when the Light Blues lost 5-1 at Aberdeen.

Ghostbusters had just been released in cinemas around the country but it was Rangers who were frighteningly bad as they suffered their heaviest league defeat in 20 years. The rout was missed by Wallace, who picked up a hiatus hernia injury in training and was advised by his doctor to stay at home.

Rangers were struggling and could only draw with Morton in the third round of the Scottish Cup at Cappielow, with Wallace once again absent. Assistant boss Totten was also in charge for the replay in which goals by Mitchell, Fraser and John MacDonald helped Rangers to a 3-1 victory. Totten said, 'It was just the tonic Jock needed while he is recovering from an operation. He was on the phone seconds after the final whistle.' Derek Johnstone – back for a second spell at Ibrox after his departure from Chelsea – scored in a league match against Morton, again, as Rangers consolidated in third spot.

Meanwhile, McClelland had moved on to pastures new at Watford and looked on from afar as the Light Blues struggled for form. He urged the hierarchy to do what they hadn't done with him, and to pay players what they were worth. He insisted they tie Cooper into a long-term and rewarding contract. On Wallace, McClelland said, 'Jock is a different breed. He is an uncut diamond, brusque and aggressive, but he was the man who dragged us back to life when he replaced John Greig. Some say he has mellowed from his earlier days at Ibrox – but that takes a bit of believing. Jock got the whole place jumping, but now he has to get the next stage right – he must have Rangers challenging for the title.'

It didn't look like happening any time soon, though, and a 1-0 defeat at home to Dundee in the fourth round of the Scottish Cup was the final insult for many. John Brown scored the solitary goal and only Cooper received pass marks. Afterwards, Wallace said, 'I'm sick. We had our chances but didn't take them.' After the match, around 100 supporters protested at the front door but were dispersed by mounted police. One fan managed to breach the heightened security to hurl his season ticket at the stadium door.

Rangers lost their next game, at Tynecastle, and the supporters voted with their feet when the Light Blues hosted Dumbarton, with just 8,424 watching Ally McCoist score twice in a 3-1 win. Wallace said, 'We've worked hard with Ally trying to get his composure right in the box, and it's beginning to pay off.'

So what better way to recharge the batteries for the remainder of the league campaign than by going on tour – to Baghdad! The Ibrox side were out of the Scottish Cup and arranged three matches, two in Iraq and one in neighbouring Jordan, while the next round of ties were being played. Wallace admitted he had one eye on the following season, and said, 'It gives us a chance to try various formations while the pressure is off. I've got to look ahead, and this is a chance to get our heads together.

'There is nothing to do out there apart from a bit of sightseeing so there will be plenty of time to talk, and we'll take advantage of that. Our problems haven't changed from day one of the season. We've caused ourselves headaches because we haven't scored enough goals.'

The Light Blues drew their first match 1-1 with Iraq's World Cup side in Baghdad, in a match watched by 22,000 spectators – and beamed live throughout the country on television. Eric Ferguson equalised for Rangers after Iraq had opened the scoring. Andy Bruce played well in goals but was injured late on and replaced by McCloy.

Wallace said, 'It took us the best part of an hour to settle on the dry, dusty pitch, but their goalkeeper saved them late on with four superb saves. Iraq were very good. They won the Gulf Cup and play quickly with plenty of one-twos.'

However, Rangers' next match – against a Baghdad select – proved a bit of a nightmare with the home side winning 4-1. Robert Prytz scored for Rangers, and Wallace said, 'The conditions were alien to us. That's not an excuse but the wind coming off the desert didn't help.'

The final match of the short tour was against a Kuwait XI in Amman, and Wallace was pleased that the match was played on a synthetic pitch rather than the bone-hard surface of the opening games. Rangers ran out 2-1 winners with McCoist grabbing the opening goal but Kuwait levelled soon after, although MacDonald came off the bench to score the winner. Wallace said, 'It was good for the players' morale and we managed to get various things sorted out. We were also able to give a few young players their chance.'

On their return, Rangers lost against St Mirren at Love Street before Dundee inflicted Rangers' fourth home league defeat of the season in a 3-1 win in which Wallace turned to youth. He said, 'Great Rangers players in great teams of the past have gone through similar and survived.'

With just a few league games left to play, Rangers headed down the coast to Greenock, where McCoist gave the long-suffering Gers fans something to cheer against the relegated Morton. He scored three times and enjoyed linking up with Gers debut boy Ian Durrant.

On the last day of the league season, Rangers lost 1-0 at Easter Road to finish joint fourth with St Mirren, and 21 points behind winners Aberdeen, but no one noticed, for 200 miles south of

Glasgow, thousands of football supporters had packed into Valley Parade to hail Bradford City, the Third Division champions. Tragically, fire engulfed a packed grandstand and 56 supporters lost their lives. It was one of the darkest days in British football.

The season was barely over when Rangers chairman John Paton revealed that the club was prepared to go 'deep into debt' to construct a championship-winning side, but he insisted: 'We will not be held to ransom by any player.

'Money is available now for Jock Wallace to buy the players he needs. We've never refused him money in the past and we're certainly not going to do so now. We showed a trading loss of over £900,000 last year, but we will go into debt to get things right. We've made what we thought was a very good offer to Davie Cooper but he has turned it down. We won't improve on that, so it's up to him.'

Wallace insisted the season just finished was far from the toughest he had ever faced. He said, 'I don't see it that way. I don't do things for Jock Wallace – I do things for Rangers. And if there is criticism in the season ahead then I'll take it.'

Wallace revealed that he had cancelled Rangers' scheduled pre-season tour of Germany, after the horrors of Heysel, where 39 Juventus fans died when a wall collapsed inside the stadium just before the European Cup Final against Liverpool. He said, 'Because of what happened in Brussels we can't take a chance before we play in the UEFA Cup. I'll take a tour in any country in the world that will make it difficult for supporters to watch us!'

21

The Party's Over

ESPITE chairman John Paton's assurances that cash was available for new players, it seemed the biggest problem was hanging on to the current ones. Six players – Cooper, Prytz, Redford, Eric Ferguson, Billy Davies, and Davie McKinnon – had failed to agree terms for the new campaign.

Wallace pressed ahead regardless and took his squad north for a short pre-season tour of the Highlands. Nairn County were first to fall and 22-year-old McCoist picked up where he had left off by scoring twice in a 5-1 rout. Rangers opened their league campaign against Dundee United at Ibrox and 28,000 watched Cooper and Russell run the show – and McCoist score the only goal of the match.

Seven days later, Rangers were top of the table for the first time in 1985 thanks to a 3-1 win at Easter Road. It was the perfect response from McCoist, on target again, who had looked likely to move away from Ibrox midway through the previous season when the goals had dried up. He said, 'Mr Wallace said he would keep me in touch about any moves. But that night I thought things through and told him I wasn't going anywhere and felt I could still make it at Ibrox.'

Hearts were despatched the following week and everything in the Ibrox garden appeared rosy. 35,000 watched the match and the only blip was a red card for McCoist, who was threatened with a heavy fine by Wallace for getting involved in a brawl. The gaffer said, 'I was disappointed with his behaviour – it was a daft thing to do. Players must handle the tension if we want supporters to do likewise.'

A penalty shoot-out win over Forfar in the League Cup preceded the first Old Firm match of the season and Super Ally was back in Wallace's good books after an encouraging performance at Parkhead. McCoist scored the opener before 60,000 spectators and only a second-half strike by Paul McStay earned the hosts a point. Rangers had retained their unbeaten start to the campaign and their mantle as league leaders, but Wallace conceded that Celtic had been the better team.

A midweek League Cup win at Hamilton was followed by a solid 3-0 Premier League win over St Mirren – and the Wallace bandwagon rolled on. It was a freezing afternoon but almost 30,000 turned up to see a team they had renewed confidence in. Wallace said, 'It is obvious we are winning more and more people back to Ibrox. To get over 27,000 for this game on such a horrible day is astonishing.'

A single goal victory over Osasuna, in the first round of the UEFA Cup, gave the Light Blues a slender advantage to take to Pamplona for the second leg, but the fall-out was a 1-0 loss at Ibrox against Dundee, their first in the league, and the players were booed off the field.

But it was just the start of an awful run that saw them dumped out of the League Cup at the semi-final stage by Hibs, before being taken apart by Aberdeen at Ibrox in a 3-0 humbling. Hugh Burns and Craig Paterson were ordered off and the Light Blues were overtaken by both Celtic and the Dons.

After exiting Europe, the gaffer opened his heart on the pressures of managing a club like Rangers and what he saw as a 'kick Rangers when they're down' mentality within certain sections of the media. He said, 'I was hurting so bad after the 2-0 defeat to Osasuna that I kept away from the players the following day because I didn't want to take it out on them. The bad publicity is really getting to me. I didn't think it would, but I'm really hurting. It's kick-the-Rangers time, and I don't understand why.

'When Barcelona or Real Madrid go through a bad time they are protected and encouraged by their press. But when we slip we are slagged off. Why is this? The press made a meal out of ten Rangers fans being arrested in Spain. But only one fan was convicted and he must have been a bampot, because he threw a bottle at a police car. But that kind of publicity does us no good whatsoever. We had no problems in Spain. The hospitality was so good and police so helpful that I would be delighted to go back there next year as part of our pre-season build-up.'

Matters improved somewhat, and after McCoist had scored to secure a point at Tannadice, Rangers were locked in a three-way battle at the top of the league with Aberdeen and Celtic. Just 24 hours beforehand, though, there had been stormy scenes at the club's AGM in which Wallace's leadership skills had been called into question by irate shareholders. As he looked on solemnly, there were attacks on team discipline, coaching and the captaincy.

However, chairman John Paton publicly backed the manager, to a point, by saying, 'Jock Wallace signed a five-year contract when he returned to Rangers in 1983 and we intend to stand by that. We are as disappointed as anyone at some of the recent results but as far as Jock is concerned, he asked for three years to sort things out – and we intend to let him see the job through.'

But while successive defeats to Hibs and St Mirren made Wallace's position just a little more unstable, Rangers remained just two points behind the top two. It was a mere stay of execution, and when they drew a blank at home to Clydebank, the daggers were out again. A four-goal show by Aberdeen's Frank McDougall against Celtic at Pittodrie left Rangers trailing – with a must-win Old Firm game looming.

A full house watched Rangers maul Celtic at Ibrox and goals by Durrant, Cooper and McMinn had bluenoses smiling from ear to ear. It was easily Rangers' best display of the season but Wallace insisted the result hadn't surprised him, and said, 'We've been threatening to do this for weeks. I thought Ian Durrant, Dougie Bell and Ally Dawson were terrific.'

But Rangers' Jekyll and Hyde form struck again the following weekend when they lost 3-0 to Hearts at Tynecastle. It was simply mind boggling, and when John Brown bagged a hat-trick at Dens Park to give Dundee a 3-2 win over Rangers, they were overtaken in the league table by both Dundee United and Hearts.

Wallace took his players to Malta for a sunshine break but missing was injured star Craig Paterson, the suspended Hugh Burns, and Bobby Russell, who was left at home due to domestic circumstances. However, their first match was put back 24 hours as Maltese fans seemed far keener to watch an Italian match live on TV. When they eventually got playing, Hamrun Spartans were beaten 4-0, with debut boy Scott Nisbet scoring twice, and McCoist grabbing the other two. Wallace said, 'Young Nisbet took his goals well and the idea of playing him up front certainly paid off.'

Nisbet was again on target in the second game, against Valletta. Rangers won 7-0 and the 17-year-old grabbed a hat-trick. Fleck scored twice and McCoist and McKinnon got the others. Wallace said, 'Everyone here is talking about Nisbet. These two games, and the performances of our youngsters, have given everyone a boost.'

Just before Christmas, 12,000 turned up to see Rangers beat Motherwell thanks to a McCoist goal five minutes after the break. The Light Blues struggled to break down a dour and defensive visiting side but were severely handicapped due to the absence of Cooper and Russell. Rather amazingly, though, the victory put Rangers just two points behind leaders Aberdeen and Hearts, the latter of whom had played a game more.

Rangers bounced back from a New Year's Day defeat to Celtic by thumping bogey team Dundee 5-0, and once again McCoist was the man of the moment with a hat-trick. Just under 14,000 also witnessed rookie striker Fleck score, but the draw for the Scottish

Cup third round saw Rangers paired with league leaders Hearts in Edinburgh.

The Light Blues had rediscovered their goal touch and scored another four the following Saturday against Clydebank, with McCoist again on target. Meanwhile, Wallace put former Dundee pair Iain Ferguson and Cammy Fraser up for sale, and said, 'I bought Cammy as a time-served professional because I thought he was right for the job. But he couldn't do it the way I wanted.'

McCoist scored for the fourth game in a row – against Hearts at Tynecastle – but the Light Blues exited the cup. In treacherous conditions, McCoist gave Rangers the lead a minute before half-time, and Durrant equalised after Hearts had gone 2-1 ahead, but John Robertson popped up with five minutes remaining to seal the win in a capital cracker. That looked like it for another season, and Wallace blamed the defeat on individual errors.

But there was a wind of change blowing through Ibrox and the corridors of power had a new name to conjure with. David Holmes took charge on Valentine's Day and despite professing his love for Falkirk, he was installed as chief executive. He insisted that Rangers would not be run from Nevada, where Lawrence Marlborough, the major shareholder in the club, was living, but from Glasgow – and made it clear that he was boss.

He added, 'It hurts me to see Rangers fans leaving 20 minutes before the end of the match just as much as it obviously hurts them. We have to stop this.' Out went directors Jim Robinson, Tom Dawson and Rae Simpson. Holmes, who had been a centre-forward with junior side Broxburn, said, 'I'm no hatchet man. I did what I had to do but I didn't flinch from it.'

One was given the immediate impression that 'Wallace's jacket was on a shoogly nail!' Rangers were 'languishing' in fifth spot in the table, eight points behind Hearts and with little chance of forcing their way into the title race. The problem was crystal clear – inconsistency. The Light Blues had been blowing hot and cold all season. Impressive wins, such as the 3-0 success over Celtic, had normally been followed by an inept display against one of the also-rans. It was a frustrating scenario for all involved.

The club received a boost with a 3-2 win over Chelsea in a friendly. Paterson, Bell – with his first goal for the club – and Burns were on target while future Ger Nigel Spackman scored for Chelsea. Pat Nevin and Doug Rougvie played for the Londoners in a match that attracted 17,512 to Ibrox on a Friday night.

McCoist grabbed another hat-trick in a 3-1 win over Hibs, but Rangers took just a solitary point from their next three league matches and trailed Hearts by 13 points with just four matches remaining. The Tynecastle side, five points ahead of both Dundee United and Celtic, looked odds-on to win the title, and with a handful of ex-Gers in their side.

Rangers, out of the Scottish Cup, made good use of their free weekend by hosting Spurs, but the players were branded 'a disgrace' by Wallace when they lost 2-0. Just 12,000 witnessed the so-called glamour game and Wallace said, 'I don't understand the attitude of players at times. For me, our performance was a disgrace. We didn't play at all and let ourselves down but most importantly we let the fans down.'

And the Sunday encounter proved to be big Jock's final game as Rangers boss as he was sacked that evening. He was replaced by Sampdoria player Graeme Souness, Rangers' first ever player-manager.

For Wallace, though, it was the first time he had ever been sacked in his rewarding, but ruthless, line of work. His luxury home in the shadow of Bothwell Castle was the perfect example of the rich trappings of the successful football manager, but the brown envelope, complete with P45, was the flip side.

At 50 years old, Wallace made it clear that he had no intention of quitting the game. He bullishly insisted he was ready to travel anywhere in the world to work. For big Jock, sitting around or tending the garden wasn't an option. He said, 'I've just been in to Ibrox to tidy up my desk but I'm still seething about that performance against Spurs. I've no intention of quitting football. Why should I? I'm an experienced manager and can work elsewhere. I've known for a couple of days what was about to happen but I kept my own counsel. Negotiations were carried out with dignity and I'm not going to say anything to spoil that. Rangers are in my blood and that will never change. I'll always have an affection for them.

'Rangers get the biggest spotlight in Scottish football and I wish the guy who takes over the very best of luck. What will I do now? Rest and play a bit of golf. But I would like to say this to the fans: Rangers will be back. I did the job to the best of my ability and leave confident that people appreciate this.'

The hangover from the Wallace sacking was evident the following weekend when Rangers lost 2-1 at struggling Clydebank – the Bankies' first ever league win over Rangers. Caretaker boss Alex Totten was furious, and pointed the finger of blame directly at the players. He said, 'Managers and coaches get the sack but players can't escape responsibility either. I felt sorry for our fans. As far as I am concerned, I was looking for a lot more from a Rangers team than I got. Players should have pride in their own display, but no one else can give them that other than themselves.'

Totten admitted it had been a difficult spell in the wake of Wallace's departure, and that some of the players, including Nicky Walker, had been in tears. Souness officially took over the reins at Ibrox 72 hours after the defeat at Kilbowie, and Totten said, 'I wish Walter Smith all the best in his role as assistant manager. He takes over my room and I left him a good luck note on his desk. For me, Rangers will always be the greatest club in the world and I reckon I've gained from my experiences with them. I won two cups and hopefully helped groom young players who will be top stars with Rangers one day.'

Souness's first game in charge was against St Mirren at Love Street, but he wasn't present. Rangers lost 2-1 although it could have been far worse. Souness had invited ex-Liverpool boss Joe Fagan to run the rule over his inherited players, and the former

Anfield supremo's verdict would have made for unpleasant reading, as would assistant Walter Smith's account of the afternoon's action.

The 1985/86 season would become the worst in the club's history. The defeat by St Mirren made it 14 losses in 34 games, meaning the best they could finish with was 36 points. Rangers' previous worst was 37.

Smith took the players to Pittodrie for the penultimate game of the season and watched his youngsters battle to a 1-1 draw, but Souness saw his charges play for the first time on the final day of the campaign. Motherwell were the visitors and a 2-0 home win meant Rangers had qualified for the UEFA Cup, despite finishing fifth. One of the other major plus points was the form of Ian Durrant, who had been struggling to shake off the effects of flu right up until kick-off, but still turned in a five-star performance.

Souness celebrated European qualification but was astonished at the morgue-like atmosphere in the Rangers dressing room. He was to learn that Celtic winning the league that day on goal difference over Hearts was the final blow for Wallace's wounded warriors.

22

Sunshine, Sangria And Soccer

JOCK Wallace awoke one morning to discover Glasgow Rangers no longer a part of his working life. They would never be far from his thoughts or his heart, but he was the type who lived to work, although an estimated golden handshake of £110,000, thanks to a two-year option clause in his contract, made his immediate circumstances a little easier. He loved football and craved a quick return to the game, and insisted he would go anywhere to get back on the managerial ladder.

At the start of May 1986, just a couple of months after leaving Ibrox, Wallace received a job offer from the United States, but turned it down as it would have seen the current incumbent being sacked.

He said, 'Since I left Ibrox the phone has been ringing regularly. I've had numerous calls from Europe asking about my availability, and have been on to contacts in England, Germany, Spain and Holland to find out what's doing. The grass won't grow under my feet. In fact, I've had an offer from West Germany and a club in northern Spain. The Spanish offer might be attractive. I might even be prepared to go down a league to begin with, which would give me time to learn the language.'

Wallace insisted he would only work in England or abroad, and said, 'Where could I go in Scotland after managing the greatest club in the world? The only way is on and up. Look, if you're on a train to Inverness, and it breaks down in Dundee, you don't just sit there. You get off and find yourself another train, or walk if you have to.'

Thankfully he didn't have to walk to his first interview. He was on the shortlist for the position as manager of Seville, one of the top five jobs in Spanish football. With a couple of British bosses already operating in Spain, Seville president Gabriel Rojas was keen to continue the trend and contacted Bill McMurdo, Wallace's agent. Big Jock said, 'It's the most attractive offer I've had and we are negotiating with them at the moment.' Seville were the second Spanish side to be linked with the former Gers boss. Osasuna, conquerors of Rangers in the previous season's UEFA Cup, had also shown an interest.

Wallace insisted the language wouldn't be an issue, and added, 'As long as there is an interpreter we will be fine. After all, I had trouble being understood in England when I was with Leicester!' But Wallace had competition for the job, and stiff competition at that. Seville announced a shortlist of just two – Wallace and his former West Brom team-mate, Don Howe, who had just been sacked as Arsenal boss. However, reports suggested Wallace was hot favourite to land the post.

The Spaniards mulled over their options for a few days before announcing Wallace as the man they wanted to take them forward. He signed a one-year contract, reportedly worth £55,000, and hopped on a flight to Bilbao, deep in the Basque heartland, to watch Seville face Athletic. He was told that should he make a success of the job, his contract would be extended by another 12 months, with an additional ten grand on top of his initial salary.

The move meant a great deal to Wallace as his 23-year-old son, John, a golf course designer, was based in Fuengirola, on Spain's Costa del Sol, just a few hours' drive from Seville. John was working alongside a famed golf course designer, the American Robert Trent Jones.

Wallace had big plans for his new employers, and said, 'My target is to make Seville a force in European football, while the job also offers a tremendous opportunity to broaden my own horizons. The big attractions for British managers now are Spain and Italy. The challenge at Seville is enormous but I've never shirked one in my life. I love Spain, it's like my second home.'

In the ten years prior to Wallace's arrival, Seville had never managed anything higher than fifth in the Spanish league, and their last title success, in 1946, was followed two years later by the Spanish Cup. It was certainly an enormous challenge and also a situation as far removed from his decision, some years earlier, to turn to English non-league football despite operating as a top keeper in the English First Division. But Wallace was joining exalted company as Terry 'El Tel' Venables was at Barcelona, while Real Sociedad had plumped for John Toshack the year before Wallace's arrival.

The first thing the new Seville boss did was to make a serious attempt at learning the lingo. He enlisted the services of Bob Chipres, a US-born Vietnam War veteran, who was a bullfighter before setting himself up as a Spanish teacher in Seville. Bob also taught the Spanish police unarmed combat, something big Jock knew a thing or two about. Shortly after taking on his new pupil, Chipres said, 'Jock's Spanish is coming along fine. It's just a question of time and practice.'

Wallace's second in command was Domingo Perez, who spoke excellent English, and said, 'Jock has no trouble with Spanish at his team briefings. But when he talks in English we all get a bit lost!'

Wallace's first season in charge at Seville saw advertising displayed on the club shirt for the first time, with Seville Expo, an international exhibition, adorning the shirt for four years.

But just a matter of weeks after arriving in Spain, big Jock's sunshine dream turned into a nightmare when he and his wife were the victims of a terrifying mugging. While their car was stopped at a set of traffic lights, two thugs on a motorbike drew up alongside the family car and one produced a brick, which he smashed through a window. They grabbed a bag full of cash, traveller's cheques and credit cards before roaring off.

A fuming Wallace said after the mugging, 'In all, we've lost about £1,500. I'm alright but Daphne was cut by broken glass. The brick just missed her and she was really shaken.' Wallace, who was house-hunting on the Costa del Sol, reported the incident to police, but they offered little hope of an arrest. Wallace immediately offered a cash reward for the return of his property, which included a top-secret dossier on the Seville players, and opponents.

Things weren't going according to plan on the pitch either with Seville managing just a single win from their first six matches, although Wallace was convinced that he was on the right tracks. The upheaval of a move to Spain, learning a foreign language and coping with a different style of football would have affected lesser men, but not this one-time jungle fighter. 'Senor Jock', as he was affectionately known, reckoned he had already won his biggest battle by convincing the players that his methods were the right ones.

He added, 'The atmosphere in the dressing room is right and that's vital as far as I'm concerned. The main problem is the language but I'm getting better at that. The players accept the training and discipline. I like Spanish players because they are good professionals. When I arrived the priority was our defence, but we've got that down to a fine art and were robbed when beaten by Barcelona. The fact they were booed off the Nou Camp pitch by their own fans tells its own story.'

The manager also had to cope with injuries to his two main strikers, and was scouring Europe for replacements, although not, as he put it, 'at fancy prices'. He added, 'I'm enjoying the experience and very confident about the future.' In October, Wallace and his wife moved into a new club villa, complete with swimming pool. There was also a luxury limousine in the driveway.

But while results were still a little inconsistent as we motored towards Christmas, two Seville players revealed how 'Mista Wolla' (The Boss) had saved them from the soccer scrapheap due to his eye for talent and ability to inspire. Right-back Ramon Nimo, 27, had been set to move to a Second Division club. His confidence was gone and his future looked bleak, but one sprinkling of Jock's magic dust and he was included in the Spanish international squad, and subsequently played for his country.

Twenty-three-year-old Jesus Choya's career was virtually over because of three serious leg breaks in two years, but Wallace used his specialist training methods to strengthen his legs and Choya was transformed into Spain's third-top goalscorer. It is not known whether or not Wallace's 'special training methods' included sand dunes, although there would be no shortage of the golden stuff in Seville.

After four months of Spanish lessons, Wallace, who still used an interpreter for press conferences, was able to have recognisable conversations with second-team coach Juan Carbacho about training schedules. He said, 'I take Spanish classes every day. Hard going, but essential. No problem with the football jargon, that's universal anyway.'

Following a home defeat to arch rivals Real Betis at the beginning of 1987, Mista Wolla knew he had to give his fans a sweetener, something to help erase the derby defeat and put a smile back on their tanned faces. He went after Ted McMinn, the unorthodox winger who had been a hit with Rangers supporters, loved for his willingness to continually run at opposition defenders, while often a great source of frustration to these same fans. But he was an entertainer nevertheless.

It was more or less common knowledge that Graeme Souness was willing to listen to offers for the player so Wallace spoke with his board and they sanctioned a £200,000 bid. But it wasn't enough and the deal stalled. Rangers were demanding £400,000, although insiders suggested the Ibrox directors would be willing to accept

£250,000. Wallace appealed for his board to go a little higher but, for the present time, they refused.

The frustrated manager said, 'I'm really sick. I had spoken to McMinn with Rangers' approval and thought I would be able to clinch a deal, but Rangers' valuation is simply more than we can offer. I'm sorry for McMinn as well because I think he would have been a rage out here.' Wallace had hoped to include McMinn in his team to play Barcelona at the Estadio Ramón Sánchez-Pizjuán, but would have to wait a little longer to get his man.

With his first season drawing to a close, Wallace was offered a new and improved two-year contract, which he signed immediately. He loved the Spanish way of life and had enjoyed his first season in charge at Seville. The contract was worth around £175,000 and Wallace said, 'It is the best deal of my career. New directors were appointed by Seville four months ago and they have given me a vote of confidence. A foreigner spending three years with a Spanish club is unusual. The youngsters at the club are coming along well. I don't bawl and shout at them but prefer to give encouragement.

'I'm not mellowing. I believe it's the best way and the method is working. It will be even more effective when I become fluent in Spanish and I am still working on that. The lifestyle is excellent and so are the people. My wife had a birthday party the other night and 30 friends turned up. I've had my battles with the Spanish press. They are very tough, much more so than at home. They can make a manager's life difficult but I think I'm winning.'

Wallace finally signed McMinn for £200,000 but disaster struck when the player broke his ankle while playing squash – as part of his training regime. As soon as he had the plaster removed, he was allowed to resume light training.

Seville were more than holding their own in La Liga and were seventh of 18, and would have been even higher had they converted a penalty kick at the Bernabeu Stadium in a match they lost 2-1 to eventual champions Real Madrid.

The 1986/87 Spanish season had been the longest in the history of the competition due to a split at the end of the scheduled 34 league games. The league was then partitioned into three sections, Championship, Intermediate and Relegation. Overall, the campaign lasted ten months and Seville finished ninth, significantly one place below Betis.

And then the shock news. Despite signing a lucrative new deal just a month or so beforehand, Wallace was sacked just weeks into pre-season. The club insisted he had failed to learn Spanish to an acceptable standard, which came as a shock to the 51-year-old, who had religiously attended lessons since arriving in the country. Club directors were also said to be unhappy at Seville's pre-season form and Wallace's alleged fall-out with star player Francisco.

The sacking came just four days before the Spanish league was due to kick off and 34-year-old coach Javier Azcargorta was asked to stand in, despite a local soccer rule preventing the former Espanyol manager from sitting in the dug-out until Wallace had received compensation in full. He hired a lawyer straight away but it wasn't until late November, almost three months after the parting, that he finally received compensation.

The matter had dragged on and on and was just about to go to court when Wallace accepted a £43,000 out-of-court settlement. Compensation terms were agreed at an 11th-hour meeting before a judge was due to rule on the issue at a Labour Court. Wallace, who was on a two-year contract, was sacked because he 'hadn't mastered Spanish sufficiently to organise his players properly'. He had initially demanded £60,000, while the club had offered £40,000.

Despite agreeing a cash settlement, he said he was still hurt by the sacking, but insisted the whole affair hadn't affected his love for Spain and that he would be willing to stay and work in the country, even turning down the chance to manage a Scottish club to reinforce the point.

His record with Seville was moderate, and read: played 44, won 14, drawn 11, lost 19.

23

The Final Insult

STILL smarting from his dismissal by Seville, Wallace was desperate to prove he was far from washed out and kept a mental dossier on Scottish football by watching as many Scottish games as he could. He was given complimentary tickets for a Celtic match by his old adversary, Billy McNeill, and enjoyed the banter with Celtic fans in the main stand. 'Hey Jock, are you joining our board of directors', shouted one punter. The teasing was relentless, but good natured, and Wallace replied, 'Look, I've been flung out of better places than this,' and the Celtic supporters loved it.

The sad thing is, one of Rangers' greatest ever managers wasn't kidding. He *had* been thrown out of better places – namely Ibrox Park. The embarrassing incident had taken place just a few days before his visit to Celtic Park. Saturday 2 April 1988, to be exact, although one could have been forgiven for thinking the event had taken place 24 hours beforehand – on April Fools' Day.

Rangers had just lost 2-1 to Hearts and Wallace was standing outside the Blue Room looking for chief executive David Holmes. He was approached by a red-faced commissionaire, who said, 'Excuse me, but I have been instructed to escort you off the premises.' Wallace asked the security man to repeat what he had just said and he did, word for word. It was at that moment that Wallace asked the question which, under normal circumstances, is the preserve of those of an egotistical nature, although fully justified on this occasion. 'Do you know who I am?' The commissionaire replied, 'Yes, Mr Wallace, I do.'

Wallace asked who had given him his instructions, and he replied, 'Mr Hood', referring to Rangers' operations executive, Alastair Hood, although he was conspicuous by his absence at that moment. A furious Wallace marched up to the Members' Lounge and told his wife Daphne they were leaving.

The irony was that assistant manager Walter Smith had left two complimentary tickets for Wallace and his wife. When the match finished, he was making his way to the top of the marble staircase, to head home, when he was stopped by a steward and asked to look into the Members' Lounge, where he met the comedian Mr Abie, former player Billy Semple, and a host of other long-standing friends. He had a cup of tea and a slice of cake and stood chatting for ten minutes, while Daphne did the same with a group of old friends.

Wallace decided then to seek out Ally McCoist, who hadn't played due to injury, and made his way to the Players' Lounge, where he met Terry Butcher, who told him that 'Coisty' was still in the dressing room. Wallace then met the club's vice-chairman, Jack Gillespie, who took him by the arm and led him into one of the executive suites. Everything was relaxed and friendly and Gillespie took him down to the foyer where he asked if McCoist was around. Gillespie said his goodbyes before rushing off to a wedding.

Wallace stood chatting to former charges such as Sandy Clark, Davie McPherson, Davie Cooper and McCoist. After a few minutes, he went back up the marble stairs, intending to return to the Members' Lounge, but bumped into Willie Waddell and his wife, and a few other familiar old faces. Again he enjoyed renewing old acquaintances.

He checked to see if his wife was okay and then went back out into the foyer to see if he could track down David Holmes, just to say hello. He met Holmes's wife and asked if she knew where her husband was, but she wasn't sure. It was at that moment that he was approached by the commissionaire and thrown out of his beloved Ibrox.

The only thing on his mind was getting the hell out of there as quickly as possible. He shouted on Daphne and told her they were leaving. She knew something was amiss and asked why the sudden rush. Wallace said, 'I've just been told to leave the premises – and that's what we're doing.'

Wallace was then reportedly forced to endure the humiliation of walking through the Members' Lounge in front of so many people he knew, under escort, to make sure he left the stadium. Later, he said, 'I have never been so angry or disgusted with anything in my life. I was flaming mad and felt so sorry for my wife, who had been such a help to me in my days at Ibrox. She didn't deserve this treatment. She was shattered when I initially told her why we were leaving.'

Wallace drove straight home and took his phone off the hook. He was in no mood to talk. He said, 'I knew more than anyone that there are several no-go areas inside Ibrox – but I had been invited into one of these areas by the club's vice-chairman. I thought it had all been an awful mistake – a blunder if you like.'

But it was no blunder and if Wallace thought he would get a personal apology, or even one through the pages of the club's official newspaper, *Rangers News*, he was sadly mistaken. On the front page of the next issue was a banner headline condemning newspapers and journalists for what they termed 'disgraceful reports'.

Wallace had always steadfastly refused to criticise Rangers, even when he was sacked in 1986, but this was different and he was in no mood to protect the club after such a humiliating experience. The regrettable events of that day didn't just leave a sour taste in the mouth of the former gaffer, but also the large number of fans present at the time – and a far greater number when they picked up their papers the following morning.

An unwritten code existed to preserve the good name of Rangers Football Club, which is all very well when the hierarchy adhere to it themselves, and aren't abusing their privileged position at the helm of a famous old institution.

More than a month had passed when Wallace decided to speak out about his experience. Perhaps he had hoped that an apology would have been forthcoming. When it wasn't, he said, 'Until now I've kept my mouth shut, but my anger will not go away – and I don't think it ever will.

'I will never again ask Rangers for a ticket for a match. I've supported Rangers since I was a kid, and was a founder member of the Tranent Rangers Supporters' Club in 1952. I've visited supporters' clubs all over the world, and have honorary memberships in places like Melbourne and Toronto.

'I have never criticised Rangers but I cannot ignore the dreadful treatment of Daph. They may have thrown me out of Ibrox but they won't stop me watching Rangers. I took Daph, my daughter and her fiance and his parents to the match with Aberdeen at Ibrox, and paid £30 at the turnstiles. The guy at the gate looked at me and said, "Mr Wallace, you should never pay to see Glasgow Rangers."

And never a truer word was spoken.

24

Off To Essex

JOCK Wallace put his house in the west of Scotland up for sale and bought into the old adage, 'have experience, will travel'. He reminded prospective employers that there was far more to his CV than running up and down sand dunes and route one football, and said, 'Players who can pass the ball win you matches. I had plenty of them, including Bobby Russell, Sandy Jardine and Alex MacDonald. And I like to think that after a few seasons working with me, John Greig was a far better passer than he was before.'

Wallace had the old fire back in the belly. He was back in the mix for a job – any job – but while awaiting the call, he headed over to Spain as part of the BBC commentary team for Scotland's European Championship qualifying match in Madrid. Prior to leaving, he spelt out the dangers to the travelling tartan army, especially as the Spanish hadn't exactly been setting the heather on fire, and were under pressure from their demanding supporters. Wallace insisted that the main threat would come from Emilio 'The Vulture' Butragueno. On the night of the match, and not for the first time, the big man soon realised that the main danger would come from a large band of Spanish louts.

Scotland pulled off a credible 0-0 draw at the Bernabeu, and the home fans were less than happy with their big-money stars – so they took it out on the Scots. Captain Roy Aitken and Mo Johnston were forced to dive for cover when a barrage of bricks came smashing through the windows of their team bus. Officials, including former Celtic chairman Jack McGinn, also had a close shave, but the real losers weren't those on the bus. As the luxury coach sped away, Spanish thugs turned their attentions to the TV men, Wallace and commentator Jock Brown.

Brown lost his glasses during the prolonged attack and Wallace scrambled to his aid. He was punched full on the face by a Spanish thug and received a nasty gash on the bridge of his nose. A Scottish Television engineer suffered cuts to his head and hands. Wallace credited his plastic glasses with saving his sight, and said, 'I would like to meet the guys who did this at some time in the future – and they would regret it!'

The following day, a newspaper report read, 'This disgraceful incident ought to be treated with the utmost gravity by FIFA. The Bernabeu is a notorious hotbed of football hooliganism and all the major Spanish cities are now festering sores of gang muggings, but this particular stadium ought to be placed out of bounds for the foreseeable future by the ruling bodies, if only on the simple premise that the only safe spectator there would be a fully-armed Charles Bronson.' A Spanish FA spokesman insisted they were trying to 'root out the National Front-type supporters'.

But the shameful incident hadn't deterred Wallace from craving a return to football and 21 years after landing his first managerial job at Berwick, he roared, 'Since parting from Seville I have done nothing, and that's not me. Football is in my blood and I would like to get back doing a job of some sort. I'm in better shape now to be a manager but if the worst comes to the worst, I'll set myself up as a Euro agent for players and tours – I need to be involved again.'

If Wallace was superstitious then he never showed it. He was announced as the new boss of Colchester United on Friday 13 January and therein began a period of just under a year in charge of the Essex club. Old Firm derbies were replaced with must-win games against Southend United, and the sands of Gullane traded for similar, if not as imposing, dunes at Clacton-on-Sea.

While at Ibrox, Wallace regularly scrapped it out with Celtic for titles but this was a completely new ball game for the self-styled Commander-in-Chief. After 22 games of a 38-match campaign, Colchester were officially the worst club in English football. Rock bottom of the Fourth Division and Wallace was tasked with keeping them in the Football League, never mind chasing silverware.

Wallace had never shirked a tackle in his life, and wasn't about to start now. He set about his task with gusto, desperate to salvage something from a rotten season. First up was a match against Tranmere Rovers, and just before kick-off, Wallace said, 'I have the hardest job in the world. Colchester are propping up the English league – but I'm back in business.'

Millionaire owner Jonathan Crisp had specifically targeted the former Rangers boss, despite Wallace admitting he knew nothing about the club. After his first training session, he said, 'I think the players are a bit apprehensive about me, but if they work hard they've no need to worry. I'm still young and hungry enough to do a good job for a team, and hopefully we can pull off a miracle.'

The 53-year-old Wallace was operating without a contract, but said, 'The fact that I don't have one doesn't worry me. If I achieve what we all want at this club then that will be reward enough.'

On his only previous visit to Essex, as boss of Leicester City, Jock had suffered the heartache of being knocked out the FA Cup by non-league Harlow Town – despite having goal machine Gary Lineker in his side. Wallace's reply to the shock of the round was to steer Leicester to the promised land of the First Division.

A fortnight after taking the job at Layer Road, big Jock almost pulled off an FA Cup shock of his own. He took his struggling side to First Division Sheffield United – and led 2-0 at one point. The match ended 3-3, but it was Wallace's troops who were left feeling deflated, despite the obvious gulf in class between the sides. However, the grit and determination he had instilled in his men in such a short space of time was nothing short of remarkable.

On the same afternoon, Wallace's former Ibrox prodigy, Robert Fleck, scored a hat-trick as Norwich thumped non-league Sutton United 8-0. The fifth-round draw would pair the Canaries with the winner of the Colchester–Sheffield United tie.

But when second-bottom Darlington pulled off a rare win, Colchester found themselves four points adrift at the foot of the table. While progression in the FA Cup was a bonus, the priority was to get points on the board, as matches were rapidly running out.

Things weren't happening quickly enough on the survival front for Wallace and he said, 'If I've got to cut a few throats to get this club back on the rails then so be it. There is no place here for losers. I want men with fire in their bellies – that's why I'm closely examining the Scottish scene.'

While at Leicester, Wallace had plundered Highland League football to sign Iain Wilson and Nicky Walker from Elgin City, as well as Kevin McDonald from Inverness Caley. With a real fight on his hands, Wallace needed warriors on his side.

On the eve of the FA Cup replay at home to the Blades, the manager sounded a rallying call, and spoke of his last major giant-killing act, while in charge of Berwick Rangers in 1967. He told his players that anything was possible, even though they hadn't won a league match in months. He insisted that the name Colchester United was still feared up north in Leeds, due to their famous cup win over the great United team of the Don Revie era. The Us had won their last three cup matches and Wallace reckoned the scalp was there for the taking. On this occasion, though, his motivational tactics weren't enough to prevent a 2-0 home loss. One positive, cried Wallace, was that the defeat would allow his team to concentrate on securing their Football League future. No distractions now.

Despite the cup defeat, the town of Colchester had been mobilised into supporting their local team. A side that had been attracting just over 1,000 people were soon drawing between 4 and

5,000 to home matches. The Essex town had become gripped by Wallace fever and a mutual desire to escape the dreaded drop into the Vauxhall Conference.

Colchester's league results had improved dramatically under Wallace. They started to score goals and win games and were soon clawing back the 11-point deficit on fellow strugglers Darlington, which had grown as Colchester focussed on the FA Cup. D-day arrived on the last Saturday in April – Darlington v Colchester, a must-win game for both clubs, and big Jock's famous 'Nae Surrender' war cry was the theme for the day. It mattered little that the Us had just sold talented Irish winger Paul McGee to Wimbledon for a club record £150,000 fee.

The match was a real battle but Wallace had managed to instil his jungle-fighting qualities into his squad and they triumphed 2-1, with ex-Whitburn Juniors ace Robert Scott grabbing the winner. It was a massive result and successive home wins over Halifax and Exeter, the latter of which drew a crowd of over 5,000, who roared the Us on to a 4-0 win, ensured the Houdini-style escape from the jaws of relegation was complete.

Wallace refused to take all the credit for the Great Escape, instead choosing to heap praise upon his trusted lieutenant. Shortly after taking over at Layer Road, big Jock had whittled down a list of possible assistants to just one. It was the name that stood out more than most: a World Cup winner with England in 1966 and star midfielder for Arsenal and Everton, among many other top-flight sides. Alan Ball had just been sacked by Portsmouth despite doing a good job under trying circumstances, and was keen to get straight back into the game. Wallace had met the tiny midfielder just once, but had been a good pal of Ball's dad, also Alan, a former player and manager.

Wallace made the pocket dynamo an offer, but after leaving Pompey, Ball had made a commitment to visit Qatar as part of 'British Week', and promised to call the Colchester boss the minute he got back. Before leaving, though, Ball decided to check the league tables and see how the Us were doing. Down the leagues he scrolled until he reached the foot of the Fourth Division table… Colchester United: 11 points adrift with 11 matches to play.

In *Playing Extra Time*, Ball said, 'When I took the job it was the beginning of something special. I never laughed so much in all my life because Jock had an enthusiasm for football and life that was incredibly rich. He was everything you wanted in a football man. He was Bill Shankly, Harry Catterick, my dad and Sir Alf Ramsey all rolled into one.'

Ball told of how the Colchester players loved Wallace like a father – while also having a fearful respect for him. But it wasn't long before the former England international discovered Wallace's passionate love for all things Rangers – and when it happened for the first time he admitted being lost for words.

He said, 'It was Colchester v Exeter on a Tuesday night and Jock was giving a rousing pre-match talk. He suddenly told the skipper, Tony English, to stand in the middle of the room and sing "Nae Surrender". The lad started murmuring "No Surrender" when Jock screamed, "It's Nae Surrender", and before I knew it the whole team was singing it at the pitch of their voices!'

But 'Bawl and Ball', as they were known affectionately by the players, pulled off the impossible. At the end of the campaign, Wallace said, 'The wee man and I are winners, and the players know it. Our target for next season is the Fourth Division championship.'

Wallace admitted that he had initially found it difficult to adapt to life at Colchester, but soon tuned in to their way of thinking. The first thing he did was build morale, make them laugh a bit, and then get in an experienced assistant. Wallace said, 'Alan Ball is world class and when I approached him to come to Colchester, he didn't even ask about wages – he just signed a three-year contract.

'When I first arrived at the club, they were well and truly in the quicksand. With that in mind, I told the players we would keep the tactics simple. Get out there with fixed bayonets and make sure they remain fixed. '

After escaping relegation, townsfolk celebrated for days, which prompted Wallace to say, 'Can you imagine a whole town covered in blue and white for days on end?' He added, 'Nothing can replace the success you can have with Rangers but I have never been happier in football. The challenge is still there for me. I'm either fortunate or daft that I can still carry on as a manager. When I stop enjoying it, I won't be doing it.' As a thank you for his efforts during his debut season, Wallace was made a director of the club.

It was soon time to prepare for the new term, and Wallace and his players headed for central Scotland, putting down roots at Stirling University. They lived in the students' quarters, which were basic to say the least. While en route to Stirling, though, the party took a short detour, and when the coach drew up outside Ibrox Stadium, it's said that the look on big Jock's face was one of sheer joy. He had arranged for the players to have a look round the stadium and trophy room before making their way on to Stirling.

The Us arranged challenge matches against Raith Rovers, Partick Thistle, Stranraer and Cumnock Juniors. Before heading north, though, Wallace proved he could still hold his own in the transfer market when he landed one of the hottest properties around. Irishman Mark Kinsella had Liverpool, Everton and Manchester United chasing him, but chose Colchester United. Kinsella played 180 games for the Us before going on to star for Charlton Athletic and Aston Villa.

Ahead of the tour, Wallace said, 'Meeting up with John Lambie at Firhill and Frank Connor at Raith will make my year.' Just over 1,000 supporters turned up at Firhill for the match against Partick, and despite Robert Scott equalising Brian Gallagher's opener, Gary Peebles gave Lambie's men a late win. The final challenge match was in East Ayrshire, against junior giants Cumnock and the part-timers gave a splendid account of themselves, holding big Jock's Colchester to a 1-1 draw.

Sadly, results didn't get any better when the English league season started, and Colchester were soon languishing in the

Fourth Division basement again. After six games, Colchester had just five draws and a defeat to show for their efforts. A 4-1 win over Maidstone at the end of September reduced the pressure a little but it proved a false dawn and by the end of October, the Us were fighting it out with Hartlepool to avoid the wooden spoon.

Then Alan Ball announced he was leaving the club. After nine months as Wallace's right-hand man, Ball had been offered the chance to become Mick Mills's assistant manager at Stoke City, and big Jock advised him to take the job. Ball said, 'Going to Colchester restored my faith in football. I always wanted to be the greatest player and got somewhere near it. Now I want to be the greatest coach and manager.'

In the month following Ball's departure, Colchester garnered just a single point and Wallace lasted just a further four weeks. Five days before Christmas, the former Rangers boss announced he was quitting the hot-seat. After losing 3-0 at home to Torquay, he was on the receiving end of some vitriolic abuse from a section of the crowd and decided enough was enough. But while he stood down as team boss, he stayed on as a director.

Former Colchester player Steve Foley was announced as caretaker boss for the second time, and Wallace said, 'I had decided to leave as manager at the end of the season, but Foley now becomes caretaker until the club find a new man. I'm staying on and will do everything I can to help the club.'

Ipswich's Scottish manager John Duncan offered to assist his neighbours by loaning them players in their hour of need. He said, 'It's no fun being at the bottom of the Fourth Division. I was there during my early days at Scunthorpe.'

During the close-season, Wallace was told that he had Parkinson's disease, and there's no doubt the condition played a part in the great man losing a little of his edge. He had bravely battled on but found it increasingly difficult to manage the team on a day-to-day basis while struggling to cope with his condition.

Alan Ball recalled the day Wallace took him aside to tell him the devastating news. He said, 'Jock poured me a drink and told me he wanted to share a secret with me. When he told me the awful news, I was devastated. When he died in 1996, I felt sadness beyond description.'

Colchester were eventually relegated from the Football League into the Vauxhall Conference at the end of 1989/90, and it took them two seasons to gain promotion back into the Fourth Division, which they clinched on the final day of the campaign.

25

The Barca Bears

WHILE researching Jock's career I was fortunate enough to meet up with many of the legendary 'Barcelona Bears' – the players who brought glory to Rangers in May 1972 when they beat Moscow Dynamo to win the European Cup Winners' Cup – the only major European trophy won by the club to this day. Each former player had only good things to say about Jock Wallace, their coach, manager, confidante and sometimes friend.

Alex MacDonald was a workaholic midfield star, beavering away in the Gers' engine room while snatching many a vital goal. He had the happy knack of being in the right place at the right time and more often than not, reserved his goals for the big occasion.

He said, 'It was Davie White who signed me for Rangers, but my first impressions of Jock, on his arrival from Hearts, was that he was a big gentle giant. I got to know him quickly because he was house-hunting in Kirkintilloch and Bishopbriggs and that was my neck of the woods. He came up to my place a few times and I took him to see some houses but he didn't move into the area because he said they weren't big enough for him!

'We had a great relationship because we were very similar. He was a worker and wanted everyone else to work, which suited me. For me, big Jock gelled the players together. Previously, we would go into our own wee groups but Jock got us socialising together and that gave us a real togetherness.

'We had a really tall team, all six-footers, so I was delighted when Jock brought wee Tommy McLean to the club. I remember one day Jock changed the training because it was pouring with rain and we went into the gym before going over to the Albion. By the time me and wee Tam got over there we were absolutely shattered. But I loved the training and I loved big Jock. He knew his players inside out. If you were feeling a bit down, he would pick up on it immediately, and say to you, "What's wrong with you, is your granny alright?"

'I remember he played me wide left in a semi-final against Celtic, and the next day we were walking across from the training ground and I said to him (we never really went to his office), "Boss, I'm not happy with this outside-left stuff." And he said, "Do you not want to play for Rangers at outside-left?" I said, "My granny would play for Rangers at outside-left, but me…" and big Jock said, "What's your granny's phone number?" In fairness, I think it was just a one-off.

'He was very thorough. Before a European tie we had the most extensive dossier you could imagine, including photos of the player we were up against, where he went on holiday, what he ate for lunch, it was incredible.

'I was surprised when he left in 1978. I didn't know his reasons but for me Rangers wasn't about the money, it was about playing for that blue jersey, which is an honour. Had I been the manager, it might have been different, but as far as I'm concerned, the blue jersey is the blue jersey and that's it.

'Away from the football, big Jock was such a gentleman but he could hardly talk to women. He was just a big bashful guy. He called everyone "kid"; me, the wife, anyone. "How you doin' kid?" that was his thing – but he was Rangers through and through.'

Another midfield star, Alfie Conn, had the distinction of playing for both halves of the Old Firm, but insisted his time under Jock Wallace was amongst the happiest of his career. He said, 'Scot Symon signed me for Rangers but I worked under Jock when he was the coach at Ibrox, and then again when he came to Motherwell. I'm not at all surprised by the success he achieved during his career because his motivation was second to none. You knew before you ran out on to that park that you were going to win. That was the mentality he drilled into you and he hated losing with a passion.

'I remember training at Ibrox one day. We were running round the park and this young boy stopped to be sick. Big Jock shot across the pitch, grabbed the lad by the scruff of the neck and started running him. He shouted, "Listen son, you're a Rangers player now, and if you're gonna be sick, you can be sick on the run!"

'That was the hard side of him, but if you had problems you could speak to him any time. He was really approachable, but if he had a problem with you then you weren't long in finding out about it. He didn't believe in allowing little problems to fester and grow into big ones.

'He had this ability to treat everyone as an equal. Showing favouritism wasn't his thing. If you were playing well you were in the team and if not, you were out, it was as simple as that. And that was the right way to do it. But I think it all stemmed from his upbringing in Wallyford and then his time in the army. Big Jock never forgot his roots.'

Colin Jackson was an uncompromising centre-half during the Wallace years and had a great admiration for his manager. He was a few months short of 20 years at Ibrox, and was a non-playing veteran of the infamous Berwick debacle of 1967.

He said, 'When it came to the technical side of the game, Jock probably wasn't the best in the world but he was an excellent man-manager. He had a real passion for the game and his team. One incident comes instantly to mind. We were training at the Albion when a player swore at big Jock in front of everyone. Nothing was said at the time, and he got on with training. When we all headed back over to the stadium, I was unfortunate enough to walk in to the boot room, and there was this player, feet just about touching the ground, and big Jock with his hand round the player's neck…

and saying "Don't you ever f****n' swear at me again and don't ever try and bring me down in front of the players."

'There was no messing with Jock. If you played the game with him then he played the game with us, and we got our days off etc. We only trained about three days a week at that time, so he was good to us. Monday was a day off, and Tuesday you got a hiding. It was always the toughest. Wednesday was quite often another day off and then you were in on a Thursday and Friday.

'When we won the first of our trebles, the team was just coming together nicely. (Willie) Waddell started it off and Jock carried it on. A few of the players, including the likes of Sandy Jardine and Willie Johnston, had been there for a while, and we had a good blend of youth and experience.

'Willie Waddell and Jock Wallace were different types of managers. Waddell was certainly better with the technical side of the game. I wasn't a great lover of him, but that was probably a personality thing. Big Jock was different and I had a lot of respect for him. He treated everyone the same and if he had favourites he hid it well. Everyone was given a chance. Quite often, it can become obvious that so-and-so is a big favourite of the manager because he's in the team every week, but that wasn't Jock's way.

'In the 1970s, Aberdeen was a hard place to go. They were starting to get a good team together – with the likes of Willie Miller and Alex McLeish – and would go on to become an excellent team. I used to get a bit of stick up there, because I had been brought up in the city and went to school there. I remember one game in particular, an evening game. We got a good result and were heading down the road when, out of the blue, we stopped at this hotel. Jock bought us all a drink and told us we were staying the night, and that we could have a few drinks but not to go over the score.

'It was his way of saying thanks for a great performance. We all appreciated the gesture and, of course, these things helped build up a camaraderie. Jock would sit and have a drink with us. He would pick up on the little things when players started to relax and tongues loosened, but never used any of it against you. He was a great man.'

Jackson was distraught when he discovered that Jock had contracted Parkinson's, and said, 'It was difficult to take in because I knew how fit he was and how well he had looked after himself.'

Goalkeeper Peter McCloy was another long-serving Ranger, and a player greatly admired by Wallace. That respect was two-way, as McCloy recalled, 'I remember my father was in hospital very ill and Jock went to visit him but never told me about it. He would just turn up at the hospital. And he would never forget your kid's names, small things like that, but it meant an awful lot to the players. It showed he was thinking about his players all the time. I think if you pay attention to the small details the big things take care of themselves.

'I'm sure Jock had his own reasons for leaving in 1978, but he never divulged them to anyone else. We all followed his career at Leicester with interest, and used to look out for their results. But he always kept in touch, which was good.

'It was a terrible shock when he got Parkinson's. It was a very sad time for everyone. He came down to a supporters' function in my home town and they had a dinner for him, but he couldn't speak at it. He was still in good form, though, and told me all about it. It was a real tragedy.'

Tommy McLean was the thinking-man's player; the winger/midfielder who could plant a cross on the head of his intended target from great distance. He would go on to achieve success as a manager in his own right but recalled his memories of playing under Wallace.

He said, 'The first time I met Jock was when I signed for Rangers. The training routines were different from anything I had been used to. Jock came across as a right hard man but he was a genuine guy and very approachable. I struggled with training at first because I was small and not great with weights, and that meant I didn't have the best of starts with Rangers.

'I eventually plucked up the courage to go and see him because I had put on about seven or eight pounds and felt it was affecting my game. I had become top heavy, which was curtailing my speed.

I was apprehensive because I didn't want him thinking I was a malingerer, but when I went to see him he was great. He was very understanding and immediately cut my weight circuits. I had been lifting the same weights as big Bomber Jackson, John Greig and all these big fellas. There was one set programme for all but once I broached the subject, he said, "Right, okay, we'll cut it in half", and from then on in it was brilliant. I had worried about his reaction, because of his fearsome reputation, but I needn't have.

'I didn't have a good start to the season, so I sat down and had a chat with Jock and he said, "You're trying to please everybody." He reckoned I was trying to be a Willie Henderson type of player, and I wasn't that type, I was more the midfield type. He said, "I want you to concentrate on pleasing me, and if you do that you will be in the team." So we had a right good discussion and he offered me some great advice.

'I know he came across as this big hard jungle-fighter type but he was a very understanding man, especially at the start of my Rangers career when I struggled somewhat. There was definitely a softer side to Jock, and one that was prepared to listen. And he definitely got me playing more as a team player than an individual.

'When Willie Waddell was the manager, he tended to keep his distance from the players, but Jock was the guy we dealt with day-to-day. He was the mainstay and the guy who gave the team talks etc.

'Jock used the word character all the time but that summed him up. He was a driven man and I'm not surprised that he achieved what he did. He saw in individuals, certain qualities that he wanted to bring out and he was good at that. He also knew what it took to knit the team together, and knew the players better than anyone else. He was a man's man.'

Willie Johnston booked his place in the Rangers Hall of Fame the day he scored twice in Barcelona to seal victory. But there was more to 'Bud' than that and he was a real fans' favourite, due to his outstanding ability to entertain. He had the unique distinction of being a maverick and a team player at the same time, and while he no doubt gave his manager a few sleepless nights, there is no questioning the affection the talented winger held for his former boss.

Johnston said, 'My first impressions of Jock were that he was man mad! We were going through a bad time and they changed the manager and brought in Mr Waddell and Mr Wallace and, as far as training went, it was just a revolution.

'Big Jock was a coach first and foremost and he was good at what he did. I fell out with him a few times but it was all through football. I felt the ball wasn't coming out to the outside-left position enough and I let him know. After the game we would have an argument but when you came in on the Monday morning everything was forgotten about. Big Jock didn't hold grudges.

'When I decided to leave Ibrox, he asked why I was going. I had just been given a ten-week suspension and Jock was at the meeting with me. I felt I had become a target and told him I wanted out of Scottish football. He was brilliant at sticking up for his players and while he backed me to the hilt, he appreciated that I'd had enough. He was a great motivator and had us in tip-top condition, and boy did he know how to get the best out of his players – that was definitely his forte.

'When big Jock became manager in his own right, Waddell was still in the background, and was there if he needed him. I don't know if big Jock was given a free hand because I left just after Barcelona.

'When I went to West Brom my manager was Don Howe. He was a great coach but wasn't so hot on the man-management side of things. At Ibrox, the players had wanted to play for big Jock – either that or you just got a doing! Seriously though, big Jock was a great man, but had one terrible habit. He would watch players as they were running out before a match and, thump, he would hit you one in the stomach. If you doubled in two with pain he would say, "Right, Johnston, in on Monday first thing for extra work on that stomach, it isn't tough enough!" But that was big Jock!'

Full-back Willie Mathieson was the unsung hero of the great Rangers team of the 1970s and was at Ibrox from 1960 to 1975, playing over 300 games. He remembered Jock with a tremendous fondness, 'The first time I met Jock was when Willie Waddell brought him in. It was an experience in itself. My first impression of him was that he was as hard as nuts. He was unbelievable but was a fit man and he made us even fitter than we already were. A lot of the success we had was down to Jock and his fitness regime. He would take you apart if you did something wrong but he was also such a fair guy and five minutes later he would invite you for a game of golf.

'Willie Waddell was the manager when we won in Barcelona, and he was the tactical brain, but a lot of it was down to Jock's training. They were a good partnership and Jock was definitely one of Willie Waddell's best signings.

'My dad wouldn't let me become a full-time footballer until I finished my apprenticeship down the mines as an electrician. I finished on the Friday and started on the Monday full-time with Rangers in 1962 along with Colin Jackson. I was in the reserves on the day of the infamous Berwick Rangers match in 1967, along with Jimmy Millar and Ralphie Brand.

'Everything Jock did was wholehearted and he was Rangers through and through. He used to tell us the story about getting a row from his mum for going to see Rangers at Ibrox when he was nine or ten. But I remember Jock and I were at a Player of the Year do at a Rangers supporters' club in Stevenson, and the chairman stood up before dinner and said that no party songs would be allowed that night. Our wives were there and when they decided to have a sing-song, big Jock got up and said, "I'd like to sing a little Dutch love song called 'Cry'," and next minute he stood up and the cry of "No Surrender" went up. The rule was broken and the hall erupted. He knew all the songs and was just a total Rangers man.

'I think Jock left Rangers in 1978 because he had reached a certain point in his career; his team was getting old and it was maybe just time to go and try something new. I loved the man to bits, he was fantastic and a very fair guy. I was gutted when I heard he had Parkinson's. For a man who was as fit as he was it was a terrible thing to happen.'

And the final words to the man voted the Greatest Ever Ranger in a supporters' poll in 1999. John Greig was a permanent fixture at Ibrox when Wallace arrived in 1970 and replaced him in the dug-out eight years later. Wallace often referred to Greig as the most valuable player he'd ever worked with, although Greig insisted that he'd never told him anything like that to his face. He said, "If he did, it wasn't without swearing!"

'Jock's strong point was his ability to motivate players. He would say that our team was that fit it didn't matter who we played because we would run over the top of them in the last 15 minutes of the game, but it didn't always work out like that, although that's what he believed.

'Jock had more to him than just character, but if you're the manager of Rangers Football Club then you're expected to win trophies, because you've generally got the best team, and Jock didn't let anyone down. He followed Willie Waddell who, in his short spell as manager, was successful because of Barcelona and other things, but we had a good squad of players then and big Jock seemed to get the best out of them. There was also a great camaraderie between the players and he fostered a great team spirit through his motivation and that definitely helped us.

'It was a shock to us all when he left. I still have no idea why he made that decision and the first I knew was when I saw it on the television. We had a good working relationship as player and manager. Sandy Jardine and I travelled from Edinburgh every day and Jock did at the start, because he lived in Tranent, but when he moved to Glasgow we only saw one another at training.

'Before he moved to Glasgow, I was bothered with an ankle injury and couldn't run on the track, so he gave everyone a Monday off and told me to meet him at his house in Tranent. We went down to the Gullane sands and he put me through a session, because it was easier to run on the sand. That was the kind of thing he would do for you.

'But I also recall a situation just before we played Bayern Munich in the semi-finals of the Cup Winners' Cup in 1972. I was injured in a cup match against Hibs on the Saturday and we were down at Gullane and he told me to go and dip my foot in the Firth of Forth. I mean, I had a stress fracture and there was no way that my fracture would get better with cold water – but I ended up with the flu!'

26

Parkinson's Disease

WALLACE'S Essex adventure was still fresh in his mind when he received a call from abroad. It was January 1990, and on the other end of the blower was a representative of Spanish Second Division side Jerez. The Andalusian club were at the wrong end of the table and wanted a 'strong man' to help get them back into the top flight. They reckoned Wallace was that man and offered him a contract to the end of the season.

However, the timing was all wrong. Wallace didn't feel right and just a couple of weeks later, announced that he was suffering from Parkinson's disease. There was no known cure for the creeping paralysis but the 54-year-old said bravely, 'I'm finished as a football manager, but I'm not looking for sympathy – I'm not that kind of guy. I first thought something was wrong when I was boss at Ibrox in 1986. I felt depressed and wanted to weep a lot. Also, I wasn't so aggressive – and anyone who has ever met me knows that's my trademark.'

Wallace, who had quit as manager of Colchester in the December, insisted his secret illness was the reason. He had described his symptoms to club physio Charlie Simpson and asked him to make an appointment with a specialist. For a month the club physio stalled, then asked the former Rangers boss to accompany him on a walk round the pitch. 'Jock,' he said, 'I've got bad news for you. You've got

Parkinson's, I recognise the symptoms.' He made an appointment with a specialist who confirmed it.

Parkinson's, known to strike men in their 50s, has no cure, and killed actor Terry Thomas after an 11-year struggle. Wallace had a course of treatment recommended by Stirling University specialists for a year, but began a new course of drugs at the start of 1990. A specialist suggested a brain operation in the US, but the cost involved was anything up to £100,000, and meant a six-month stay and delicate after-care.

The advice from his neurologist at Chelmsford was that he should hold off on surgery, but Wallace insisted he was going to the US for an examination around Easter. He said, 'I have to face up to the fact that the illness is serious. There's nothing I can do but keep up morale and fight it, although that shouldn't be too difficult as I've always been a fighter.'

He admitted that the ravages of the illness had taken him close to the edge more than once, and that there were times when he just wanted to cry. He said, 'A major symptom of the disease is depression. You want to weep, and for a guy like me that is hard to handle. I was questioning myself, feeling like a big Jessie and even then, at that stage of the illness, I didn't know what was wrong.'

But after learning to cope with the diagnosis and disease, and convinced that he had overcome its most acute symptoms, Wallace emerged as a virtual one-man crusade, and took time out to help and encourage other sufferers such as the wife of former Celtic and Scotland player Bobby Evans.

He said, 'Rene Evans is a wonderful woman. Any time I'm over from Spain I look her up. It's vital we stick together and encourage one another because this illness can be beaten. We have to fight it all the way by keeping ourselves as fit and supple as possible. The medical people reckon there is no cure as such, but it can be controlled and that's the message of hope I want to give to fellow sufferers.

'What I would say to them is this – accept you are unwell but never give in. Fight the depression and the pain and you can win. I'm one of the lucky guys because I was able to visit a top neurologist, John Markham, who works out of the University College of Los Angeles. He has put me on a course of medication that allows me to lead a normal life. I feel for those who can't get access to a man such as Markham but that's no reason to allow the illness to win.'

Wallace reckoned his new medication would allow him to get back into football. He knew his time was up as a manager, but appealed to clubs to take a chance on him as an assistant or on a consultancy basis. He felt he had too much to offer to just let go.

Once he made his condition public, the good luck messages flooded in. The football world may have been stunned by the news that he had Parkinson's but the man himself was adamant that the condition would not finish him off. He said, 'I've kept it secret for three years and now I'm glad it's out in the open. I've always been a fighter and I've no intention of giving up now.'

Celtic manager Billy McNeill said, 'It's very distressing to find out about Jock's illness,' while Hearts chairman Wallace Mercer, who once tried to sign Jock as manager, said, 'Like everyone in the game we are very sad to learn of his illness.' Former Motherwell chairman Ian Livingstone, who signed Jock as Fir Park boss, said, 'He is very popular and I would be surprised if most clubs didn't rally round.'

When it became clear that Wallace wouldn't work in football any more, he started a campaign to raise funds and awareness of Parkinson's. A group of west of Scotland businessmen set up a testimonial fund. Ian Livingstone was part of the group and announced that a dinner would be held in Glasgow's Hospitality Inn. Many football clubs and fans indicated their support for the testimonial.

Wallace had already said that if he could be treated at the Los Angeles clinic it could cost him his life savings. He would have to stay in hospital for several months, and costs could work out at around £80,000. At the time he was commuting between his homes in Spain and Colchester, where he was still a director of the club.

In June 1990, Wallace returned to Glasgow to launch the charity named after him – the Jock Wallace Parkinson's Disease Appeal. He insisted he wasn't merely living out his dying days on the Costa del Sol, but had never felt fitter and played golf every day.

He said, 'I want to help people who have the disease and that's why I'm getting involved in this appeal. It will mean spending a lot more time in Scotland in future but that's what I want to do.'

It was decided to turn the testimonial dinner into the launch pad for the appeal, and organisers spoke to the likes of Archie Macpherson, Billy Connolly, Andy Cameron and Lawrie McMenemy about getting involved.

A spokesperson for the charity said, 'Jock is playing golf and getting bored. He's not capable of sitting in Spain just resting. He wants to get involved again, especially in football. He is adamant that money raised should go to individuals rather than any organisation. He wants to meet some of the people who will be helped, even to the extent of escorting them to where they can be treated.'

But Wallace received a major setback at the end of June when he was attacked by a drug-fuelled mugger just a stone's throw from his luxury home in the small town of Los Boliches, in the resort of Fuengirola. He had been out for a stroll with wife Daphne, and friends, when the attacker plunged a knife deep into his side. He battled to protect his wife but as the Spaniard ran off, Wallace collapsed in a pool of blood.

A police car rushed him to a local clinic but the wound was so bad that he was immediately transferred by ambulance to a larger hospital in nearby Malaga. He spent two days being treated for a four-inch deep stab wound and was told that the blade had narrowly missed one of his kidneys.

A man was arrested two hours after the incident, and Wallace said, 'I'm glad it's all over. We were on our way home after dinner with friends when suddenly this guy appeared. He attacked me and I struggled with him. I get my stitches out in a couple of days then I'm off to Britain.' A Costa del Sol detective said, 'He picked the wrong man to try to rob. Senor Wallace put up so much resistance that he fled.'

It later emerged that the young Spanish mugger was punched so hard on the nose by Wallace that he was still dazed when police caught up with him. A detective said, 'We thought the mugger had a broken nose. He had a lot of blood on him – and it turned out to be his own. It must have been quite a punch.'

Just over a fortnight later, Wallace was back in the UK and working hard on the launch of his charity. Organisers were tasked with tracking down as many of Jock's former players at Rangers as possible, especially those who had taken part in the gaffer's treble wins. The dinner was an instant sell-out, and tickets were as scarce as briefs for an Old Firm cup final – 850 tickets at £35 a head was a great start for the charity.

Motherwell, Hearts and Colchester booked tables, while the manager and assistant from Berwick Rangers confirmed their attendance. Celtic also took a table, as did Rangers. On the eve of the dinner, reports surfaced that Wallace had thrown his hat in the ring for the vacant Blackburn Rovers job, but again, nothing came of it.

At the beginning of 1992, and with Rene Evans in desperate need of treatment, Wallace became personally involved and paid for her to fly to London to see one of the country's top specialists. He insisted on meeting all the couple's expenses from the fund.

At the time, the Evanses lived in a sheltered housing complex in East Kilbride, and Bobby said, 'The doctor who looked after Jock has recommended a new treatment for Rene. She was treated like a VIP and it has given her a real boost. Before Jock volunteered his help she felt so helpless that she cried a lot. Now she feels there is hope. We can't thank Jock enough.'

The big man celebrated Burns Night with a charity function, and the evening included 'A toast to loyal Wallace – O would, or I had seen the day; That treason thus could sell us; My auld grey head had lien in clay; Wi' Bruce and loyal Wallace!' Burns enthusiasts got together at the Moat House in Glasgow and one said, 'Jock is the kind of guy Burns would have liked. Big, honest and a great believer that a man's a man for aw that.'

Despite his illness, stories appeared in the national press linking Wallace with the vacant manager's jobs at Spanish Second Division sides Real Betis and Malaga, but he seemed to be focussed more on winning his personal battle with Parkinson's. He said, 'This is supposed to be an illness you can't beat, but believe me, it won't get the better of me. There's one thing I know for sure – I won't die from Parkinson's disease.'

Wallace was back in Scotland for the Scottish Cup Final between two of his former clubs, Rangers and Airdrie, in 1992, and said, 'I have fought this problem until it has come to a standstill and now feel strong and fit. Physically and mentally I feel great. You must keep working and fighting it and establish a fitness pattern to combat it. For the past two years I've worked like hell on my physical fitness.

'Now I feel sharper than at any time in the past eight years. I play golf regularly, I get to football matches. I live like anyone else on a day-to-day basis. I was fortunate that I was treated by one of the world's top neurologists and he has told me to get back into football. It was wonderful to hear that I'm fit enough to work again.'

But Wallace was convinced that the pressures of management were taking years off the lives of leading football bosses and that the stress and strain of managing at a high level had contributed to his illness. He said, 'Look what it has done to Kenny Dalglish and Graeme Souness. They are two tough, very single-minded professionals – two Scottish lads who never knew what it was to accept second best as players. But they go into management and look what happens. Kenny suffered what I would term a nervous breakdown just before he quit Liverpool, and Graeme has had major heart surgery.

'I'm pretty much convinced it was the pressures of managing Rangers during my second spell with the club that brought it on. Running a football club can be a great life, but as the three of us have discovered, there can be a hefty price to pay.

'I'm not saying I wouldn't have developed Parkinson's had I been in some other walk of life. I just don't know. All the same, I have been told by the medical people that it is accelerated by stress and I reckon the pressures of managing Rangers brought it to a head. Believe me, it's very difficult to cope with.

'I'd been eating sloppily. I found my hands were shaking. I had pains in my legs and especially my calf muscles. I had recognised what I now know to be the early stages of the illness but when I went to Seville the problems disappeared for the most part. It was a more laid-back job over there.'

Rangers rolled out the red carpet for Wallace in 1993 with Ibrox chairman David Murray approving plans for a testimonial year. It was the first time a Rangers manager had been honoured in such a way, and Wallace said, 'At last I have been recognised by Rangers. For them to welcome me back to Ibrox in this way is fantastic. I want to personally thank David Murray for this gesture. It is great news.'

It was hoped that a series of dinners, golf matches and quiz nights, to be held the following year, would help towards costly medical bills. To kick-start his special year, Wallace was the guest of honour at Ibrox for a league match between Rangers and Aberdeen. Ally McCoist said, 'It was Big Jock who made a man of me. He gave me a really tough training schedule and I had to work harder than I'd ever done. He always had his own ideas, like murdering us on Gullane sands, but he's quite a guy.' Before the match, Wallace said, 'I'm really looking forward to going out to meet the fans.'

It was also announced that Wallace would be honoured by his home town of Wallyford at the beginning of 1994. Before that, though, there was a glittering evening in big Jock's name at Victoria's Nightclub, in the centre of Glasgow, as the football world came together to help ease his financial burden.

But in October 1994, big Jock, the former iron man of Scottish football, was reduced to tears when he came face-to-face with his former fighting colleagues, the Gurkhas, after a day of celebrity golf and a testimonial dinner in his honour. He sat speechless as an officer appeared in full uniform and presented him with a ceremonial kukri, the Gurkhas' fighting knife. Guests included Gary Lineker, who had flown in from Japan, Southampton manager Alan Ball, Frank McLintock, Andy Gray and former boxing champ Henry Cooper.

The presence of so many sporting greats merely underlined the high esteem in which Wallace was held and the dinner, staged in the small hamlet of Princes Risborough in Buckinghamshire, was a great success. The Gurkha involvement had come, quite literally, out of the blue. One of the organisers had received a phone call from a former British Army officer, just two days before the event, to say that the Gurkhas wanted to contribute to Jock's year. At the dinner the regiment's highest-serving officer in Britain, Captain Balcrishni Guru, handed over one of only two such knives commissioned annually for presentation to those respected by the Gurkhas for their help and friendship during the war. Jock was visibly stunned and recalled, 'At times in Malaya it was pretty hairy but many good friendships were made. The presentation was incredibly moving and brought back a lot of memories.'

He added, 'Parkinson's can often hold you back. Symptoms include worsening speech, which is very frustrating. I also have problems writing. People ask for autographs, but after a short while just signing my name becomes difficult. I used to jog every day, but can't any more. Old weaknesses from my football career are made far worse by the trouble. I still enjoy golf but getting round the course is difficult, so I have to use a motorised buggy.

'I keep hoping that medical advances will find a cure. Luckily I've always been fit – and a fighter. In the US they use conventional medicines along with a strict regime of physiotherapy. You need to be disciplined, which isn't a bother to me. I'll try anything that might help. I've been to a world-renowned herbalist, which did me a bit of good. I refuse to give up – I know I must keep pushing to improve my health. If I stop trying, even for a short time, I'll never make that ground back up again.'

27

Jock Wallace:
Rangers Legend

I N July 1996, Wallace headed over to the UK to visit his daughter Karen and her family. It was to be his final journey. While at her home in Hampshire he died of a heart attack, although it later emerged that he had visited a doctor the day before his death. The family had enjoyed a meal and big Jock had complained of feeling unwell. He was under the impression that it was merely indigestion but decided to get it checked out nevertheless. The doctor agreed with the former Rangers manager's prognosis.

Sadly, just 24 hours later, he slipped away while dozing in an armchair as the family tried in vain to awaken him. An ambulance was summoned but the strapping 61-year-old died on his way to hospital. He had just arrived from Spain to spend time with Karen, her husband Stephen and their three children.

As news of his death started to filter through, Rangers supporters made their way to Ibrox to lay scarves and other mementoes as a mark of respect for one of their own, a true Rangers man and a genuine fan of the club. The growing red, white and blue shrine also included the colours of rival football clubs, including Celtic, as fans put rivalries to one side to pay tribute to one of the great characters of the Scottish game.

And tributes were soon pouring in from those who had played under the successful manager, as well as rival managers and players. Derek Johnstone, the man Wallace rated as the best he had ever coached, said, 'There was no bigger Rangers fan than Jock and the fans will be very sad.'

Walter Smith, who was Rangers boss at the time, said, 'Jock was always the first to phone if we had a bad result and would offer sound advice. He was one of the most successful and respected figures in the entire history of Rangers Football Club.

'To win two trebles means that his football side needs no justification whatsoever, but as a human being he was everything he seemed to be – an honest, straightforward man who was a good friend to have. It speaks highly of him that although his second spell at the club did not reach the enormous heights of his first, his legend was never lessened by that fact.'

Alex Totten said, 'When I was manager at Kilmarnock, big Jock called and said, "Totts, can I come down for a game?" I said to him, "Gaffer, that would be great." We were playing Hearts and he travelled to the game with Jim Jefferies. I took him into the dressing room and he met all the players, and they were saying, "Wow, it's Jock Wallace."

'He then asked if he could take training on the Tuesday. I agreed, thinking it would be great for the players to have a wee change. He called me on the Monday and said, "Sorry Totts, I cannae make it, I'm at Gleneagles playing golf, but you know I think the sun shines oot your erse," and that was the last time I spoke to him. He was a great man.'

Alex MacDonald, who was managing Airdrie at the time of Jock's death, said, 'I am absolutely devastated. It is a sad day for Scottish football and for everyone who knew big Jock. My own dad died last month and I feel I have now lost two fathers in the space of a few weeks. He was a wonderful man and a great manager.'

Scotland boss Craig Brown said, 'Big Jock had tremendous integrity and was a very honest man. He was admired for this alone. And he always took the time to assist young managers. I phoned him many times in my Clyde days and he was always very helpful. He was a fine man, and devoted to Rangers.'

Wallace's lion-hearted skipper John Greig said, 'We all knew Jock was ill but his death was still a shock. Players respected him and the fans adored him. I'm finding news of his death difficult to take in and I'm thinking of his wife and children in their time of sadness.'

Gary Lineker, who played under Wallace at Leicester, admitted to being distraught at the news. Lineker was given his big break by Wallace before going on to play for Everton, Barcelona and Tottenham. Shortly after Jock's death, he said, 'When you're a young lad with a lot of spare time and a few bob in your pocket it's so easy to go off the rails. I had a solid upbringing but even so it would have been easy to hit the slippery slope into oblivion when I was just a kid at Leicester. But Jock, to his eternal credit, made sure I stayed firmly on the straight and narrow.

'When he was managaer at Leicester and I was just 16 he taught me how to live properly and how to cope with the glamour and demands of football. I owe him a lot. He took a close interest in me even though I wasn't as talented as some of the other players at the club at that time. Then he gave me my first chance and – equally as important – he stuck by me. He was always keen to give youngsters their opportunity and did the same thing with plenty of others. He was great with us and encouraged us on and off the park. He taught me how to dedicate myself properly to football.

'Mind you, maybe it was fear of the big man that made sure you didn't put a foot out of place! Overall, though, he was a tremendous early influence on me. Jock was a great man. He was hard and strong but always fair – and his bark was worse than his bite. He was very caring and I remember, even as a 17-year-old, how much trouble he took to look after the young players.

'He was a great motivator who knew exactly how to get the best out of the lads. He had a great knack of knowing when to shout at someone or put his arm round them. I'm just glad I listened to him and I was saddened by the news of his death.'

Work commitments at the Olympic Games prevented Lineker from attending Wallace's funeral but he made it clear that his thoughts would be with Jock's family.

Former Rangers winger Tommy McLean said, 'Big Jock was an honest, down-to-earth type, who never used a million words when just two would do. All of us who played for him will have happy memories of Jock.'

Former Celtic player and manager Billy McNeill said, 'To me big Jock was one of the good guys – wholehearted and larger than life. You knew what you were getting with him and it's very sad to see him go.'

The final word goes to Rangers great Sandy Jardine, who said, 'I had been trying to break into the Rangers first team around the time of the famous defeat in Berwick. So while the result was bad news for the club, it was a blessing for me. And it was big Jock who showed faith in me when my form dipped later on in my career. He moved me to right-back and that made me a first-team regular.'

Jardine added, 'When he first arrived at Ibrox, I think a few people said "Jock who?" But they soon knew who he was because of the 45 players who started out lapping the track on his first day of pre-season, only half-a-dozen were still standing at the end. It needed someone to sort us out at that time – and we had just found the right man.

'But there was so much more to him than an iron fist. You need to ally skill and ability to hard work to get anywhere and Jock's teams were all outstanding ones. He was a very caring man who always asked about your family. He knew when players should work hard and when they should relax. It was good for team spirit and there were so many good days. His managerial record was extraordinary and I would never have achieved what I did without him.'

Jock Wallace had lived his life to the full. He had fulfilled his childhood dream of becoming a footballer before going on to make his mark in the competitive field of football management. Suddenly, he was gone, but his was one name that would never be forgotten.

Bibliography

Football is the Wallace Religion by Graham Clark

Playing Extra Time by Alan Ball and James Mossop

Stairway 13 by Paul Collier and Donald S. Taylor

Various editions of the *Daily Record, Sunday Mail, Evening Times, The (Glasgow) Herald, Daily Express, Daily Mail* and the *Berwick Advertiser.*

USEFUL WEBSITES

http://www.herefordunited.co.uk/club/history/

https://sites.google.com/site/bedfordoldeagles/home

http://www.youtube.com/watch?v=2AClvoDorrQ

The Jock Wallace Song

Now you'll have heard about the Yankees being first upon the Moon,

And how the Russkies plan to visit Venus very soon,

But here's a little story that I'll tell you for a lark,

It's all about the songs they sing in the stands of Ibrox Park.

Singing Ee Eye Addio run and tell the boys, tell them that the Big Jock's back.

Singing Ee Eye Addio run and tell the boys, for he's as welcome as the Union Jack.

Now we've had Gallus Alan Morton, Dougie Gray and Tigers Shaw,

They tell me Torry Gillick was a genius on the ba'

We've had Slim Jim Baxter, Willie Henderson an aw'

But the mighty Big Jock Wallace is the greatest of them aw'.

Singing Ee Eye Addio run and tell the boys, tell them that the Big Jock's back.

Singing Ee Eye Addio run and tell the boys, for he's as welcome as the Union Jack.

Singing Ee Eye Addio run and tell the boys, tell them that the Big Jock's back.

Singing Ee Eye Addio run and tell the boys, for he's as welcome as the Union Jack.

Now we've had Gallus Alan Morton, Dougie Gray and Tigers Shaw,

They tell me Torry Gillick was a genius on the ba'

We've had Slim Jim Baxter, Willie Henderson an aw'

But the mighty Big Jock Wallace is the greatest of them aw'.

Singing Ee Eye Addio run and tell the boys, tell them that the Big Jock's back.

Singing Ee Eye Addio run and tell the boys, for he's as welcome as the Union Jack.

Listen to the song on the link below

http://www.youtube.com/watch?v=2AClvoDorrQ